THE CEl

GREAT CELTIC CHRISTIANS
alternative worship from the community of Aidan and Hilda

RAY SIMPSON

kevin
mayhew

The Celtic Prayer Book is published in four volumes:

Volume One
Prayer Rhythms: fourfold patterns for each day

Volume Two
Saints of the Isles: a year of feasts

Volume Three
Healing the Land: natural seasons, sacraments and special services

Volume Four
Great Celtic Christians: alternative worship from the community of Aidan and Hilda

The hymns in all the volumes will be included in *The Celtic Hymn Book* to be published by Kevin Mayhew Ltd in 2005.

First published in 2004 by

KEVIN MAYHEW LTD
Buxhall, Stowmarket, Suffolk, IP14 3BW
E-mail: info@kevinmayhewltd.com

9 8 7 6 5 4 3 2 1 0

ISBN 184417 233 3
Catalogue No 1500697

Front cover: St John and his symbol, from *The Lindisfarne Gospels* by Janet Backhouse. Reproduced by courtesy of the British Library
Cover design by Angela Selfe
Edited by Marian Reid
Typesetting by Louise Selfe

Printed and Bound in China

For the Churches and households of Britain,
Ireland and the English-speaking world
from The Community of Aidan and Hilda

Acknowledgements

Bible references, where not paraphrased, are from the New Revised Standard Version of the Bible, copyright © 1989 by the Division of Christian Education of the National Council of Churches in the USA. Used by permission. All rights reserved.

Contact The Community of Aidan and Hilda,
The Open Gate,
Holy Island,
Berwick-upon-Tweed,
TD15 2SD

aidan@theopengate.ndo.co.uk
www.aidan.org.uk

Contents

* The material for the saints listed in bold type is arranged in the form of morning, midday, evening and night prayer.

A Calendar of Great Celtic Saints Celebrated in This Book*

13 January	Mungo (Kentigern)
16 January	Fursey
1 February	Brigid, *also 24 March, 10 June*
11 February	Caedmon
1 March	David of Wales, *also 6 November*
2 March	Chad
17 March	Patrick, *also 24 March, 10 June*
20 March	Cuthbert, *also 4 September*
16 May	Brendan
3 June	Kevin of Glendalough
9 June	Columba of Iona
4 July	Martin of Tour, *also 11 November, 12 November*
28 July	Samson
31 July	Joseph of Arimathea and Glastonbury saints
5 August	Oswald, *also 8 October*
25-31 August	The Aidan and Hilda Week
31 August	Aidan, *also 8 October*
9 September	Ciaran of Clonmacnoise, *also 8 February, 6 March, 6 June*
16 September	Ninian of Whithorn, *also 26 August*
26 October	Cedd, *also 7 January*
1 November	All Saints
6 November	Illtyd
17 November	Hilda of Whitby, *also 25 August*
21 November	Columbanus, *also 23 November*

---

* See overleaf for additional dates included in the calendar of the Community of Aidan and Hilda

In addition to Celtic saints' days, the Community of Aidan and Hilda includes the following in its calendar:

17 January	The Desert Fathers and Mothers (Antony)
24 June	John the Forerunner, *also 7 January, 29 August, 23 September*
27 December	John the Loved, *also 6 May, 3 September*
4 July	Independence Day (US) – in order to embrace our sister community in that land
12 July	Healing the Land

Mary

8 December	Her conception
1 January	Her role in God's plan
2 February	Presenting Christ in the temple
25 March	God's messenger told her she would conceive Jesus
31 May	Her visit to her cousin Elizabeth
15 August	Her assumption into heaven
8 September	Her birth

Preface

Who this book is for

The material in this volume may be used by groups who want to organise an event around a saint or particular theme (themes are listed on page 431 at the end of the book). It may also be used by:

1. Individuals who follow a daily pattern of prayer and who wish to observe the great Celtic saints' days. The material is arranged so that it can be used as morning, midday, evening and night prayer.

2. People of all ethnic backgrounds. This volume gives insight into one of the most positive shapings in the history of Britain and Ireland, one which provides a sound foundation for a multi-ethnic society. The Celtic saints in this volume came from different races and lived in the fifth to seventh centuries after Christ. They lived in what we now call Britain and Ireland. Some welcomed visitors from other continents and some emigrated north, south and east. In Britain, there is currently a debate about introducing tests of 'Britishness' for those who apply to become citizens. In order to know the nation we are part of, we need to know where it has come from, and the forces which have shaped it.

3. Churches who seek an alternative to one of their normal services. *Great Celtic Christians* is of interest to those in liturgical churches as well as those in new churches.

Introduction

In a recent poll, TV viewers rated television soaps top and religious programmes bottom for their value in giving helpful insights into life and how to live it. *Great Celtic Christians* sides with the TV viewers. The stories (the original 'soaps') loom large, and religion is taken out of its box and placed at the heart of life.

This volume invites us to revel with God's celebrities from the world's western isles. These early announcers of the Christian Faith did not think of the people as aliens to be conquered, but as lamps to be lit. They did not push for a place at some religious top table – they gave away their love and remained true to themselves.

As centuries passed, many of them tended to get squeezed out of the churches' liturgical top tables. But the worshipping public now tires of politically correct liturgies that blanket over the familiar, friendly ways of our spiritual parents. They, and people who don't go to churches, want to celebrate real people who touched – and still touch – the hearts as well as the minds of ordinary people; who lived at the edges, uncocooned; who had their own endearing idiosyncrasies; who excited others to holy living; who show us how Christianity can be lived in a natural way, in the outdoors as well as indoors, at work and play, with the passion and poetry that Celtic people have in abundance, and even in the shivering silence of a lonely hour. They want to celebrate their own saints in a homespun way, and invite them back to the meal table, altar or countryside as familiar friends.

The point of this is not to be nostalgic. These great Celtic Christians beckon us to open our eyes to God in our present situation, to be real, and to develop as God's partners. As we celebrate their special days, they will put questions into our minds. Aidan refused a horse: what high horse do I need to dismount from? Cuthbert's need was for food: what is my need? These saints were accessible: where do I need to be accessible? They leaned on Providence: for what do I need to lean on Providence?

So here are some twenty-four most notable God-guided personalities from the early centuries of Christianity. They are loved by people in their respective lands or localities – and now they are shared more widely.

The book begins with extended material on Aidan and Hilda since *The Celtic Prayer Book* series comes from the Community of Aidan and Hilda. This is a worldwide movement of Christians who seek to cradle a Christian spirituality for today, renew the Church, and heal the lands. To earth that commitment they draw inspiration from Celtic saints and, in particular, Aidan and Hilda. Aidan (d.651), because he is the people's saint; from his mission base at Lindisfarne this Irish Christian spread the Faith to English-speaking people through love rather than fear. He is seen as a model of a gentle, unthreatening but prophetic Christian who lays down his life for others. Hilda (d.680), because she was the first English woman to lead both men and women in a large community of prayer and mission; she fostered callings among rich and poor, sent out missionaries, and crossed the divide between the Roman and Irish missions. The two are a sign of soul-friends of different race and gender working together for the common good. 'Explorers' apply the Community's Way of Life to their present circumstances with the help of a soul-friend. 'Voyagers' take first vows. It is possible to take life vows as a 'Long

Voyager', or as a 'Monastic Long Voyager'. The Community is developing an e-mail Celtic Christian Studies Course. Community households are appearing, and it is possible to become a link church or a 'skete'.*

In an article in *The Guardian* on 26 August 2002, Ian Bradley called for Aidan to become Britain's patron saint. He wrote:

> Billy Bragg's alternative national anthem, 'Take Down the Union Jack – It Clashes with the Sunset', which made the singles chart in those distant days before the (Queen's) Jubilee Weekend, acutely observes of Britain 'it's not a proper country, it doesn't even have a patron saint.'
>
> There is a strong Christian argument for the United Kingdom as an embodiment of the principle of unity through diversity, and a model of the Trinitarian doctrine of perichoresis, the interpenetration of the constituent parts of a body so that they retain their identity but also contribute to a bigger whole. The fact that it lacks a patron saint is undoubtedly a drawback in this age of corporate branding. It is time we identified a suitable candidate for the role . . . [Aidan] came from Ireland, spent many years as a monk in Scotland, and did his greatest work in England . . . Aidan had several characteristics which make him an ideal patron saint for Britain in the twenty-first century. He was famous for reproving those with money and authority who abused their power and wealth.
>
> He was notably pro-women, persuading Hilda to set up her monastery at Whitby. Above all, he was a model of Christian humility and gentleness . . . preferring to walk and meet the people at their own level.

---

* The Community has its retreat house and office at The Open Gate, Holy Island, Berwick-upon-Tweed TD15 2SD. Its websites are www.aidan.org.uk and, in the US, www.aidantrust.org.

After the Aidan and Hilda section comes material on the most notable Celtic Christians, in alphabetical order. The angels, and three biblical personalities whom Celtic Christians celebrated with especial rapport are also included: John, the loved, John the Forerunner, and Mary, the mother of Jesus.

The prayers, poems, stories, dialogues, creative activities and readings are primarily a resource bank from which anyone may draw in order to create their own celebration. However, the material for the saints listed in bold type in the index is arranged in the form of morning, midday, evening and night prayer. This enables those who keep daily patterns of prayer to observe these saints' days in this traditional form. When used in this way, the storytelling may be omitted. Extra material is sometimes added after the Night Prayer.

The index of themes enables groups to facilitate themed celebrations drawing material from various sections. The term 'Alternative Worship' used in the title applies to both liturgical and new churches. Many liturgical churches now provide 'alternative worship services' for people who tire of prescribed forms. Indeed, the Archbishop of Canterbury is calling for 'a mixed economy Church': 'alternatives' are set to become mainstream. These alternative services are often prepared by groups and use various media. On the other hand, some Pentecostal and new churches, who have no prescribed forms of worship, provide an alternative to the songs/prayer/preach sandwich which some worshippers feel lack an awareness of the unseen but ever-present world of the angels and saints. In both old and new churches alternative worship can also take the form of turning justice and green issues into prayer events.

The following extract from an article in the magazine of the US Order of the Community highlights why alternative forms of worship are so needed:

I am an Episcopalian, and I am keenly aware as I pray our prayer book how supremely reasonable and logical our prayers are. We are not alone. The same is true of the Roman Missal, the Lutheran Book of Worship, the Presbyterian Book of Order, and most other prayer books in our Western world. We shape our prayers within the rules of logic and rationality. One could perhaps argue about some of our premises, but our reasonability is still obvious. And so our prayers are of course reasonable. But I am also quite aware that while those reasonable prayers express the mind, they do not touch the soul. They use words to limit and shape reality. But by their nature they rule out and hold at bay the majority of my life and the vastness of the presences that surround me.

Celtic prayer, it seems to me, sings along with the music of what is happening in my world. Our Western world has become so science-based and so reason-ordered that much of our reality is ruled out. In his book, *The Mountain Behind the Mountain*, Noel O'Donoghue begins to point to those excluded parts of reality: the presences of history, of other times and places in this very place, of memories and even cultural memories, and of the liminal (the boundary experience of another world shining through). Along with him my soul seeks not so much to tell God what I think, but to listen to the Presence, feel it, touch it, breathe it in.

The language of reason (prose) reduces and limits; the language of poetry and metaphor includes and suggests. And it also takes me beyond the self-serving prayers of asking into the wider realms of searching, experiencing and conversing.

And in the poetic metaphor of Celtic prayers I learned that the least of prayer is beseeching God for goodies, and that the greater part of prayer is opening myself to his presence in the nooks and crannies of my life as well as in the blue, cloud-studded skies that overshadow me.

Jack Bowers, Anamchaide, *Vol.4, No.2, Spring 1998*

Storytelling – A Magnet Then and Now

Storytelling is a jewel in the crown of the Celtic tradition. In early Celtic societies, storytelling formed part of the life of households. Poets of high rank who visited a royal house would tell a tale on their first night there. In an Irish story written down in the eighth century, the learned poet Forgall recites a story to Mongan, an Ulster King, every night from Samhain to Beltane (1 November to 1 May).

Storytelling could be well- or ill-used. A court storyteller's praises could be used to affirm a good king or collude with a bad king. His satire could have prophetic force. As with Jesus' parables, the implication of stories might be understood by some and not by others.

Great care was taken to safeguard the authenticity of the tradition which stories preserved and handed on. The apprenticeship of the Druid was long and arduous: everything had to be committed accurately to memory. The poets were the historians. A colophon on the most famous Irish Saga of *Cu Chulainn* in the twelfth-century Book of Leinster echoes the end of the Book of Revelation: 'A blessing on everyone who will memorise this with faithfulness and will not put any other form upon it.'

The art of storytelling was prized by the Church in Celtic lands. At the end of a tale called *The Fosterage of the Houses of the Two Mothers*, it states that 'St Patrick ordered that there should not be sleep or conversation during this story, and not to tell it except to a few good people so that it might be better listened to.' Columba campaigned to maintain, under due regulation, the institution of the bard in Irish society. Bede's account of a typical social gathering in a large barn in the grounds of Hilda's Whitby monastery suggests that each person present was expected to take a turn in either singing or reciting something. This account is a story in itself, a story of Caedmon, the illiterate cowherd whom God inspired to turn Bible stories into popular songs. St Caedmon's-tide, around 11 February, is a good time to gather for storytelling.

A brief account of a typical Scottish gathering in a crofter-storyteller's house was given by Alexander Carmichael at the close of the nineteenth century. A peat fire was in the middle of the floor. The house was full, with girls crouched between the knees of fathers and friends, and boys perched wherever they could climb. The host's family and neighbours kept their hands busy with sewing and other crafts, and conversation flowed around the storytelling. A visitor would be invited to sit next to the host, and follow the host's opening story with one of their own.

Similar descriptions could be given of house gatherings in Ireland. Some of the stories were myths from prehistory which came in different versions. Others were of historical events rehoned in the telling, and some were the story-teller's own experience.

In recent years, the value of the story has been rediscovered alongside the limits of rationality. Psychologists have found that recourse to 'this treasure house of archetypal forms' is invaluable for the cure of psychological illnesses.* Christians

---

* c.f. C. G. Jung, *Collected Works,* Vol. XII.

are once again realising that Jesus chose to communicate his message through stories because they convey meanings and reach levels of understanding that a sermon or preachment cannot.

Storytelling is part of our Judaeo-Christian heritage. The Haggadah, the Hebrew service book used in Jewish households on Passover Eve at a festive meal to commemorate the exodus from slavery in Egypt, literally means 'narration'. Its purpose was to enthral the young: education through entertainment. The Golden Haggadah, an extended version made in Spain in 1320, includes poems and pictures too.

Members of the Community of Aidan and Hilda on Lindisfarne encourage households and groups to gather during winter months for storytelling evenings. The storyteller features in most of the material in this book which can be used as it is for morning, midday, evening and night prayer, or as one piece for such gatherings. The storyteller may prefer to create his or her own story from the storytelling sources listed at the end of the book.

The concept behind this volume resonates with movements such as Godly Play – an approach to spiritual formation that is based on creating a sacred space in which to tell a faith story from memory, wonder about it together, and then allow open-ended opportunities, usually with art supplies, for children to engage with the story on their own terms.

It is a way for parents to tell the stories of faith in the home. After a story is presented, the children and the storyteller wonder together about aspects of the story that draw their interest. For instance, with the parable of the Good Shepherd, they might wonder together how the sheep felt as they followed the shepherd. Or whether the sheep have names. Or how it might feel to be inside the sheepfold.

After a time of exploring the story with wondering, the story is put away. The children choose the art supplies they would like to work with, and they spend some time creating whatever they choose, in response to what they feel is most important in the story, or most interesting. Stories of great Celtic Christians may be used in this way. The Bowthorpe workshops, which supply wood figures for godly play in the UK (www.Godlyplay.com), also provide templates for some of the Celtic stories in this volume. They are at Saint Michael's Cottage Crafts, Bowthorpe Hall Road, Bowthorpe, Norwich NR5 9AA, Tel. 01603- 746106. The principles of Godly Play apply to adults as much as to children.

Symbols and Actions

In the Celtic tradition 'the five-stringed harp', that is, the five senses, is used in worship, for each of the senses is God-given. Since, however, Christians from different Church streams have different approaches to how they should be used, the suggestions here should merely be taken as options.

A Focal Display Feature

In buildings to which people come throughout the day, a display illustrating the theme of a forthcoming act of worship generates interest and feeds the imagination. In the pages that follow, we provide a display suggestion for each great Celtic Christian.

Making the Sign of the Cross

Making the Sign of the Cross upon oneself is a reaffirmation of one's baptismal vows, believing in Christ as Saviour and following him as Lord. When the hand is held with the middle finger, the index finger and the thumb together, it expresses faith in one God who exists as three persons, the Holy Trinity. At the same time the ring finger and little finger are held down to the palm, which expresses faith in the one person of Jesus Christ who exists in two natures, fully God and fully human.

In some traditions it is thought to be appropriate to make the Sign of the Cross as an expression of this living faith in the one true God and his Son, our Saviour Jesus Christ, whenever the Name of God – Father, Son and Holy Spirit – is invoked at the end of the Creed, and whenever invoking the Name of Jesus who lives and reigns with God the Father and the Holy Spirit. When the Gospel is read, some Christians trace the Sign of the Cross on their head, lips and heart to remind themselves that God's Word should be in our mind, on our lips and believed with all our heart.

This symbolic gesture is rich in meaning and expresses our faith in God: Father, Son and Holy Spirit; the incarnation and death of our Saviour Jesus Christ on the hard wood of the Cross for our sins, and his glorious resurrection and ascension. The movement from head to heart reminds us of Jesus Christ coming into the world – God becoming man – to live and die as one of us by being born of the Virgin Mary. The movement from the heart to the right shoulder reminds us of his resurrection and ascension to God's right hand. As we trace the Sign of the Cross on our head, heart and shoulders, we remind ourselves that we are to be enlightened by the gospel, believe it with all our heart, and bear the yoke of Christ, his Cross, loving others as we love ourselves.

Physical Postures in Worship

The idea that worship is simply a mental exercise is not a Christian idea at all but in fact denies the principal of incarnation. Worship is not entertainment. The focus of worship is God alone. Since we come into the presence of God through worship, standing is appropriate. We stand in God's presence out of awe, respect and reverence. We stand to sing, to confess our faith, and sometimes to pray. We sit to listen to instruction in the faith. We kneel to confess our sins and to pray. Some bow out of respect for the altar, the cross and the precious signs of the body and blood of our Lord Jesus Christ which are sometimes reserved by the altar. Scripture teaches us that every knee shall bow and every tongue confess that Jesus Christ is Lord to the glory of God the Father. When we come to church and face the altar, or when the cross passes us in procession, some bow in anticipation of that day. The very word 'worship' is indicative of the physical posture of prostration, just as a dog might lick its master's hand.

Incense

'For from the rising of the sun to its setting, my name is great among the nations, and in every place incense is offered to my name . . . says the LORD of hosts' (*Malachi 1:11*).

Incense represents the finished work of Christ and our prayer which is offered to the Father in Christ's name. The sacrifice of Christ on Calvary obtained our eternal redemption. The merits of Christ's death on the Cross rise to the Father as a sweet smelling aroma, a propitiatory sacrifice. Our prayer is acceptable to God by virtue of the blood of Christ, the merits of which are reckoned to us by faith. Those who incense the altar, the Gospel Book, the Eucharistic elements, the ministers and one another believe that they

21

bathe themselves in the prayers of Christ our Great High Priest and the apostles and saints throughout history, and the prayers being offered in Christ's name all around us.

'The twenty-four elders fell before the Lamb, each holding a harp and golden bowls full of incense, which are the prayers of the saints' (*Revelation 5:8*).

Candles

Candles symbolise that our Lord is the Light of the World. Two candles represent the two natures of Christ who is fully God and also fully human. A beautiful meaning attached to candles used in worship is that the wax, which comes from the virgin bee, symbolises Our Lord's body, born of the Virgin Mary; the wick symbolises his soul; and the flame symbolises his divinity, thus setting forth the mystery of the Incarnation.

Intercessions

Requests for intercessions may be written on a church prayer board, prayer tree, website, or put into a prayer box during the week. During worship these may be projected on to a screen which also depicts the saint of the day; while music is quietly played, the worshippers offer these to God.

Aidan and Hilda

Aidan (d.651), is the people's saint who brought Christianity to English-speaking people through love, not fear, so that it took root in their hearts. An Irishman, he established the mission community and the first recorded school for English children at Lindisfarne. The school was also open to Britons and the catchment area embraced both England and Scotland as they are today. Aidan is a model of a gentle, unthreatening but prophetic Christian who creates a hate-free, prejudice-free, greed-free environment and who lays down his life for others.

Hilda (d.680) was invited by Aidan to pioneer women's ministry among the English and became the first British woman to lead both men and women in a large community of prayer and mission. She fostered callings among rich and poor, sent missionaries far and wide and crossed the divide between the Roman and Irish Missions. She was known and loved as a spiritual mother far beyond the bounds of her own country.

Together, Aidan and Hilda are a sign of soul-friends of different race and gender working together for the common good.

The Aidan and Hilda Week is August 25–31

On 25 August Hilda's remains were placed in a shrine and her life was celebrated. Aidan died on 31 August.

Other Aidan and Hilda dates

8 October – this is believed to be the day when some of Aidan's bones were taken from Lindisfarne to, eventually,

Innis Boffin in Ireland. Other bones were said to be placed in Cuthbert's tomb at Durham. It is likely that a few of his bones would have been left on his own island of Lindisfarne at the time of the Viking invasion.

17 November – St Hilda's Day*

11 February – The day of Caedmon, Hilda's protégé

Some Prayers Used by the Community of Aidan and Hilda

Lord Jesus, simplicity and a deep love for people
shone out of your apostle, Aidan.
Grant that, like him, we may be gentle in our loving
and bold in our speaking;
that we might inspire others to learn your ways,
and so pass on the fire of faith.

You made Hilda to shine like a jewel in the land.
Help us, like her, to encourage others to their callings,
to reconcile those who are divided,
and to praise you with our whole being.

May your churches be true to their birthright.
May they be places of prayer and eating,
living and learning, work and celebration;
the fire of Christ in their midst
drawing people to you.

*The Church of England's Common Worship calendar, diverging from the tradition of Christendom, currently transfers this to 19 November, two days after Hilda's death.

Kindle in us the adventure of obedience, the single eye,
the humble and generous heart, which marked Aidan,
Hilda and your Celtic saints.

Prayers Based on the Ten Elements of the Community of Aidan's and Hilda's Way of Life

Leader   For my shield this day I call:
a mighty power,
the Holy Trinity!
Affirming threeness,
confessing oneness,
in the making of all
through love.

Study

First   Implant your Word in our hearts,
that we may move deeper into your love.
Embed your Word in our minds,
that we may think your thoughts.
Increase our hunger to know you
in the lives and the words of your people,
that we may grow in the wisdom of Christ.
All   Renew us in your Spirit
with the gift of understanding.

Soul-Friending

Second   Deliver us, O Lord,
from soul-limiting self-sufficiency.
Open our hearts to those you appoint
as our companions on the way.

Create in our hearts a place of hospitality
that we may share your joy with others,
and receive their blessing in return.
May we offer the joy of soul-friendship
to an orphaned world.

All   Renew us in your Spirit
with the gift of a soul-friend for the journey.

Rhythm

Third   Lord,
we are a people bent out of shape.
The yoke of our self-appointed burdens
chafes our shoulders and wounds our souls.
We have filled our time
with things that starve our hearts.
Restore in us the balance of work, prayer
and recreation,
and the Sabbath rest that re-energises.

All   Renew us in your Spirit
with the blessing of creation's rhythm.

Intercession

Fourth   God of all the earth, manifest in us
your love of the whole human family.
Move our hearts with compassion,
that we might storm the gates of heaven,
crying mercy for a world lost in illusion, greed
and war.
Deliver us from praying our own agenda,
that we may seek your best for all.

All   Renew us in your Spirit
with a passion for intercession.

Simplicity

Fifth Father, free us from the demand
to build empires to our own glory.
Remind us that the one who dies
with the most possessions
may die without you.
Help us to exchange the costumes
of worldly honour
for the garments of humility.

All Renew us in your Spirit
with an attitude of simplicity.

Creation

Sixth God of creation, your Spirit brooded over the chaos
and brought a universe to birth;
you rejoiced at each day of creation,
delighting in its goodness before the hosts
of heaven.
You breathed your life into all creatures
and your Spirit into us,
and so made a marriage of heaven and earth in us.
May we treasure our kinship with all creation
which finds its liberation with ours in Jesus Christ.

All Renew us in your Spirit
with tender care for all creation.

Wholeness

Seventh Triune God, Eternal Three, Eternal Unity,
you created us to be integrated beings.
Deliver us from the fragmentation we have brought
upon your Church and ourselves.
Heal us, that we may lay healing hands on those

who are broken by the disorder of sin
and the groans of creation.

All   Renew us in your Spirit
with the gift of wholeness and healing.

Openness

Eighth   Spirit of God,
you come to us as wild wind and gentle breeze,
you speak to us in tongues of fire and as a still,
small voice,
you call us to venture out on the wide ocean
of your love:
may we be ever open to speak forth in prophecy
and launch ourselves into mighty wind.

All   Renew us in your Spirit
with openness and vulnerability.

Unity

Ninth   Lord Jesus Christ,
you prayed that we all might be one
as you and the Father are one:
give us a spirit that repents
for the divisions in your Church,
fosters love and truth among your people,
and lays down its life for the hurting parts
of the human family.

All   Renew us in your Spirit with the love of unity.

Mission

Tenth   Lord Jesus, you sought us out
in the ordinary places of our lives;
you visited the respectable and disreputable

to reunite them to your Father;
you confronted what was wrong:
remove our fear of walking into uncomfortable
places,
move us to reach out to those
who have lost their way;
strengthen us to confront the injustices
of our times,
and help us to light up for people the connections
between their lives and your truth.

All   Renew us in your Spirit with a zeal for mission.

For my shield this day I call:
a mighty power,
the Holy Trinity!
Affirming threeness,
confessing oneness,
in the making of all
through love.

Day by day, dear Lord:
teach me from your Word and your world,
lead me on my pilgrimage of life,
free me to live in your rhythms,
spur me to overcoming prayer,
strip from me all that clutters,
cherish through me your creation,
heal through me what is broken,
blow me to places on the edge,
inspire me to foster unity,
reach out through me
with your justice, truth and love.

Aidan

Focal Display Feature

A picture or icon of Aidan handing on a torch of flame like an Olympic athlete, with other runners waiting to carry it forward.

Preamble

Routine acts of worship begin with 'Those Who Trust in God'

There may be music, and incense may be burned

Reader   I saw the Lord sitting on a throne, high and lofty; and the hem of his robe filled the temple. Seraphs were in attendance above him; each had six wings: with two they covered their faces, and with two they covered their feet, and with two they flew. And one called to another and said:

'Holy, holy, holy is the LORD of hosts;
the whole earth is full of his glory.'

The pivots on the thresholds shook at the voices of those who called, and the house was filled with smoke. And I said: 'Woe is me! I am lost, for I am a man of unclean lips, and I live among a people of unclean lips; yet my eyes have seen the King, the LORD of hosts!'

Then one of the seraphs flew to me, holding a live coal that had been taken from the altar with a pair of tongs. The seraph touched my mouth with it and said: 'Now that this has touched your lips, your guilt has departed and your sin is blotted out.' Then I heard the voice of the Lord saying, 'Whom shall I send, and who will go for us?' And I said, 'Here am I: send me!'

Isaiah 6:1-8

Storyteller

That happened to the prophet Isaiah some six hundred years before Christ. About six hundred years after Christ, something not all that different happened to a man on the island of Iona, on the north-western shore of Britain, at a council of the community founded by the great Columba.

Further south, the pagan Saxons had colonised the largest English kingdom, Northumbria.

Oswald, who as a boy had sought refuge at Iona and became a devout Christian, pledged to God that if ever he got back Northumbria's throne, which rightfully belonged to his family, he would invite Iona to send a mission to his people. Oswald did regain the throne and Iona sent a mission. The mission failed. 'Those Northumbrians are too rough to take to Christ's ways,' Corman, the leader of the aborted mission, reported to Iona's council. 'Brother,' said Aidan, 'perhaps you should have given them the milk before you gave them the meat of God's word, and perhaps you should have put yourself in their shoes rather than trying to force them into our mould.' That was how the community decided to make Aidan a bishop and send him instead. Aidan, in the words of Isaiah long before, said, 'Here am I, send me.'

There may be singing, such as 'I, the Lord of land and sea'

Those Who Trust in God

First   Those who trust in God are like a mountain
that lasts for ever.
As the mountains surround Jerusalem,
so you surround your people from this time on
and for evermore.

Second   The rule of wickedness shall not prevail in the land
you give to the godly.
Do good, O God, to those who are good,
to those who are right in their hearts.

First   Peace be upon the land.

Echoes Psalm 125

We Go Forward

Storyteller

So a band of twelve, Aidan at their head, set out on foot and by boat on the journey from Iona to Northumbria.

The following may be acted out by twelve people who march as they speak

Leader   We go forward into the unknown
with God as our Helper.

All   Your kingdom come.

Leader	We go forward in the strength of the mighty Three in One:
All	Your kingdom come.
Leader	The Father who cares for us; the Saviour beside us; the Spirit who makes us strong.
All	Your kingdom come.
Leader	We go forward in light of sun, in strength of earth, in flowing of water.
All	Your kingdom come.
Leader	We go forward with the desert hermits and the holy martyrs, with blessed Columba and all the holy and risen ones.
All	Your kingdom come.
Leader	We go forward with the word of the apostles and the wisdom of the seers; with the angels above and the prayers of all God's people.
All	Your kingdom come, on earth as it is in heaven.

*If the Preamble is omitted there may be an
Old Testament reading such as Psalm 125,
followed by silence*

Reader	Matthew 28:16-20
First	Aidan, what vision was in your heart on the long journey from western isle to eastern shore? What bridge did you fear to cross? What weakness filled you with doubt?

A living flame is brought by Aidan

Aidan   My friends, we who are weak
are made strong in Christ.
We came bearing the torch of living flame.
The light I bring is the light of Christ.

Aidan hands the living flame to another

The Light of Christ Is Among Us

Leader   The light of Christ is among us:
All   In the gentle touch,
in the listening ear,
in the patient toil,
in the concern for the poor,
in the challenging of wrong.

There may be singing, teaching or storytelling

Intercession

Aidan   We weep for the hungry without any bread,
the children who need to be fed.
We weep for mistreated ones, strangers to love,
those oppressed by force from above.
All   We cry out for peace in a world full of wars.
Heal all the ancient scars.
We plead for your justice to fill all the lands,
as the waters cover the sands.
Aidan   We pray against cruelty, hatred and pain,
ignorance, and greed for gain.
We pray for hostages, may they go free.
Forgive the sinners, starting with me.

Andrew Dick

Each of the following stanzas may be mimed

Leader	God of Aidan of the gentle touch,
All	Give us the gift of gentleness.
Leader	God of Aidan of the generous heart,
All	Give us the gift of generosity.
Leader	God of Aidan of the ceaseless prayer,
All	Give us the gift of prayer.
Leader	God of Aidan of the burning faith,
All	Give us the gift of faith.
Leader	God of Aidan of simple dress,
All	Give us the gift of simplicity.
Leader	God of Aidan of the friendly meeting,
All	Give us the gift of meeting.

There may be free or silent prayer and singing

Leader   From today, and always, may we:
look upon each person we meet
with the eyes of Christ,
speak to each person we meet
with the words of Christ,
and go wherever we are led
with the peace of Christ.

Aidan   May the raindrops fall lightly on your brow.
May the soft winds freshen your spirit.
May the sunshine brighten your heart.
May the burdens of the day rest lightly upon you
and may God enfold you in love.

35

AIDAN MIDDAY PRAYER

Storyteller

As Aidan came to Lindisfarne, and made it the cradle of Christianity for the English people,

All So we welcome you into this place, into our hearts and into the lives of our people.

There may be silence and singing

Leader With loving kindness Aidan brought
Christ's message of forgiveness and hope.
With gentleness of heart he showed the people
a new way through their fears
and out of the darkness;
a way of light and hope through Christ.

Reader Psalm 119:9-16

All Help us to think your thoughts, pray your prayers,
and speak words that bring life to others.

Leader Through dedication, self-discipline and study,
Aidan showed his pupils a life of service
and learning.

All We will strive for wisdom in the service
of Christ's Way.

Leader We give thanks for the school Aidan founded
on Lindisfarne.

All We pray for teachers and pupils that they may be
inspired by God.

Reader What does the Lord require of you?
To do justice, to love kindness,

and to walk humbly with your God.

From Micah 6:8

Leader   Aidan bought slaves their freedom,
confronted those who abused power,
was fair to all and frugal in his habits.

All   Where there is despair, may we bring hope;
where there is wrong, may we bring right;
where there is darkness, may we bring light.

Echoes the Prayer of St Francis of Assisi

Leader   Aidan made silent retreat
that he might advance the kingdom of God.

All   Restore our hearts to stillness.
Expand our hearts to love.

*There may be free prayer, the Lord's Prayer
and singing*

Leader   Aidan brought the light of Christ to brighten
a dark land.
Help us to pass on that light –

All   To warm cold hearts,
to illumine ignorant minds,
to guide straying feet.

Leader   May compassion move in places of power.
All   May we walk in the Way which Aidan opened up;
the Way that is gentle and true.
May we walk as friends to neighbour and stranger,
and bring Christ's light anew.

AIDAN EVENING PRAYER

Leader This evening we thank God
for the life and witness of Aidan
who brought Christ's faith to the English people.
God has called us to share in the inheritance
of the saints;
therefore we pray:

All Open our eyes to your presence.
Open our ears to your call.
Open our hearts to your love.
May you be our All in all.

There may be singing

Storyteller

Aidan came to Oswald, the leading English ruler.
He met with the royal advisers, and prepared for
his great mission.

God's Word

Reader Psalm 47

Storyteller

Aidan chose Lindisfarne as his base, and it became
a 'cradle of Christianity'.

Leader Ebb tide, full tide, praise the Lord of land and sea.
All Barren rocks, darting birds, praise God's holy name!
Leader Poor folk, ruling folk, praise the Lord of land
and sea.
All Pilgrimed sands, sea-shelled strands,
praise God's holy name!

Leader	Fierce lions, gentle lambs, praise the Lord of land and sea.
All	Noble women, mission priests, praise God's holy name!
Leader	Chanting boys, slaves set free, praise the Lord of land and sea.
All	Old and young and all the land, praise God's holy name!

These words may be said or sung*

Leader	Let us recall God's blessings in creation and friendship.

Blessings may be named by any present

Storyteller

Aidan went out with faith-sharing teams to tell the people the good news of Christ. He listened to the people, gave money to the poor, and bought slaves their freedom.

Reader	Isaiah 61:1-3

Leader	We are told that Aidan was 'above anger and greed'. Let us confess the seeds of anger and greed that still lie within us.
Leader	Lord, have mercy.
All	Christ, have mercy.
Leader	Lord, have mercy.

There may be silence

---

*Included in *The Celtic Hymn Book,* Kevin Mayhew Ltd, to be published 2005.

Dedication

Leader	Aidan served you with all his powers.
All	We will serve you with all our minds.
Leader	Aidan served others with all his love.
All	We will serve with all our hearts.
Leader	Aidan schooled his body and soul.
All	We will serve you with all our being, every day and night of our lives.

There may be singing

The following may be omitted in routine acts of worship

Storyteller

Aidan took a summer retreat on Farne Island, overlooking the king's headquarters at Bamburgh. He had built a little hermitage where he could pray alone and undisturbed. During that time Penda, the pagan tyrant of Mercia, reached the royal city, besieged it, and began to set fire to it. Pulling down all the neighbouring villages, he carried vast quantities of roofing thatch and wattled walls to Bamburgh, piled them high around its walls, and when the wind was favourable, set fire to them. When Aidan saw all this, tears flowed from him. He raised his eyes and hands to heaven and said, 'Lord, see what evil Penda does.' No sooner had he spoken than the wind shifted away from Bamburgh, and drove the flames back on to Penda's troops, injuring some and causing such panic that they abandoned their assault on a city so obviously under God's protection.

More things are wrought by prayer than this world dreams of.

Intercession

One or more of the following sections may be used

1.   **Prayer 'blowing' activity, following the example of Aidan on Farne Island.**

Leader   See, Lord, what destruction is being wrought on your world.

All   Blow your winds that the destroyers may change or retreat.

Leader   See, Lord, what is being done to _____
          (examples may be named).

All   Blow your winds that the destroyers may change or retreat.

2.   **A Commonwealth of Aidan's Children.**

Leader   Aidan knit together in a commonwealth of love once-hostile peoples of four races.

All   Knit together in your love the peoples of the Commonwealth (*or* _____).

Leader   Aidan left his own beloved country and laid down his life for another.

All   Help us to leave behind what is past and lay down our lives for those who are different from ourselves.

Leader   Aidan's folk were spiritually formed by wanderers for the love of God from Africa.

All	God bless Africa: guard her peoples, guide her leaders, and raise up many saints.
Leader	An archbishop from Asia lifted up Aidan's spiritual son, Chad.
All	Lift up your children in Asia, and let them lift us up in turn.
Leader	Aidan rejoiced when the rich gave their food to the poor.
All	Teach us that there is enough for everyone's need, but not for everyone's greed.
Leader	Aidan used gifts of money to buy the freedom of slaves.
All	Heal the scars of slavery, and free today's slaves in ships and wealthy strongholds.

3.   Aidan's Ways.

Leader	Aidan cultivated peace.
All	Peace of Jesus, fill our hearts.
Leader	With loving kindness Aidan brought Christ's message of forgiveness and hope. With gentleness of heart he showed the peoples of the land a way out of their darkness; a way of light and hope through Christ.
All	God, give us compassion in our dealings with those we meet on our journey.

There may be free prayer or silence

Leader	Through self-discipline and study, Aidan showed his pupils a life of service and learning.
All	May we who seek to follow his way shine as lights in the dark places of fear,

	bring healing where there is hurt,

bring healing where there is hurt,
bring hope where there is despair.

Leader May God bless you with the divine flame;
may that flame burn brighter even than the flame
brought in our forebears' hands.

All Amen.

AIDAN NIGHT PRAYER

There may be singing

Storyteller

The king sent a priest named Utta to bring back
King Edwin's daughter from Kent to become the
queen of Northumbria's King Oswy. Utta was so
concerned that he begged Aidan to pray for their
safety as they brought back the Princess on the
long and dangerous sea journey.

Reader I pray to you, O Lord. Do not let the waters
engulf me or the depths swallow me up, or the
pit of death close its mouth over me. Answer me,
O Lord, out of the goodness of your love.

From Psalm 69:13, 15, 16

Storyteller

Aidan blessed Utta's group and gave them a flask
of holy oil. He prophesied:

Aidan You *will* encounter storms and contrary winds,
but remember to pour the oil on to the sea
and it will become calm.

Storyteller

All this happened as Aidan had foretold. The waves swept over the ship, it began to fill with water and death seemed imminent. Then Utta recalled Aidan's words and poured some oil on to the raging sea. At once, as Aidan had predicted, the sea became calm and they were saved.

Leader Lord, you call us to pour oil on troubled waters. Pour generously upon those
we name before you now.

All Calm us all, and help us rest in you.

Leader We bring to you the troubles in our places of work

There may be a pause, during which any may name troubles of their place of work

All Calm us, and help us rest in you.

Leader We bring to you the troubles in our households.
There may be a pause, during which any may name troubles of their household

All Calm us, and help us rest in you.

Leader We bring to you the troubles in our church.
There may be a pause, during which any may name troubles of their church

All Calm us, and help us rest in you.

Leader We bring to you the troubles of the world.
There may be a pause, during which any may name troubles of their world

All Calm us, and help us rest in you.

Leader Spirit of wisdom and peace, permeating all creation, move in the unconscious waters of their lives and ours this night.

There may be singing

Reader   Matthew 11:28, 29 or Philippians 4:5-7
             or Peter 3:3, 4

Leader   And now, let us place the day that has passed and
             the night that is ahead into the hands of our God.
All   Here be the peace of those who do your will.
             Here be the peace of each serving other.
             Here be the peace of praise by night and day.

There may be silence

Leader   In gratitude for Aidan we lay down in peace.

All   The day's turmoils are stilled,
             the birds cease their songs.
             As gentle rain falls on tender grass,
             may your grace fall on our sleep.

CELEBRATING ST AIDAN

**The Aidan Way of Outreach: Play readings and
actions for use by weekly groups or as a single-day
event, with a break after each 'week'.**

Week 1

Christian   I am a new Christian and I live in a land of
                many faiths but mostly none. The fire of Christ
                burns in me, but there seem so few of us in
                the church – so many outside it who drift
                through life and know nothing of Christ. I
                know nothing about how to pass on this fire
                to them. Can you enlighten me?

Anamchara* It has to start with an invitation. Jesus advised his disciples 'Go where they invite you'. A great mission to convert the pagan English started with an invitation.

Christian Tell me about it.

Anamchara Young Oswald, king of the largest English kingdom, invited the Christians of Iona and their colleagues in Ireland to evangelise his people.

Christian Why did he invite them?

Anamchara People only give invitations to people they like, perhaps because they have been good to them. And those Iona Christians had been good to Oswald when he was in a hole. He and his brothers and sister had to flee Northumbria when the king, their father, was killed. Otherwise they would have lost their heads too. 'Where, in this cruel world,' they asked themselves, 'can we go that will be both safe and welcoming?' The answer was – to the Christians, and especially to the Christian sanctuary of Iona.

Christian So we can't evangelise until we get an invitation? And we won't get an invitation unless we make friends?

Anamchara Yes.

There may be a dance or song about friendship, such as 'Shalom, my friend'. A group of Christians arrive, some of whom speak as follows:

---

*An anamchara is a mentor or soul-friend

First	We've just come back from knocking on every door in our street to tell them about our big meeting next month. We might as well not have bothered, they wrote us off as if we were some marketing group.
Second	Actually, I didn't go with them. I was with the Combat for Christ group, 'prayer-bombing' the city. The trouble is, I get back from these prayer-bombing sessions and can't handle the explosions at home.
Third	I don't know why you waste your time on all this stuff. I'm happy staying at home and surfing the net.
Christian	So, soul-friend, what advice do you give to these Christians?
Anamchara	I think you know, Christian. We need to live in such a way that sooner or later we get an invitation. Tell them the story of Oswald and Iona and his inviting the people of Iona to bring a mission to his people.

Christian mimes the telling of the story, pauses, and the anamchara claps his/her hands

Anamchara	Now, I have a challenge for each of you. What is the potential 'Iona' in your life and what is the potential 'Iona' in the Christian church or network you are linked to? I mean by that, how do you become a place of welcome and prayer, a safe place with its own godly rhythms? A refuge and a magnet for sincere people who seek help? A place which both an ordinary person and a famous person could

trust and be at home in? It won't be like that first Iona. What will it be like? Come back and tell me next week.

Each person takes ten minutes in silence to listen to God for the answer, then their inspirations are shared in groups of four, for ten minutes

A scribe from each group will report its inspirations in the coming week

Week 2

Anamchara This week a number of people who have reflected on the challenges I gave them last week will share with us their inspirations.

Inspirations are shared

Christian These things are really important. They are foundations, and I realise we need to work at them for a long time to come. Nevertheless, I'm impatient to learn what happened when King Oswald invited a mission team. It must have been a fantastic experience.

Anamchara Not at all. It was a dismal failure.

Christian Really? What happened?

Anamchara They sent a priest named Corman with a faith-sharing team of twelve. He got nowhere, so he returned to Iona and announced that the English were uneducated hooligans, not civilised enough to understand or accept the gospel.

First Uneducated hooligans. That's what my mate calls the people who live on his housing estate.

Christian	What did Corman do wrong?
Anamchara	The Iona community called a meeting to discuss this. One of them suggested Corman should have been more gentle, given them the milk before the meat of God's Word, and not imposed his own standards and culture on them.
Christian	It seems to me that's exactly what Christians do nowadays.
Second Christian	Give an example.
	You name it. The jargon we use and the books we hand out in church. The style of our services and gatherings. You could say we've hundreds of 'populations', made up of different ethnic and age groups, who would not feel at home in a church.
Anamchara	I know what you mean. But let me continue with the story, for Corman was not the last word. The man who had suggested the 'softly softly' approach was named Aidan, and they sent him over in place of Corman, with a second faith-sharing team. His approach was quite different, and it worked. Though it was *nearly* hijacked right at the start.
Third	How's that?
Anamchara	The king had a huge ambition for Northumbria, which was much the largest of the English kingdoms. He naturally wanted to reach the greatest number in the shortest possible time, just as do most Christian organisations today. So he offered Aidan the equivalent of a presidential helicopter. In his case, it was a royal

horse. But Aidan refused to ride a horse. He insisted that he and his team would walk everywhere. This might have infuriated Oswald, but it probably didn't, because he was a rare kind of top person – humble, and God-honouring.

Third I wouldn't walk everywhere if I could have a helicopter. What's the point?

Christian I can see a point. Didn't Jesus walk everywhere? I mean, he took time to talk with people; he was on a level with them.

Anamchara Exactly. And the point is that it worked for Jesus and it worked for Aidan. He made himself vulnerable, after all he could have been attacked. He took an interest in people, he spent time with them, listened to them and then shared his own faith with them. A record of those times states that the people in all the villages grew to love those Christians from Lindisfarne. They ran out to meet them, asked them to pray for them, to heal them, to teach and baptise them. So many wanted these things that, instead of doing ten people's work themselves, Aidan's folk sent for ten times as many people to come over from Iona and Ireland to do the same thing. Soon there were friendly faith communities all over the country from the Firth of Forth down to the Humber.

First It couldn't happen now.

Second I agree. Doors don't open like that these days.

Anamchara Unless you have a key.

Christian What sort of key?

Anamchara	The key for Aidan was to get off the high horse. I think that is the key for us today, too.
Third	What do you mean?
Anamchara	I want you to find out what I mean. My challenge to you for this week is this: What does it mean for you personally to get off your high horse? And what might it mean for the church or Christian network you are linked with to get off its high horse?

Each person takes ten minutes in silence to listen to God for the answer, then these inspirations are shared in groups of four, for ten minutes. All reconvene and a scribe from each group reports its inspirations

Week 3

Anamchara	Welcome everybody. I hope, after last week, that none of you have come on a high horse! Have you any questions?
Christian	Yes. What we heard about Aidan, the way he walked everywhere and made friends with people, was great. But some of us have honestly tried to serve others outside our churches. After a time you get weary. Lots of ministers seem to burn out, and then it's easy to give up. Why didn't that happen to Aidan?
Anamchara	They key difference is this: he offered not only a message, but a model. The model was the mission community at Lindisfarne. Aidan formed a community that maintained a rhythm of prayer, practical work, study and hospitality.

51

Anamchara	By living this way they could set a certain number free to go on faith-sharing teams, knowing that others would keep the home fires burning, and knowing that they would return and be part of the community rhythm again.
First	How did they divide up the different responsibilities at the home base?
Anamchara	Some were set aside to lead the daily times of worship. Others would be responsible for the refectory and for welcoming visitors. Others, including married people and their families, would attend to the cattle, the crops or the fishing. The scholarly types would teach, and so on.
Second	That's all very well, but they lived together in a godly village community, we don't. Once you get outside your church environment you go back to the old ways. How did those Aidan missionaries who spent weeks on the road avoid losing the plot?
Anamchara	First of all, they learned to keep their tongues from idle chatter.

A group ostentatiously place a gobstopper in their mouths and then place a finger over them

Anamchara	They used every spare minute to memorise the Scriptures. First they learned the psalms, then the Gospels.

The group each hold up a text to their eyes; then they remove the text and keep repeating it aloud

Anamchara	Of course, when you do that you meditate on them. Then, when you meet someone, you

have the right word for them, as Aidan did. His words, his attitude towards them, his love and attentiveness, touched them and they took him to their hearts and to their homes.

Pause

Third   I can see what you're getting at. It's quite revolutionary, really, having *both* a faith community *and* an inner life that really reflects God. But isn't there still something missing?

Anamchara What's that?

Third   I was thinking of people at the bottom of the social pile out there in the sticks – they'd never get to Lindisfarne and they wouldn't know about the inner life of wandering missionaries. They were oppressed. Neglected. Justice was the only language that they could hear. And there are millions like that today.

Anamchara I couldn't agree with you more. And I am sure Aidan would have agreed with you, for we know of at least three ways in which he stood for justice. First, he spoke out against abuses of power by those in high places, which took courage, since their boss, the king, was also Aidan's sponsor.

This may be mimed

Anamchara Second, if wealthy people gave him donations, he refused to use them for the church – for silverware, or the church buildings, for example. He gave the money to those in need, or he

53

went to the slave market and bought a slave his freedom.

This may be mimed

Third What was the third way?

Anamchara He encouraged his sponsor, King Oswald, to take practical action to care for the most needy sections of society. As far as we know, Oswald was the first English ruler to appoint a member of staff whose role was to care for the poor. It was the beginning of a social revolution. And we know that when that staff member informed Oswald, who was enjoying an Easter Day banquet, that a crowd of hungry people were outside, Oswald ordered their own food to be taken to them, and also the silver dishes to be broken into pieces and distributed to the poor.

This may be mimed. Nuts and biscuits may be given to people near the back

Anamchara Aidan was so moved that he raised the king's arm and prophesied that it would long be blessed.

First I think I can see what you're getting at too. Didn't someone say 'The medium is the message'? That's what you're saying, isn't it?

Anamchara Yes. But the point of saying it is that all of us learn to live it. So this brings me to my challenge. In the first week, we tried to find out what our own 'Iona' is. In the second week, what 'high horse' we need to get off. This week, the challenge is: how will you

model God's justice to people who will never
believe through words alone?

*Each person takes ten minutes in silence to listen
to God for the answer, then these inspirations
are shared in groups of four for ten minutes. All
reconvene and a scribe from each group reports
its inspirations. If these are shared at a fourth
weekly meeting, the Aidan Evening Prayer may
follow*

TWO STORIES AIDAN MAY HAVE TOLD

Suitable for family and group occasions

Child   I've heard stories of what Aidan did when he
               came to the English people, but I'd like to
               know what he did when he was a boy.

Anamchara The only certain facts we have are about his
               time in Britain. But stories were told about
               what he did before that. We know that he
               came from Ireland. Some say from the middle
               of Ireland somewhere near the Shannon river.
               He most likely was sent to a nearby monastery
               founded by Columba, and that could have
               been Durrow.

Child   What do we know about Durrow?

Anamchara We know that Columba visited it and found
               that the apples from the orchard were so sour
               that the local people complained. So he prayed
               over them and asked God to bless them. From
               that time onwards the apples tasted sweeter.

You can still see the great High Cross at Durrow, and the famous Durrow Gospels, which were transcribed or kept there.

Child   Where else do you think Aidan went before he left Ireland?

Anamchara   There is another story that he became the spiritual leader of Scattery Island. If so, he would have heard the tales they told about the first Christian to live there, Senan, who established a hermitage more than fifty years before Aidan arrived. Senan was a very determined man.

Child   In what way?

Anamchara   An angel showed Senan the island in a vision when he lived in another place, and told him: 'That will be the place of resurrection for you and a great number of saints. No wicked deeds have been done there, because a horrible sea creature has frightened off anybody who might have lived there.'

So Senan, using faith and prayer as his weapons, overcame his fears and made it his island home of prayer. Mind you, he thought it was *his* island and was rather rude to a woman who wanted to join him.

Child   How do you know that?

Anamchara   Because one day a lady named Canair also had a vision which told her she must go there. In her vision she saw a pillar of fire rising above every faith community in Ireland, but one of them was taller than all the others. That was the one over Scattery Island. 'That island will be my place of resurrection,' she told herself. So off she walked until she arrived at the island.

'You can't live here,' Senan told her, 'women aren't allowed here.'

'How can you say that?' Canair said, as she stood knee-deep in the sea. 'Jesus welcomed women, he stayed in their homes, he healed them, and they were the first to see him after he rose from the dead.'

'You will not live one night on this island, and I believe that's what God has told me,' insisted Senan.

'Well, I am equally certain that God has told me I will set foot on this island and that I will receive Holy Communion here,' she retorted.

Child   What happened?

Anamchara   Senan allowed Canair to stand just a little way up the beach and did give her Holy Communion. Then she died and went to heaven. So both of them were right!

A KONTAKION FOR AIDAN

*A Kontakion is a hymn used during worship in honour of a
particular saint, and may be addressed to the saint.
Often chanted by one person or a group who fit the words
to a chant. The following setting is by Jacynth Hamill*

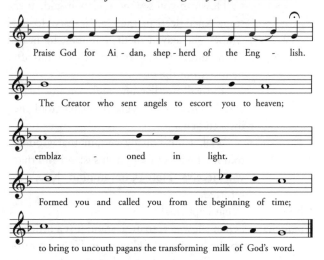

Praise God for Ai-dan, shep-herd of the Eng - lish.

The Creator who sent angels to escort you to heaven;

emblaz - oned in light.

Formed you and called you from the beginning of time;

to bring to uncouth pagans the transforming milk of God's word.

All   Aidan, the Creator of angels who sent them
to escort you to heaven, emblazoned in light,
formed you and called you
from the beginning of time
to bring to uncouth pagans
the transforming milk of God's word:

Praise

You, who were chosen by the Chief Shepherd,
Jesus Christ, to be the shepherd of the English,
counsellor to rulers, friend of the poor,

tireless teacher and protector of the North,
sender of missions to the peoples of the South,
rejoice and know that the meek shall inherit
the earth:

Praise

You, who from an early age
established yourself in doing God's will,
who from your youth ceased to chase
the surface pleasures of this world,
renounced your own kin for the good
of the English:

Praise

Iona, seeing your wisdom, consecrated you and
sent you forth to a people
to whom the Gospel was like a foreign tongue.
You, who chose the holy island of Lindisfarne
as a spiritual cradle for the English people,
submitted in obedience and humility:

Praise

You were ascetic in the line of the desert fathers,
shepherd-like in the line of faithful pastors,
missionary in the line of evangelists
of the Gospel,
intercessor, memoriser of Scripture,
defender of truth and right,
champion of the poor . . .*
rejoice and enter into the joy of your Lord:

Praise

---

*Repeat second line of chant

You, who poured oil on troubled waters,
teach us to bring your peace to a troubled world.
You, who established the first school
for English boys,
teach us to learn true wisdom.
You, whose raised hand caused the invading
tyrant to withdraw,
raise your hand still.
May we, your children, live in the spirit
of that raised hand:

Praise

We thank our God for your trusted partnerships
with Kings Oswald and Oswin,
your soul-friendship with blessed Hilda,
your encouragement of women's gifts.
The spiritual children through whom
you have blessed the world:

Praise

Illumined by the rays of the True Sun,
you brought light into the darkest corners
of the kingdom.
Forsaking the vain glory of earthly battles,
you entered into the spiritual battle against evil
and ignorance.
Fasting from food and fastidious company,
you taught us how to subject the flesh to the spirit.
Learning stillness, you put to death
the rampant noise of human strife:

Praise

Rejoice, pillar of the Church,
who entered into joy through many sorrows.
Rejoice for the healing,
rejoice, bearer of light, for the light that shines;
filled with the grace of the Holy Spirit,
fill us with that same sweetness.

Praise

In our lowliness, may we receive
from that treasure house which you bequeathed;
may we learn from you
to have speech seasoned with the right
and good word for everyone,
and the Name above all names
unceasingly on our lips
so that all glory will be yours
through the ages of ages.

All   Amen.

A KONTAKION FOR THE LINDISFARNE GOSPELS

Leader   All glory be to you, O God,
for the Gospels of Lindisfarne,
jewel shining in the dark ages,
transcribed by Bishop Eadfrith.
Blemishes were removed,
beautiful letterings were made.
Billfrith the anchorite
wondrously enriched it with gold
and smiths bound it in shining metal.
Enriched by the wondrous work of smiths,

by inspiration from Ireland, Italy
and the Anglo-Saxons,
the Gospels give honour to you.
Praise be to God,
honour be to Aidan, Cuthbert, Eadfrith, Billfrith
and the community of Lindisfarne.

All   Alleluia!

The Mantle of Aidan of Britain

Leader   Aidan, you had the vision of a population
transformed in Christ.
You had the faith to come.
You had the gentleness to win the hearts
of king and everyday folk.
You were father to the poor.
You ministered in power and patience
to the sick and dying.
You created teamwork.
Your visits to tell people the good news
gave your team a pattern to follow.
You loved the people of the island.
You lived simply and prayed much.
You prepared a mission to the kingdom.
You influenced many to reach others for Christ.
You are like Christ for the nation.
You are apostle to this land.
You are in pain that people here
are heedless of your Lord.
You will not rest till they are won.

All   Father, put the mantle of Aidan upon us.

Hilda

Focal Display Features

- A picture or icon of Hilda
- A bowl lined with fine cloth with imitation jewels in it.
- A gold-coloured drape placed across a table – symbolising Hilda's radiance
- Ammonite

HILDA MORNING PRAYER

Leader	Wisdom lights up the land.
All	She calls us to walk her ways.
Leader	Wisdom has built a house.
All	She calls us to learn her ways.
Leader	Wisdom is more precious than rubies.
All	We desire her above all things.

Leader   O God, our vision,
in our mother's womb you formed us
for your glory.
As your servant Hilda shone like a jewel
in the church,
so we now delight to claim her gifts of wisdom
and nurturing.

The following hymn (to the tune 'Ode to Joy' by Beethoven), or another, may be sung

All   Come, you faithful, through God's gateway
to the door of Wisdom's home,
enter in with hearts receptive,

making faith and truth your own.
Never doubting, never ceasing,
to your Saviour homage give.
Come, you people, be upstanding,
ceaseless praises ever sing.

Reader   Psalm 33:1-5, 20, 21; Psalm 34:1-10 or Psalm150

Reader   Blessed are you, God of the planet Earth,
you have set our world like a radiant jewel
in the heavens
and filled it with activity, beauty, suffering,
and hope.
Blessed are you, God of this land,
for giving Hilda as a radiant jewel
to light up our darkness,
faithful in both achievement and adversity,
constant in disappointment,
wise mentor, generous host,
counsellor of rulers, friend of cowherds,
encourager of talents,
able teacher, noble in bearing,
unceasing in praise.

All   Blessed are you for Hilda,
a radiance in our darkness.

There may be creative activities or singing

Reader   Isaiah 61:10; 62:5

Leader   Hilda was constant in faith throughout her life.
All   Forgive us, Lord,
for the times we have been faithless.
Leader   Hilda offered guidance to high and low alike.

All	Forgive us, Lord, for prejudice towards others.
Leader	Hilda fostered excellence in all that was done.
All	Forgive us, Lord, for being content with the second rate.

There may be silence

Reader	Philippians 4:2-9

Leader	Blessed are you, Guardian of Truth, because you need us.
All	Blessed are you, Protector of your Church, because you trust us.
Leader	Blessed are you, Father and Mother of us all, because you give us people to love and work to do.
All	Blessed are you in all the peoples who live here, in all the lessons we have learned, in all that remains for us to do.

There may be singing

Intercessions

Any of the following may be used

Reader	Almighty God, who gave to your servant Hilda the rich gifts of vision, love and wisdom: grant that we, inspired by her life and teaching, may walk as one family in the paths of love and obedience, and attain to the reward of the poor in spirit.

From the Order of the Holy Paraclete, Whitby

Reader	O God, who endowed Hilda with gifts of justice, prudence

and strength to govern as a wise mother
over the members of her large household,
and to become a trusted and reconciling friend
to leaders of Church and people:
give us grace to accept the varied gifts you bestow
on your children, that our common life
may be enriched and your will be done.
You gave your servant Hilda grace
to turn away from the privilege of her royal birth
and to use her gifts in generous leadership.
We thank you for the many who have given up
comfort and privilege for the sake of the gospel.
We pray for all who by their lives
challenge the values of our society
and help others to choose the way of Christ.

Reader Eternal Wisdom, Father and Mother of us all,
may the honouring of your name
echo through the universe,
may your just ways be followed
by the peoples of the world.
In times of temptation, strengthen us,
from the grip of evil, free us.
Send us out in the steps of Hilda and your saints
to welcome in the glory of the power that is love.

Echoes in part a prayer from
The New Zealand Book of Common Prayer

There may be specific petitions and singing

Leader Hilda stands as a sign of peace and reconciliation.
All Peace between those who disagree.
Females Peace between men and women.

Males	Peace between rich and poor.
All	Peace towards all,
	that we may pass from death to life.
Leader	Let us go in this peace of Hilda and the Lord.
All	Thanks be to God.

HILDA MIDDAY PRAYER

Leader	Worn by the cares of the day,
All	We offer you our praise.
Leader	Buffeted by trials,
All	We will not cease to return thanks to you.

There may be singing or naming of blessings

Leader	Be with us now, Lord, in the middle of the day.
	Keep us generous towards others,
	constant in praise,
	and may we have forgiveness in our heart
	towards all.
All	May all we do be a labour of love.

Reader	God of life, help us to trade
	with the gifts you have given us.
	Bend our minds to holy learning
	that we may escape
	the fretting moth of littleness of mind
	that would wear out our souls.
	Brace our wills to actions
	that they may not be the spoils of weak desires.
	Train our hearts and lips to song
	which gives courage to the soul.
	Being buffeted by trials, may we learn to laugh.

Being reproved, may we give thanks.
And having failed, may we determine to succeed.

Echoes 'A Homily of Hilda', author unknown

Reader Psalm 119:33-40

Reader Do not be grudging in your work,
but do it to the Lord
with a sense of responsibility towards those you
work for. *Echoes Ephesians 6:7, 8*

Leader As we thank you for Hilda
and her mentoring of a rising generation
we offer you our skills and pledge
to build others up for the common good.

First I give my gifts to you, Lord,
and everything I do.

Second I give my love to you, Lord,
and everyone I serve.

Third I give my tongue to you, Lord,
and everything I say.

Fourth I give my being to you, Lord,
and everything I am.

All We give you worship with our whole life.
We give you praise with our whole tongue.
We give you love with our whole heart.
We give you honour with our whole being.

There may be silence and singing

Leader I give you my best thought,
my deeds, my words, my will, my understanding,
my intellect, my journey, my end.

After Carmina Gadelica

All	Praise to you, Giver of Light.
	Praise to you, Source of Love.
	Praise to you, Spirit of Wisdom.
	Inform us, inspire us this day.

HILDA EVENING PRAYER

Leader	Now let us praise the Maker of Heaven,
	the Crafter of the starry skies,
	the Keeper of Eternity.
All	Now let us praise the Birther of Glory,
	the Guardian of the human race
	who binds the universe in one free bond of love.

There may be singing

Reader	Psalm 100; 103; 145:1-13; 146; 148; 149 or 150

Leader	As a mother comforts her child,
All	So you take us in your loving arms.
Leader	Be our refuge from the strife of tongues.
All	Inspire us by Hilda's saintly life.

Reader	Proverbs 8:1-16; Wisdom 6:12-20, or a reading about Hilda.

Leader	You are the treasure I most desire.
	Uncreated Beauty,
	I long for you more than all things.
All	Your face Lord, will I seek.

There may be silence and singing

Reader	Philippians 4:4-9

There may be teaching, sharing, creative activity or singing

Intercession

either

1. Praying the Seeds into Flower

Leader	As Hilda drew out the songs the cowherd dared not sing,
All	Bring the dormant seeds to flower in your people. *Anyone may mention examples*
Leader	We pray for those with no one to encourage them. *Anyone may mention examples*
All	Bring the seeds of confidence in them to flower. *Anyone may mention examples*
Leader	We pray for those who are trapped by their circumstances.
All	Bring the seeds of freedom in them to flower. *Anyone may mention examples*
Leader	We pray for those who find it difficult to learn.
All	Bring the seeds of understanding in them to flower. *Anyone may mention examples*
Leader	We pray for those at the bottom of the social pile.
All	Bring the seeds of empowerment in them to flower. *Anyone may mention examples*
Leader	We pray for those who lack food or friendship.
All	Bring the seeds of abundant life in them to flower. *Anyone may mention examples*
Leader	We pray for those who are weak or nearing the end of their earthly journey.
All	Bring the seeds of praise in them to flow. *Anyone may mention examples*
	There may be silence, music or singing

2. Spiritual mothering or nurturing

Leader	We pray for a recovery of spiritual motherhood.
	We pray that you will raise up those who:
First	Instil a confidence in Christ that energises
	and frees the other to leave childish attachments
	and face the world with love.
Second	Through patience and sensitive listening
	allow healing to come.
Third	Enable creativity to be born and talent to blossom.
Fourth	Kindle the desire for holy living.
Fifth	Accept that we are incomplete
	and bear one another's pain.
Sixth	Embrace and reconcile those of clashing views.
Seventh	Teach us to drink deeply from the wells of wisdom.
Eighth	Model for us ordered lives,
	sustaining relationships and lifelong learning.
Ninth	Inspire in us the practice of reflection
	and the habit of praise.
Tenth	Nurture a nation and shape it for God.

There may be free prayer and singing

Leader	May the blessing of God and of Hilda go with you.
All	Thanks be to God.

HILDA NIGHT PRAYER

Leader	Companion of our souls
All	We come home to you.
Leader	In the evening of life as in the morning
All	We give praise to you.

Reader   Psalm 119:145-149

There may be singing

Storyteller

After tending the community at Whitby for many years, that devoted servant of Christ, Hilda, suffered the trial of a long bodily illness, in order that, like the apostle Paul, her strength might be made perfect in weakness. A burning fever tortured her continually for six years, yet she never ceased to give public thanks to God night and day and to instruct her flock. She taught them in health, to serve the Lord with all their energy, and in sickness, always to return thanks to God. In the seventh year of her illness she received Holy Communion, called her sisters to her, urged them to preserve peace among themselves and towards others, and while she was still speaking, passed from death into life.

That same night a sister named Begu, who lived in the daughter monastery thirteen miles away at Hackness, was sleeping in the dormitory when she heard the bell which was rung to summon the community to prayer or to gather them when one of them had died. She saw the roof rolled back, a light pouring in, and Hilda being borne to heaven in the middle of the light, attended by angels. She woke up, but realising that none of the sisters had seen or heard this, she ran to the sister in charge and told her that Hilda was dead. This sister called all the community to church to pray and sing psalms, which they did throughout the night. Only at dawn did brothers come from Whitby to inform them of her death. Thus by a beautiful harmony of events, it was divinely arranged that while some watched Hilda's departure from this life, others watched her entrance into life everlasting.

Echoes Bede's account
in the Ecclesiastical History *4:23*

Leader We give thanks for your saints
All Who shine, like Hilda, in radiant brightness.
Leader May the saints and the angels light up our night
All And urge us on to heavenly virtues:
Leader The virtues of peace and love,
All Devotion to you and justice to all,
Leader Wise friendship and a constant life,
All Faithful work and constant praise.

There may be singing

Leader Many called Hilda mother
because of her grace and wise counsel.
Females May her gifts of wisdom and inspiration
be reflected in the believers of our age.
Leader Her strength was made complete in weakness.
Males May the strength of those in trial
be made complete in weakness.
Leader Rejoicing in the fellowship of Hilda,
we commend ourselves and our dear ones
to your safe keeping.
We remember especially this night:

Any may name loved and needy ones

There may be silence, singing, or sharing

Reader	Proverbs 9:1-6; Philippians 4:4-9 *or*
	Matthew 13:31-33

First	When tumults increase,
	lead me into the peace of your presence.
Second	When shadows increase,
	lead me into the light of your presence.
Third	When trials increase,
	lead me into the joy of your presence.
Leader	Teach us to live nobly and die gratefully.
All	That we may receive heaven's glorious rewards.

Storyteller

Hilda was succeeded as abbess first by the widow of King Oswy and then by her daughter. We know nothing more about her community until it was completely destroyed by the invading Vikings in 867. According to the records of Glastonbury, Hilda's remains were taken to that great abbey. England was blessed but Whitby was truly bereft. In local legend, however, whenever the sea birds fly over the abbey they dip their wings in her honour.

There may be music and reflection

Leader	Attended by angels and the company of Hilda and of heaven
All	In quiet we lay down our heads.
Leader	In you alone may we live secure,
All	Watching with Christ while awake,
	resting in him while asleep.
Leader	Father, Mother of us all
All	Your name be hallowed this night.

| **Leader** | Earth mover, Pain bearer, Giver of life |
| **All** | In joy we lie down to sleep. |

CELEBRATING ST HILDA

A Dramatic Narrative of Hilda

The following two paragraphs may be mimed

Storyteller

Hilda was born in 614 into the pagan royal family of the largest English kingdom, Northumbria. Her father, a great-nephew of King Edwin, was a Saxon and she was given the Saxon name Hild, which means 'struggle'. Breguswith, Hilda's mother, had a dream while she was pregnant in which her husband was taken away. She searched for him everywhere but could not find him. She did, however, find a precious jewel hidden in her garments. It gave such a brilliant light that the whole land was lit up by it. This dream was prophetic, for it is thought her husband was killed by poisoning, and Hilda indeed would light up the land.

Woman

In our losses come much grief and many tears. But never let us think that is all. For treasures are to be found in beds of nails. Even as we rise up and fold our clothes tightly round us in a vain attempt to hold in the pain, jewels are hidden in their folds. Shake out your clothes. Open up your lives. See what treasures are there to be found.

Reader	Into our despair,
All	Come with your hope.
Reader	Into our hurts,
All	Come with your healing.
Reader	Into our emptiness,
All	Come with new life.

There may be music, dancing or singing

Storyteller

It is likely that Hilda was brought up at King Edwin's court. When Edwin's fiancée, Ethelburga, came up from Kent, which was where Augustine had come from Rome to set up a Christian mission, she brought with her the Italian monk, bishop Paulinus. So into the life of eleven-year-old Hilda came the black-haired, hook-nosed, stooping missionary Paulinus who taught the Christian Faith to the king and his household.

The story may be told of the sparrow flying through the lighted hall, and the advice given to Edwin at his council, narrated in Bede's Ecclesiastical History *2:13*

Storyteller

Two years later, in 627, King Edwin took the momentous step of accepting the Christian faith, as did Hilda. They and many others were baptised on Easter Day, 12 April, at York.

Baptism promises and immersion may be re-enacted

Storyteller

It was usual to marry from that age on. Did Hilda marry, or did she resist pressure to do so, and cherish a desire to one day be a bride of

Christ? We do not know. When Hilda was nineteen disaster struck. King Edwin was killed in battle and Christianity went underground. If Hilda, like Edwin's immediate family, had to flee, she most likely joined her sister who had married East Anglia's king.

At that time, the girl Etheldreda, a devoted Christian who one day would come to Northumbria and later would found the great Christian community at Ely was also at the East Anglian court. Who better than Hilda to turn to as her mentor and soul-friend? For Hilda was without doubt dedicating herself to the best possible education, and was already growing in the wisdom that would become her trademark.

The following imaginary conversation between Hilda and Etheldreda may be narrated.

Etheldreda

Hilda, you seem like a mother to me.

Hilda I'm glad to hear you say that, my dear, for I have been thinking much about spiritual motherhood. Our nation needs spiritual mothering so much. We lose so many of our men in these senseless battles. Then their wives become withdrawn and hard. God does not want that.

Etheldreda

I would like to be a spiritual mother one day, but I'd like to know what it really involves.

Hilda Once I went to a place where fragments of broken objects had been dumped on the ground. I picked some of them up, washed them, and looked for beauty in their shape, texture and colour. Then I turned them into a mosaic. A spiritual mother brings out the beauty in broken lives and brings the fragments together.

There may be a group exercise as follows: what questions would you like to ask Hilda? Write these down as a group. A senior person takes the part of Hilda and offers answers that Hilda might have given

Storyteller

Within two years of Edwin's death there was again a Christian king on Northumbria's throne, – Oswald, a nephew of the late King Edwin. Sooner or later Hilda returned, and met the man who changed her life. Oswald had invited Bishop Aidan to bring a mission from the Irish monks at Iona to his people. Aidan and Hilda met. When, where and how we do not know. Whenever it was, they struck up a friendship which continued for the rest of their lives. Hilda probably journeyed to and fro between the East Anglian and Northumbrian courts. During this period she not only continued her education, she began to think about her vocation. And Aidan began to give thought to the spiritual needs of the kingdom. Nearly all the monastic churches were staffed by male monks. But Aidan knew that a male–female balance was essential. He had ordained a few women to take vows as nuns, but there were none who could pioneer the great work that was needed and Aidan continued to ponder these things.

The following prayer may be said or sung by a lone voice and may be preceded by a bugle call

Lone voice

> Call, call, call, King of the highest hills.
> Call, call, call, Christ of the farthest paths.
> Call us, Counsellor of the near gate.
> Set our spirits free to soar where you climb.
> Set our feet free to follow where you go.
> Set our mouths free to teach what you command.

Storyteller

> Hilda's sister was widowed, as were so many women in those days of endless battles; perhaps Hilda was, too. Her sister decided to become a Christian nun, and to train at a monastery at Chelles, in modern France, which followed the Rule of Ireland's great wandering pilgrim, Columbanus. Hilda, back in Northumbria, eventually decided she must follow suit, returned to her uncle, King of the East Angles, and prepared to sail to Chelles.

> If she had followed her sister to Chelles we might never have heard of her again. But news of her plan came to the ears of Aidan, and he had another plan, a plan which he truly believed was of God.

Aidan

> Hilda, your own country needs you. We need women who will develop communities for women as well as men, places of education, prayer, hospitality, outreach and creative activity. Villages of God. You, more than any other woman I know, can play a key part in all this.

Hilda	But I have not been trained in the monastic life. I am not even a novice yet, and, as you know, there are no communities in our own land where I could be trained.
Aidan	I know. But we are in a missionary situation which requires us to take risks for God. I and my colleagues will train you. We will visit you frequently. And there is a little community by the banks of the river Wear. This can be a little laboratory. We will support you with frequent visits, conversations, prayer and teaching.

Storyteller

So it was that Hilda began her calling as the first real woman leader within the English Church. Aidan arranged for her to have a plot of land on the north side of the river Wear.

After one year there Heiu, the first woman Aidan had ordained as a nun, who had founded a small women's monastery at Hartlepool, decided God had called her to be a hermit. In 649 Hilda was asked to take her place. She built up the foundations and disciplines of that community, helped by Aidan and other godly leaders who loved her for her innate wisdom and devotion to God's service. She worked hard at developing a Rule of Life for the community. No doubt she drew on the Rule of Columba which Aidan had brought to Lindisfarne; and probably, too, she drew on the more detailed Rule of Columbanus adopted by her sister's monastery at Chelles. And no doubt she used her practical insight to adapt and extend the Rule to suit the conditions of Northumbria.

A bell is rung. A group kneels in prayer. The bell is rung again. The group sits and studies. The bell is rung again. The group does manual work such as sweeping. The bell is rung again. The group prays. The bell is rung again. The group eats. The bell is rung again. The group meets in pairs. The bell is rung again. The group prays. The bell is rung again. The group sleeps

Storyteller

August 651 was a month of great sadness for Hilda. Her distant relative Oswin, the saintly king of northern Northumbria, was killed through the treachery of his cousin. Eleven days later Aidan, his devoted friend and hers, also died, perhaps of a broken heart. Never again would the simple and Christ-like spirit of those two leaders be the dominating influence in Hilda's world. The new king, Oswy, built a monastery in expiation for his crime, and continued to build churches. A superstitious man, he and his queen Enfleda vowed that if he won the battle against Penda, the heathen king of Mercia, he would dedicate their child, Elfleda, to the religious life. He won the battle, and asked Hilda, at Hartlepool, to foster the child. It was he who asked Hilda to develop the monastery at Whitby, and who no doubt gave her land for that purpose. It grew quickly and became a large community for both men and women, based on the same Rule. Hilda directed the studies. Each member had to devote prime time both to study of Scripture and to practical service of others.

Mime nuns taking clothes, food, money and a gospel book to poor people

Storyteller

In 664 Oswy, nudged by his vice-regent son Alcfrith, called a synod at Whitby to decide whether the ways of the Roman or the Irish Mission should be followed. Clergy and monks of every rank gathered there. What old and new friends would Hilda have talked to there? Surely she would have conversed with Cuthbert, who was then prior of Melrose; but who, after the Synod, would be sent to introduce the Roman ways to Lindisfarne?

Oswy supported the arguments of the prelate Wilfred and ruled in favour of the Roman regulations. Hilda, who had the unenviable task of hosting this significant, most political event, must have felt the pain of the Irish participants from Lindisfarne who, under Aidan's successor Colman, decided to leave for Ireland with all the Irish and thirty of the Saxon monks, never to return.

There may be music of lament or the chanting of Kyrie eleison

Hilda continued to lead the Whitby community, as before, in a most impressive way. She was willing to operate under the new framework, while remaining true to the spirituality she had learned from Aidan. She maintained friendships with people from both the Irish and the Roman persuasions.

Hilda stands between a Celtic monk and a Roman prelate and holds the hand of each.

All may sing a hymn about the universal nature of Christ's Church

Storyteller

Hilda's world was changing. On Oswy's death his widow Enfleda, a supporter of the Roman rules and of the turbulent prelate Wilfred, joined the abbey where she would later succeed Hilda as abbess. Whitby was very much under the royal influence, and would become a mausoleum for Northumbria's royal family.

Turf wars broke out in the Church, which was now the most powerful ally of the State. Many of these power disputes involved Bishop Wilfred. We learn from Eddius's *Life of Wilfred* that representatives of both Hilda and Archbishop Theodore presented evidence at an enquiry in Rome headed by Pope Agatho in 679. They took the trouble to stand up for people who were being misrepresented. Wilfred, however, did not just have representatives, he was there in person. He succeeded in getting back control of the See of York against their advice. Yet even Eddius, who was Wilfred's public relations man as well as his biographer, in recording this episode calls Hilda 'holy'.

Whitby's godly village expanded and replaced Lindisfarne as the major spiritual centre of this largest of English kingdoms. Buildings had to be extended. The scriptorium and library and hospice, the dormitories, spinning and other workshops and the estates of cattle and crops – all had to be maintained. No less than five of Hilda's monks became bishops. And people came from beyond the bounds of her own kingdom to consult with her. She had truly become the mother of a nation.

Mime people of many backgrounds seeking out Hilda

All   Hilda, jewel in the darkness,
              mother of the Church, pray for us.

All sing Blessed Hilda, holy mother,
              friend of Aidan, Christ's own stalk.
              Born to honour, stripped of father –
              finding faith, baptised at York;
              shining as a radiant jewel,
              lighting up our darkened walk.

              Taught of God by Wearside river,
              daring, learning, steeped in prayer;
              you became a guide to many –
              friend of folk from far and near;
              drawing out the cowherd's talents,
              held by earth and heaven most dear.

              Faithful host and reconciler
              staying true through shifting ties,
              thankful in success and trial
              always fair and always wise;
              meditator, motivator
              wisdom's jewel, and heaven's prize.

              May be sung to the tune of 'Blessed city, holy Salem'.
              There may be prayer

Storyteller

According to Glastonbury records, when the Vikings destroyed Whitby in 867 its abbot fled to England's ancient spiritual home with Hilda's relics, where they have remained. Hilda is included in the eighth-century Calendar of Willibrord and perhaps in the ninth-century list of those whose names are to be remembered at the altar at Lindisfarne. With us, however, it is our hearts on which she is inscribed.

All

Hilda, jewel in the darkness, mother of the Church, may we honour you by fostering Christ-like ways in our lands today.

Questions About Hilda

A storyteller sits by a fire with four or five others sitting around

First

Storyteller, what do you think Hilda was really like?

Storyteller

I think she was quite a woman! Aidan knew that. Why else was he so keen to get this woman above all others to change her plans to emigrate?

Bede had no place in his record for things that did not fit into his conventional framework. So when he tells us that Hilda was a woman of great energy, we may imagine her as like the wind: a breath of fresh air. She breathed an air of naturalness and was not afraid to make deep friendships with people of both genders nor to trust her intuitions.

We have to ask why she had such a rapport with Aidan and the Irish Mission. Was it their genuineness? Their authentic spirituality? Their love of the people? Their finding glory in looking up at the stars at night more than in building great basilicas?

She was certainly a good listener. We know this from the trail worn to her door by ordinary people who came to consult her, by rulers who sought her advice, and by holy men who came to give her their advice.

Second   What do we know about Hilda's spiritual children?

Storyteller

The story of how the cowherd Caedmon, who could not read, became the first great poet and singer of the English, is well known and will be told another time. Today, I will tell you of six of the monks Hilda trained who became great and caring bishops. Each exercised a particular calling which Hilda must have encouraged and believed in herself. Aetla became bishop of Dorchester. Bosa became bishop of York after the king sacked Wilfred; Bosa shone with holiness and humility. John became a priest at Beverley and then bishop of Hexham; he loved people and healed the sick. Oftor became a Bible teacher and missionary bishop to the Middle Angles. The younger Wilfred became bishop in the see of his controversial namesake. Tatfrith, a man of learning and energy, was consecrated a bishop but died before he took office. All these had great merit and holiness.

Third   What can we learn from Hilda?

Storyteller

I will choose two things from many. First, we can learn faithfulness. Hilda persisted in an age when many did not. Some who had been baptised with her gave up when King Edwin was killed. More gave up when bubonic plague came. Hilda persevered, finally, through six years of a painful terminal illness. In our fickle age, when fashion is more important than faithfulness, Hilda calls us to stand firm.

Second, we can learn from her the art of encouragement. Imagine a princess and an abbess in charge of a huge set-up, who actually listened when an illiterate farm labourer claimed a gift of song. She listened, encouraged and then enabled him, and so gave to the English-speaking people their first Christian poet.

Fourth   What do you think is the legacy of Hilda?

Storyteller

To assess this, we have to take note of scholars. A notable Anglo-Saxon historian observed: 'No woman in the Middle Ages ever held a position comparable with that of Hilda of Whitby.'

We also should not ignore legends, which tell us about the impression made on later generations. People say that the ammonite fossils found on Whitby's shore were once snakes which plagued the area, which Hilda turned to stone. People sensed her great authority long after her death.

From the late nineteenth century until the present time there has been a revival of interest in Hilda. With the development of education for women she has become the patron of schools and colleges, as well as of churches, all over the world. Since 1915 there has been a community of Anglican sisters at Whitby – the Order of the Holy Paraclete – which draws inspiration from her monastic and educational ideals. The movement for Women in the Church has taken Hilda as a symbol, and an icon of Hilda, sponsored by Churches Together in Britain and Ireland, was unveiled in Durham Cathedral for the third millennium, thus superseding a millennium when women had little place. In 1994 the worldwide Community of Aidan and Hilda began. At the same time an interest in expanding spiritual direction to embrace soul-friendship and spiritual mothering has brought the relevance of Hilda's life to the fore.

LIVING IN THE SPIRIT OF HILDA
An Interactive Meditation

Different people may read any of the following thoughts, gathered from members of the Community of Aidan and Hilda, on what living in the spirit of Hilda is about, keeping a pause before they read

1. Having a big enough heart without being anyone's fool.

2. Enabling much to come to birth, without that which has already come to birth dying out through lack of a secure, affirming framework in which to grow.

3. Being true to the Faith in a multi-faith society, yet also being true in friendship to people of all faiths.

4. Maintaining consistency; standing with the marginalised without losing our own identity.

5. Continuing to give to others even when we ourselves are exiled from home comforts and in a hard place.

6. Being like a great tree which, because it has roots deep in the soil, can bend with changing winds without being uprooted.

7. Being an enabler – so that things can happen through us.

8. Embracing huge changes imposed by circumstances without being diminished as a person.

9. Having a heart and mind open to the working of the Spirit.

10. Being fair, firm and gracious to all, yet refusing to be shoved around.

11. Being earthy, rounded, in touch with wildness, able to stride across the moors, and not be sanitised or confined to a rarefied atmosphere.

12. Valuing and fostering an inclusive community.

After a time of silent reflection, invite those present to add to or amplify this list.

Now invite those present to meditate on the following questions, or to divide into five groups and each group to meditate on one of the following questions:

If Hilda were here today,

1. What wisdom would she share?
2. What challenges would she give?
3. What teaching would she impart?
4. What people would she associate with?
5. For what would she shed tears?

Share thoughts and close with a prayer

A GATHERING ON THE THEME
'IN THE HEART OF HILDA'

*Nobody has ever measured, even poets, how much a heart can
hold* Zelda Fitzgerald 1900–1948

Before and as People Gather

*Create touches that speak of the homeliness and creativity of
the 'godly village' which was Hilda's Whitby, of creation and
the varied types of people who came for counsel.*

Thanksgiving

Psalm 135

Each takes a shell or ammonite

Sorrow

Give us tears for the rending of your Body;
give us ears for the cries of the dispossessed;
give us compassion for the overlooked;
give us mercy for those whose lives are warped by strain.

There may be pipes of lament

Listening and Learning

John 15 (The True Vine)
As we make a habit of listening to God, our hearts become as God wants them to be.

Or: Matthew 5:1-6

Or: Luke 24:13-49 (The Emmaus couple)
Jesus listened as a couple poured out their hearts to him. God speaks through ordinary, everyday things such as breaking bread at the meal table.

Visualisation Exercise

Hilda is often depicted holding a church building to her heart. But it was people, not buildings, which she treasured most.

Reader   Hilda, mother and friend, what do you hold in your heart? Tell us.

Hilda   These things I will keep within my heart:
joy of soul-friendship;
sorrow for the havoc wrought
by clashing human wills;
praise;
hope;
the unity of Christ's people;
welcoming communities;
the wisdom of creation;
God's forgiveness for warring clerics;
the fostering of hidden gifts;
the teaching of believers;
the healing of a land.

During an extended period of silent meditation people visualise what might replace the church building that is traditionally depicted in Hilda's heart. Insights may be painted or shared.

Leader   God says: In my hands your tears become
diamonds of joy;
their brilliance radiates to damaged ones
near and far.
I will draw out their splendour
and remake them into wholeness.

Intercession

Compile a prayer-letter from another part of the world which begins: 'Our need for prayer support here is great: we need you to hold us in your hearts and in God's heart. We need training, equipping; pray that the killing fields may become heaven fields as happened in your land.'

Finale

There may be singing and this final prayer

All   Thank you for Christ, the True Sun;
for Light flooding Hilda in her mother's womb –
the light of the Gospel and the Lindisfarne Gospels
dedicated during Hilda's life;
for the light shining in this place and in our hearts.
May we go forth fortified by the life of Hilda,
trusting that you will scatter the darkness
from our path.

A KONTAKION FOR HILDA

Blessed are you, mother of the Church,
radiant jewel lighting our darkness;
faithful in achievement and adversity;
disciple of Aidan;
teacher of bishops;
fosterer of nuns;
wise mentor, generous host;
friend of creation;
counsellor of rulers, patron of cowherds;
encourager of talents;
able teacher, noble in bearing;
constant in disappointment;
devoted to prayer, unceasing in praise.
Like a tree whose roots go deep, you bear the secret
of growth and the fruit of wisdom;
you seek to heal the wounded nations.
All glory to the Three of Tender love
outpouring on you, outpouring on us;
one God, who mothers us all.

Two Prayers Suitable for Schools

Schools and colleges in many countries are named after Hilda

Leader   Father, as Hilda shone like a jewel
in her mother's womb,
may we know that each of us is special
and can shine for you.
Jesus, as the birds saluted Hilda at Whitby,
may we honour you as she did.
Spirit, as Hilda drew out the songs

that were locked in shy Caedmon's heart,
draw out from us the talents that lie buried.

Leader   Eternal Wisdom,
help me to learn from the likes of Hilda:
to be reliable;
to grow in understanding;
to study, work and pray hard – but not too hard;
to treat every person with respect
and none with contempt;
to maintain steady faith, good balance,
and true friendships.

Brendan

16 May
Any occasion whose theme is pilgrimage, journey, adventure

Also Sea Sunday

Focal Display Feature

A photo, projection or model of a coracle or boat on a windswept sea. Sea music may be played.

Preamble

This may precede Morning Prayer at a day event

Storyteller

Brendan was born at Annagh, Tralee Bay in southern Ireland in about 486, and he lived to be over ninety. On the night of his birth Erc, the local bishop, saw the village 'all in one great blaze', with angels in shining white garments all around it. Realising this was a child marked out for a special destiny, he asked a nun called Ita to foster Brendan. When Brendan was old enough, Erc himself taught him the Bible, and Brendan learned all about the saints who were the glory of Ireland. He founded several monastic communities, including the great Clonfert monastery, which attracted three thousand brothers. He wrote an inspired Rule of Life which was used for several hundred years. Brendan had flaws, however. He also went on sea voyages. Reading between the lines, it seems that Brendan's romantic ideals became cut off from the realities of everyday life. But by going on these voyages, he came to realise this. At first he became angry, but he later mellowed, and was used by God into old age.

Four centuries later, the historical Brendan was used as the hero of a series of sea voyage fables which had great symbolic meaning. Like the stories of the grail in other lands, these were about the desire to search for the perfect community under God, unsoiled by the frailties of human nature. They were set in the framework of the Church's year, and brought fresh insight into the Christian seasons.

BRENDAN MORNING PRAYER
The Call to Journey

Leader We come into the presence of the sending Father.
We come into the presence of the pilgrim Son.
We come into the presence of the blowing Spirit.
We come into the presence of the Three in One.

Leader	High King of land and sea,
All	Wherever we go is yours.
Leader	You led our forebears by cloud and fire,
All	You lead us through the days and years.
Leader	You led St Brendan by sign and sail,
All	Your presence goes before us now.

There may be singing, for example, ' Spirit of God' (Skye Boat tune)

Reader Psalm 107:1-9, 23-31

Response after every three verses

All   We thank you, God, who leads your people on.

Lament

Leader   Brendan was willing to leave all and sail out into the unknown.

All   Forgive us for putting safety first.

Leader   Brendan first waited long on God.

All   Forgive us for rushing in where angels fear to tread.

Leader   Brendan looked to God when others gave up hope.

All   Forgive us for our lack of faith.

Leader   Father, we thank you for Brendan's adventures for Christ on sea and land; and for his founding of communities of faith. Kindle in us a spirit of endless adventure and loving community.

God's Word

Reader   Jonah 2

There may be a Proclamation or the following poem.

Background sea music may be played

Brendan   Shall I abandon, O King of Mysteries,
the soft comforts of home?
Shall I turn my back on my native land,
and my face towards the sea?
Shall I put myself wholly at the mercy of God,
without silver,
without a horse,
without fame and honour?

97

Shall I throw myself wholly on the King of kings,
without a sword and shield,
without food and drink,
without a bed to lie on?

Shall I say farewell to my beautiful land,
placing myself under Christ's yoke?
Shall I pour out my heart to him,
confessing my manifold sins
and begging forgiveness,
tears running down my cheeks?

Shall I leave the prints of my knees
on the sandy beach,
a record of my final prayer in my native land?
Shall I then suffer every kind of wound
that the sea can inflict?

Shall I take my tiny coracle
across the wide, sparkling ocean?
O King of the Glorious heaven,
shall I go of my own choice upon the sea?

O Christ, will you help me on the wild waves?

Early Irish – sometimes attributed to St Brendan

Meditation

Sea music may continue.

There may be meditation on this theme: what is God calling me to leave behind and to embark upon?

There may be singing

Reader   Acts 27:14-26

We Journey in Your Love

Reader   Forgetting what is past,
             we look to the things unseen.
All   We journey in your light.
Reader   The sun shall not strike us by day,
             nor the moon by night.
All   We journey in your light.
Reader   We look not to right or left,
             but straight towards your way.
All   We journey in your light.
Reader   The rough places shall be smoothed
             and the pitfalls shall be cleared.
All   We journey in your light.
Reader   The proud shall be brought low
             and the humble shall be raised up.
All   We journey in your light.
Reader   The hungry shall be fed
             and the poor shall have good news.
All   We journey in your light.
Reader   No final home have we on this life's passing seas.
All   We journey in your light.

Storytelling

*A story may be told of a sea journey or of Brendan,
such as the following*

Storyteller

Once Brendan asked his friend Barinthus, grand-son of the great King Niall, to encourage him with some words from God. Barinthus told how his son had walked out on him, but had stumbled upon an island of monks, and now God was working miracles though him. Barinthus had visited his son there. The monks lived in separate cells, but they would come out of them like a swarm of bees to welcome a stranger; there was no divisiveness in their talk, or in their friendship. While they were there, Barinthus and his son learned of an island of saints radiant with the light of Christ. This they briefly visited, but they were told not to stay.

Brendan was captivated. He took fourteen brothers into a retreat to wait on God, and his family fasted and prayed too. They all agreed God wanted Brendan to sail to this 'land of Promise'. Eventually sixty people left in three large coracles piled with necessities. After skirting round or visiting various islands, some inhabited by holy hermits who prophesied over them, circumnavigating whirlpools and riding on dolphins, Brendan and his crew returned to Ireland. They gathered strength for a second voyage, which included hair-raising experiences, illness, death, fellowship with island hermits, and a charming rapport with creatures of sea and land.

There may be coracle making (miniature ones can be made out of half-nuts, matchsticks and card), sea journey painting and singing.

Intercession

Leader God, who saved Noah and the creatures of earth from the great flood,

All Save us.

Leader	God, who through a whale rescued Jonah from the ocean bed,
All	Save us.
Leader	God, who stilled the storm when your friends began to sink,
All	Save us.
Leader	God, who guided Brendan through frightening seas to a safe homecoming,
All	Save us.
Leader	Father, be with us on every road.
All	Jesus, be with us on every mound. Spirit, be with us through every stream, headland and ridge and round.
Leader	Be in each sea, each town, each moor, each lying down, each rising up.
All	In the trough of the billows, in the wastelands of sin, each step of the journey we take.

There may be free prayer and singing

Leader	In stillness or storm, be always vigilant, trusting and thankful. Sail forth across the seas of life knowing both the frailty of your craft and the greatness of your God.

BRENDAN MIDDAY PRAYER

Leader	When we are pressed by work
All	the Father is present with us.
Leader	When we are tossed by storms
All	Christ is present with us.

Leader   When we are all at sea

All   the Spirit is present with us.

Storyteller

Brendan and his crew spent three months sailing across the vast ocean, with only the sea and sky for company, not knowing in what direction they were moving. They ate only every third day. One day they saw a great column rising from the sea. It was what we call an iceberg. It was so big they could hardly see the summit. It was clear as glass and hard as marble and when it was sunlit it shone like silver. 'Let us inspect this wonderful creation of God's,' Brendan said. They spent a whole day sailing around the column, marvelling.

Leader   We pause in the middle of day
and are mindful of God's wonders.
May we perform our heavy tasks,
aware of their setting in God's creation.
With every breath we take,
with every bite we make,
may we marvel, Lord, at your works.

There may be silence

Reader   Psalm 103:1-4

There may be singing

Storyteller

As they sailed on they caught sight of a rocky island which filled Brendan with foreboding. They tried to avoid it but the wind carried them towards it. As they drew nearer they heard a horrible noise, like the blowing of bellows followed by hammering. Brendan made the sign of the cross and prayed, 'Lord Jesus Christ, deliver us from this evil island.' A man grimy with fire and smoke hurled a huge piece of blazing slag at the coracle, then all the islanders did the same. The sea all round them was hissing like a boiling cauldron. 'Soldiers of Christ,' Brendan called to his brothers, 'put on your spiritual armour and stand firm in the faith; for we are at the very gates of hell.' At last the wind turned southwards, and they sailed away.

Reader   Ephesians 6:14-18

Reader   Dear God, be good to us;
             your sea is so wide,
             and our boats are so small.
             Prayer of the Breton fishermen

Reader   Protect those who work on the seas,
             those who travel by night,
             those who serve us in space,
             and our brothers or sisters
             who are making difficult journeys of faith.
Leader   Thank you for the many people who,
             through their work,
             enable us to ride or drive, to fly or sail.
All   God bless them all.
Leader   Thank you above all for giving us two legs
             that enable us to walk and run.
All   Let all bless God.

There may be free prayer, the Lord's Prayer and singing

Leader	The God of life be our champion and leader.
All	We shall not be left in the hand of the wicked;
	we shall not be bent in the court of the false;
	we shall rise victorious above them
	as rise victorious the crests of the waves.
All	Amen.

There may be sea music, movement or singing

BRENDAN EVENING PRAYER

Storyteller

The Brendan crew were on an island teeming with birds. As the time for evening prayer approached the birds began to sing as if with a single voice, beating their wings against their sides. These words from Psalm 65 are what this combined human and winged chorus chanted: 'Praise is due to you, O God, our vows to you we'll prove' (Echoes Psalm 65:1).

All chant Praise is due to you, O God, our vows to you we'll prove (*repeat*)*

Storyteller

After seven hard years Brendan and his crew found an island – on which lived a holy man, clothed, like Adam, in naked innocence – which they took to be the island of paradise. This holy

---

* Music for this chant is included in *The Celtic Hymn Book*, to be published in 2005 by Kevin Mayhew Ltd.

man helped them understand that if they settled there, they would spoil the innocence of the island, and bring speech, and with it sin; he urged them to return home. One senses Brendan returned a chastened, even angry man. It seems it took some years for him to come to terms with his 'shadow' side, and there are stories of his 'taking it out' on others. His soul-friend Ita wisely advised him to travel abroad. God began to work miracles through him, and he may have founded monasteries in Britain and Gaul. During various visits home and away it is said he met with both St Brigid and St Columba who perhaps acted as spiritual guides.

Reader   The great sea has set me in motion.
Set me adrift, and I move as a weed in the river.
The arch of sky and might of storms
encompass me
and I am left trembling with joy.

An Eskimo song

There may be a recording or simulation of storm sounds

God's Word

Reader   Genesis 12:1-3

Reader   Columba is thought to have preached on this passage as follows: God counselled Abraham to leave his own country and go on pilgrimage into the land which God had shown him, to wit the 'Land of Promise' – Now the good counsel which the Lord had enjoined here on the father of the faithful is incumbent on all the faithful, that is, to leave their country and their land, their wealth and their worldly delight for the sake of the Lord of the Elements, and go in perfect pilgrimage in imitation of Him.*

There may be music or silence

Reader   John 21:1-14

There may be group discussion of this passage and singing

Storyteller

Brendan and his crew arrived for Pentecost on an island called The Paradise of Birds. The abbot said: 'It is time to say Compline and then to return to our cells.' After Compline each brother took one visitor to share their cell for the night. But Brendan and the abbot remained in the church. Brendan asked him, 'How is it possible for your community to have maintained silence, apart from the worship, for so many years?'

'For eighty years', the aged abbot told him, 'we have communicated through sign of finger or eyes, except when we are praising and praying to God. What is more, there has been no sickness of body or spirit during all that time.' Tears welled up in Brendan's eyes. 'I wish we could stay here a whole year,' he said, without much thought.

---

* Quoted in David Adam's *A Desert in the Ocean* (SPCK, 2000, p.20).

'You could do,' explained the wise abbot, 'but the important thing is to find out what is God's calling for you.' Then he prophesied with unerring insight: 'The fourteen of you who first set out from Ireland are to return home, for you are needed there. One of the two who joined you later will go on pilgrimage to another island. And the other will go to his death, for he is cut off from God.' All this came to pass.

Intercession

First   Out of the depths of life's torrents
I weave a prayer of stillness
and enter into God's Presence.

Second   Afloat in an ocean of need
I weave a prayer of direction
and steer towards God's port.

Third   May Father aid me,
may Son aid me,
may Spirit aid me
on sea and land,
in the shielding of the city everlasting.

*Carmina Gadelica**

Free prayer

There may be singing

---

* A collection of prayers and chants handed down by western islanders of Scotland over many centuries, and recorded by Alexander Carmichael in the nineteenth century.

Leader   God of the elements, glory to you
for being our radar in the ocean wide.
Your hand be on our rudder,
your love be over the mast on the heaving foam.

All   God be with us at every leap;
Christ be with us on every steep;
Spirit be with us in every deep;
each step of the journey we go.

BRENDAN NIGHT PRAYER

There may be singing

Storyteller

Brendan mellowed. He became a major (though unsmiling) Christian leader. He died while on a visit to his sister Brig. At Holy Communion the Sunday before he died, he said: 'God is calling me to the eternal kingdom; and my body must be taken to Clonfert, for angels will attend there, and there will be my resurrection.' A prophet spoke of 'the age of Brendan who was without crime, who was sage, and prophet and priest; ninety-three years exactly; he lived among great peril'.

Leader   Jesus who stopped the wind and stilled the waves
grant you calm at night.
Jesus of the purest love, perfect companion,
bring guarding ones around you.
Jesus of the lakeside breakfast
guide you finally ashore.

Reader   Jesus said: Father, I would like you to take this trial from me. However, not my will, but yours be done.

Leader   In the steep common path of our calling,
whether it be easy or uneasy to our flesh,
whether it be bright or dark for us to follow,
may your own perfect guidance be given us.
Be a shield to us from the ploys of the deceiver,
and from each hidden thought
our minds start to weave.
Be our director and our canvas.
Even though dogs and thieves try
to wrench us away from the fold,
be our Shepherd of glory near us.
Whatever matter, issue or problem
that threatens to bring us to grief,
hide it from our eyes
and drive it from our hearts for ever.

Carmina Gadelica

There may be silence

Reader   Psalm 124:1-6

Reader   Be vigilant, for your adversary the devil prowls around like a roaring lion seeking someone whom he may devour. Be firm in your faith and resist him, because you know that your fellow believers in all the world are suffering similar temptations. But after you have suffered for a while, God, who calls you to share the eternal divine glory, will personally make you complete, firm, strong and securely established. To whom be glory for ever.

Echoes 1 Peter 5:8-11

All   Amen.

Leader   Keep us watchful, dear God.
All   Keep us watchful over our tongues
and our temptations.
Leader   Forgive us the sins of this day.
All   Forgive us our thoughtless deeds and words.
Leader   Keep our dear ones in peace this night,
especially those we now name.
Any may speak the names of loved ones

There may be singing

Leader   Awake, may we watch with Christ.
Asleep, may we rest in peace.

All   God be a smooth way before us,
a guiding star above us,
a keen eye behind us,
this and every night.

Brigid

1 February – her main festival

24 March – on this day in 1185 St Malachy thought he had discovered the remains of Brigid, Patrick and Columba at Downpatrick

10 June – her remains were placed in a shrine with great rejoicing

Also suitable for gatherings where the theme is hospitality, house blessing, faith or outreach

Preamble

This may precede Morning Prayer at day events

Storyteller

According to *The Annals of Ulster**, Brigid was born in 452, and therefore before St Patrick died. She has been called the spiritual midwife who helped bring to birth Christian Ireland, and 'the most celebrated Irish woman of all time' (Alice Curtayne). She is a potent Christian symbol of womanhood. When she was on her way to a synod at Leinster, the bishop, likening her to the mother of Jesus, said 'I see Mary coming', and she became known as 'the Mary of the Gael', that is, 'the people's Mary'. Through her compassion, energy, and healing powers, everything she set her hand to used to increase.

Her large monastery at Kildare, in the central

---

* *The Annals of Ulster*, now only existing in late medieval manuscripts, seem to have been copied from originals which record events between 431 and 565.

plain of Ireland, replaced the influence of pagan kings. Her father, Dubhtach, was a pagan chieftain of Leinster and her mother, Broicsech, was a Christian who was for a time made the slave of a pagan Druid.

Even though, in her early life, Brigid suffered great privations, she was always cheerful and kind to people and animals alike.

In later times Brigid was imagined to be the midwife, or the wet-nurse, present at Christ's birth, and she was made a symbol of the Bride of Christ. She became the guardian of the poor who work the land, and the patron of those who study. Beautiful prayers have come down to us which reflect these traditions.

St Brigid's Day falls on 1 February, the day of Imbolc, the Celtic season that marks the coming of light after the dark days of winter. In Celtic lands it marks the start of the 'lambing' season, but for all of us it can signal the appearance of new life from apparent barrenness.

Brigid Morning Prayer

Leader   The things of the season of dark are falling away.
Hidden from public gaze
the Lord is now revealed and comes to us as light:
the light that streams to us through soil and saints
and makes all it touches fertile.
In union with your servant Brigid we shout:
'Welcome to you, the Light of the world.'

All   Welcome to you, the Light of the world.

Lament

Leader	For the things of the dark months of which we are ashamed,
All	Lord have mercy.
Leader	For the places in our lives that have become no-go areas for you,
All	Christ have mercy.
Leader	For the sins which have made us hard and frigid,
All	Lord have mercy.

There may be a period of silent self-examination, or any may speak out examples of things to be confessed after each 'Lord have mercy'

Leader On St Brigid's Day each year a cross is blessed and placed in homes and outhouses as an extended prayer to ward off the dark powers of evil and hunger. This custom stems from the account of how Brigid nursed and witnessed to a pagan Druid. To help make the gospel clear to him, she made a cross from the rush matting, and he subsequently became a Christian. Those who observe this custom may take rush crosses to their home after this service and use prayers of blessing for a home.

Reader Psalm 128

All The ever excellent woman,
the brilliant, sparkling flame;
the bird alert on the cliff-edge,
the healer of sick and lame.

She never was half-hearted
about the love of God;
she never craved for profit,
but loved her bounteous Lord.

A midwife of the Faith was she,
a farmhand and a nun,
as she gave glory to her Friend.
So we praise the Three in One.
Echoes Ultan's seventh-century hymn to Brigid

God's Word

Reader   Joel 2:21-27

Making Brigid Crosses

Materials needed:

- 12 (or 16) straws (if using real straws, soaking them in water for a while will enable you to bend and fold them)
- matching raffia, or thread
- 4 rubber bands to hold the 4 arms of the cross while making it

Method:

Traditionally this cross is made from straw; it is a cross with equal-length arms. Each fold should be in about the centre of the straw, but rather than a true 'V' shape, it should be a narrow 'U' shape so that the base of the 'U' folds around the other straws. Fold two straws, loop their 'U' ends together, and arrange them so that the arms are at right angles to each other. Take a third straw and fold it. Position it around both arms of one of the first straws, and pointing in the opposite direction from the second straw. Take a fourth straw and fold it. Place it around the third straw, pointing in the opposite direction to the second straw. This forms the first 'round' of the cross. For the second round, take four straws and fold them in a 'U' shape in the middle. It may be necessary to use small rubber bands to hold the arms in position together. Place the first one around one arm of the cross, parallel to an inside one, and facing in the same direction. Place the next straw over the two straws, facing round the cross. Do the same with the third and fourth straws, but slip the final straw through the 'U' of the first straw (rather like threading a needle). The third, and if required, fourth, rounds of the cross are done in exactly the same manner as the second round. Tie raffia or thread round the arms to stop the cross falling to pieces.

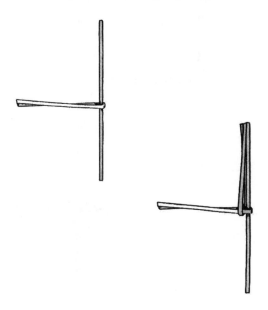

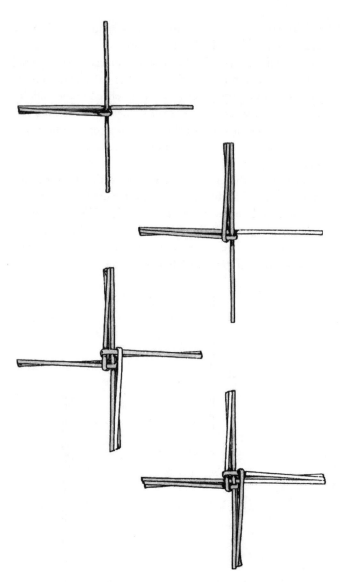

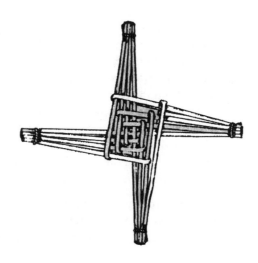

Reader Luke 5:1-11

Storyteller

Brigid took hospitality and raised it to a divine art. As a girl she visited her mother and, because her mother was unwell, churned the milk and made it into butter for her. She divided the curds into twelve portions, and put a thirteenth in the middle of the table. 'Why are doing that?' asked the cart driver.

'There were twelve apostles who gathered around Jesus Christ the Lord, who was the thirteenth,' she told him. 'One day God will send thirteen poor people, then I will give the butter to them, and by doing this, I will be giving it to Christ himself.'

The wife of the pagan Druid who employed Brigid's mother as his slave, brought large baskets to be filled with butter. But there were only one and a half churns left – not enough. Yet the baskets were filled and the Druid's guests were delighted with it. In fact, something about all this touched him so much that he gave Brigid's mother her freedom and became a Christian. This is an example of what Jesus meant when he said: 'The more you give, the more you shall receive.'

Reader Brigid is the woman of hospitality.
All Homemaker God, open our hearts and our homes until they reflect the welcome of your generous heart.

A tablecloth is laid on the ground or on a table and a picnic or symbols of a meal are placed upon it

All I would prepare a feast
and be host to the great High King,
with all the company of heaven.
The sustenance of pure love be in my house,
the roots of repentance in my house.
Baskets of love be mine to give,
with cups of mercy for all the company.
Sweet Jesus, be there with us,
with all the company of heaven.
May cheerfulness abound in the feast,
the feast of the great High King,
my host for all eternity.

Traditional Irish

There may be singing

Intercession

Brigid crosses may be distributed

Leader   As we go to our homes, we pray that they,
             like Brigid's, may be places of hospitality
             and holiness,
             with the cross of our Saviour Jesus Christ
             at their heart.
             The cross of Christ be in outhouses,
             caravans and boats, box rooms and cupboards
             and neglected areas of our lives.
             May foul things that have accumulated during
             winter be gone.
             May we be opened to growth and light,
             beauty and generosity, adventure and love.

Reader   You who put beam in moon and sun,
             you who put fish in stream and sea,
             you who put food in ear and herd,
             send your blessing upon me.
             Bring forth the warmth, the tears, the laughter,
             from our repressed and frozen ground.
             Bring forth loving, healing, forgiving,
             to our fretting, festering wound.
             Bring in light and truth and singing
             after dark and frigid years.

Blessing

Leader   You who made Brigid fruitful,
             make us fruitful, too.
             May we go in the strength of God
             the ever-fruitful Three.

Brigid and Stones

Suitable for **MIDDAY PRAYER** *and pilgrim visits*

Five readers hold a stone each. The first reader places their stone in the middle of the circle

First   The first Brigid stone represents the earth.
Brigid is the woman of the earth.
Holy people draw the earthly things to themselves.
Jesus says, 'The meek shall inherit the earth.'
May we enter into our earthiness.

All   From earth we come, to earth we go.
Your kingdom come on earth, as it is in heaven.

Pause or creative activity

The second reader places their stone in the middle of the circle

Second   The second Brigid stone is for peace.
Brigid is the woman of peace.
Jesus says, 'Blest are the peacemakers' –
may we be peacemakers.

All   Deep peace of the quiet earth,
deep peace of the still air,
deep peace of the setting sun,
deep peace of the Son of peace.

Pause or make a sign of peace

The third reader places their stone in the circle

Third   This is the stone of work. The Bible calls us to do our work as if we do it for God. Brigid used to help her mother, a hard-working slave, in the kitchen. A song she sang as she churned the butter for her mother and their many visitors is recorded in *Lives of the Saints from the Book of Lismore*: 'Mary's Son, my friend, come to bless this kitchen. May we have fullness through you.' Through Brigid, the Lord multiplied the butter as he once multiplied loaves and fishes.

Third	Mary's Son, my friend, come and bless our kitchens.
All	May we have fullness through you.
Third	Mary's Son, my friend, come and bless the soil.
All	May we have fullness through you.
Third	Mary's Son, my friend, come and bless our work.
All	May we have fullness through you.

Pause or singing

The fourth reader places their stone in the circle

Fourth The fourth stone is for healing.
Brigid is the woman of healing.
Jesus calls us to heal the sick.

Brigid laid healing hands on blind eyes.
All Open blind eyes through us.
Fourth Brigid healed closed hearts.
All Open closed hearts through us.
Fourth Brigid, may we be the healing hands of God.

The leader blesses a white cloth for healing, cuts it into pieces, and gives each person a piece. Each person turns outward, kneels, and lays the cloth on the ground for the healing of the world in a moment of silent prayer.

There may be a song or music

Fifth   This is the stone of blessing.
             Brigid is the woman of blessing.
             Jesus says, 'It is more blest to give than to receive
             . . . bless even those who persecute you.'

All   May we become blessers of the world.

Leader   Let us each think of a way we wish to bless
             a person, place or thing.

             *Each or any person may sing, play music, display a
             picture, recite a poem, tell a story, light a candle, or
             offer a prayer, creative art or something they have
             cooked or brewed*

             There may be dancing, music or singing

             *To conclude, gather in silence in a circle, holding
             hands, and walk sunwise three times*

Leader   The encompassing of God and of Brigid be with us;
             the encompassing of God who mothers us all.

All   The encompassing of God be with you
             and with every person we shall meet.

BRIGID EVENING PRAYER

Storyteller

             The *Book of Lismore* records that St Brigid was
             'abstinent, she was innocent, she was prayerful, she
             was patient, she was glad in God's commandment,

she was firm, she was loving, she was a consecrated casket for keeping Christ's Body and his Blood, she was a temple of God, her heart and mind were a throne of rest for the Holy Spirit'.

Reader Come, Holy Spirit, this evening hour.
Brigid was your dwelling place;
make us your dwelling place, too.

Reader Psalm 84:1-4

Silence or singing

First Her heart contained no poison,
no snake lurked within her breast.
She nursed no grudges, harboured no resentments.
In the spiritual field where she sowed,
the weather was always right.

Second When she sowed the seeds of the gospel
in people's hearts,
the soft rain would fall so the seeds would sprout.

Third When she taught Christians how to grow
in the image of Christ,
the sun shone in the day, and the rain fell at night,
so the fruits of good works would swell.

Fourth When she welcomed the sick and the dying,
the weather was warm and dry
to prepare their souls for God's harvest.

Fifth Now in heaven she intercedes for us,
sending upon us the gentle dew of God's grace.
A medieval Irish hymn to Brigid

Leader   'Put me to the test', says the LORD of hosts;
              'see if I will not open the windows of heaven for you
              and pour down for you an overflowing blessing.'

Malachi 3:10

There may be singing

Reader   Do not store up for yourselves riches here upon
              earth, where moths and rust destroy,
              and robbers break in and steal.
              Instead, store up riches for yourselves in heaven,
              where moths and rust cannot destroy,
              and robbers cannot break in and steal.

Echoes Matthew 6:19, 20

Storyteller

Brigid's monastery brewed ale for the churches
round about and, as Christianity spread, Brigid's
faith-sharing teams went out to churches far and
wide. Easter was an opportunity to minister to
the increased numbers who came, and in one
church a blind person, a consumptive, a leper
and a mentally ill person were healed through
Brigid's ministry.

Once Brigid visited a place where the Christians
feared to preach God's Word because a madman
was about. Brigid challenged the madman to
preach the Word of God himself, which he did!
She told nuns who saw the Devil: 'Make Christ's
cross on your face and on your eyes.'

Leader   Jesus said, 'Blest are those who show mercy.
              God will show mercy to them.'

Echoes Matthew 5:7

Storyteller

When Brigid was made a nun, she took as her special text these words of Jesus: 'Blest are those who show mercy.' Let us pray for God's mercy.

First   Have mercy on the places in our lives
that have slipped away from the light
and from fruitfulness.

Second   Have mercy on shady businesses;
may they move into the light of integrity.

Third   Have mercy on shoddy workmanship;
may it move into the light of excellence.

Fourth   Have mercy on shallow spirituality;
may it move into wisdom's riches.

Fifth   Have mercy on sleazy government;
may it move into the nobility of service.

Storyteller

In groups or together, let us pray for people who are in particular need of God's mercy.

There may be free or silent prayer

There may be singing

Blessing

Leader   May the road rise up to meet you;
may the wind be always at your back.
May the sun shine warm upon you face,
the rains fall soft upon your fields,
and, until we meet again,
may you be held in the hollow of God's hand.

BRIGID NIGHT PRAYER

Leader   I am under the keeping
of the Friend of Brigid
early and late,
each light, each dark.
I make Christ's cross over my eyes. +

All   I make Christ's cross over my eyes. +

Leader   Each day and each night
that I place myself under Christ's keeping:

All   I shall not be forgotten,
I shall not be destroyed,
I shall not be imprisoned,
I shall not be harassed by evil powers.

Leader   Nightmares shall not lie on me.

All   Black thoughts shall not lie on me.

Leader   No ill-will shall lie on me.

Reader   Psalm 16:1-3, 7-11 or verses from another psalm.

Leader   Keep me as the apple of your eye.

All   Hide me under the shadow of your wings.

There may be silence and singing

Reader   John 15:1-5

Each of these petitions may be followed by a pause

Leader   May we abide in Christ.

All   And be fruitful in our being.

Leader   Mary's Son, our Friend,
may these for whom we pray
have fullness through you.
Any may recall names aloud or silently

Storyteller

When Brigid was but a little girl she sometimes stayed with her mother who, although a Christian herself, was in the enforced employment of a pagan Druid. Once the Druid had only just gone to sleep when he woke with a start to see three Christian priests in white robes baptising and naming the infant. He heard them give her a name that he knew well, for it was the name of the most loved goddess of his people. Brigid was the goddess of poetry, the daughter of Dagda, the Good god, and she had two sisters of the same name who were the patrons of smithwork and healing. The Druid approved of this name, but why did the priests and the infant's mother choose it? Perhaps it was their way of saying what Jesus said, 'It is the meek who shall inherit the earth', and what Mary had said, 'God will bring down the mighty ones and raise up the lowly.'

It was midnight. The Druid watched the stars overhead. Suddenly he saw a column of fire rising from the house high into the air, bathing everything in light. He rushed over to tell his uncle who was a Christian and who was staying nearby. What did it mean? 'It means,' his uncle told him, 'that she is a holy girl.'

It is no accident that artists have depicted the aura that surrounds holy people as a halo of light.

Leader   O God, who brought fresh light
into a dark place through little Brigid,

make this night holy,
and bathe us in the light of your presence.

Storyteller

When Brigid was but an infant the Druid, who later became a Christian, saw her lying asleep with her arms stretched out in the shape of the wooden crossbeams to which Christ was nailed. The Druid realised that she wanted to pray day and night, when awake, and when asleep.

Leader   Let us each say
All   I make the sign of the Cross of Christ. +
My Christ, my Shield, my Saviour;
each day, each night, in light, in dark,
my Treasure, my dear One,
my eternal home.

Leader   Now let the day's work cease.
Let the world move into silence.
But before the day is over,
let God's holy name be praised.

There may be singing

All   Ever-shielding Father,
ever-loving Son,
life-giving Holy Spirit,
ever Three in One:
rain grace on us and heal us
and we shall lie down in peace.

BRIGID'S TIDE – A SERVICE OF LIGHT

This is for use on the evening of 1 February,
St Brigid's Day. This is the first day of the Celtic season of
Imbolc, which welcomes the coming days of light and is the
eve of the Festival of Light (Candlemas) which celebrates
the presentation of Christ. It is suitable for use on the
Sunday following, but may be used at any time

> *Two readers enter and face the people: the first holds*
> *a lighted candle*

First   I sing a song of light that is glorious,
            coming to greet the cold, dark days.

Second   The frozen days now melt away
            and frozen hearts become warm.
            Creative rays shine through our souls
            and revive the tired and torn.

First   I sing a song of light
            that leaps across the barriers of pride.

Second   A light undimmed by the weary years,
            by prejudice and fear;
            a blazing radiance that lights the world
            and brings the Saviour near.

> *The candle is placed in a holder*

> *All may sing the Taizé chant 'The Lord is my light,*
> *my light and salvation, in God I trust, in God I*
> *trust' from Psalm 27, or another song*

Reader Genesis 1:1-19 or 1-5, 14-19

First   Ultan's seventh-century hymn to Brigid,
            one of the oldest in the Irish language,
            begins with these words:

Brigid, woman ever excellent,
golden, radiant flame,
lead us to the eternal kingdom,
the brilliant, dazzling sun.

Reader   John 1:1-5 and 8:12

*A song of light may be sung or the following
may be sung or said*

All   Light of the world, in grace and beauty,
mirror of God's eternal face;
transparent flame of love's free duty,
you bring salvation to our race.
Now, as we see the lights of evening,
we raise our voice in hymns of praise;
worthy are you of endless blessing,
sun of our night, lamp of our days.

Leader   Let us name the darkness we face.

Females   So we can hail the coming source of Light.

Males   Shine through the mists, the deadening heavy clod.

All   Hail, gladdening Light
of God's pure glory poured,
holiest of holies, Jesus Christ our Lord;
may the blessing of light be on you.
Light without light and light within.
May the blessed sunlight shine upon you
and warm your heart
till it glows like a great peat fire
so that strangers may come
and warm themselves at it,
as well as friends.
And may the light shine out of your eyes
like a candle set in the windows of a house.

Blessing

Leader   May the Light that streamed from Mary
             light up your life.
             May the light that shone through Brigid,
             shine through you.
             May its goodness preserve you,
             its energy enliven you,
             its rays heal you
             and lead you to the heart of the Three in One.

All sing 'Hail, gladdening Light'

People Who Met Brigid
A Play Reading

Boy   Why did God bring Brigid into the world?

Girl   No one can know the answer to that question.

Attendant

             I know why – as far as I am concerned, anyway.
             She saved my life when she was only a small girl.
             We were on a journey from the house of her
             father, a chieftain, to visit her mother, when I was
             taken ill. I felt like death. Little Brigid ran off to
             a nearby farm and brought back some water in a
             jar. She prayed over it, and poured it down my
             throat. Instantly, something inside me told me
             that I would be all right. And so I was. We arrived
             late, of course, but apart from that you wouldn't
             have noticed anything different from usual.

Chief   I am Brigid's father and I employ the man who has just spoken. As I've got old, I've often asked myself why Brigid was brought into the world. She caused me nothing but trouble. First of all, she insisted on adopting her mother's religion. That was unsettling enough for us pagans. I never knew what she'd be saying to my Druid and my other advisers. Then she would keep giving things away. My things. She had this infuriating habit of giving food and clothes, *and* other things, to any wretch she came across. She used to say I'd never miss them, since we had so much. But in my opinion that was not the point. So I determined to stamp it out. I decided she must marry as soon as she was thirteen. I had a handsome young prince all lined up for her – and a sizable dowry. Politically, it was exactly what we needed; it would have created an alliance which would have done us nothing but good. But the stupid girl refused. She absolutely refused. I knew it was no good fighting her. She was indomitable. So I agreed to give the dowry to set her up as a nun. I have to admit that what she's done since then is more than I ever imagined. In one way she's got nothing, but in another way she seems to have everything. All Ireland's gone after her, and I feel as if I and our old ways are being left behind.

Man in the Street

I don't know a lot. I can't read or write, but I do know this: Brigid saved my life. I'm a rough and ready sort of bloke. One day I saw a fox. So I killed it. Well, foxes muck things up. They're pests.

132

How was I to know that this particular one was the chief's pet fox that did tricks in front of his guests? I found out that they all used to laugh when that fox performed, and the king wasn't half pleased.

Anyway, when he found out what had happened, he was out of his mind with fury. He sent his security people down and they took me away from my family and clapped me in prison. He ordered our house to be taken and my wife and kids to be sold as slaves. I was for the chop. I waited in that prison, dreading the day when they would take me out and chop my head off.

But of course, all that reckoned without our saint, Intrepid Brigid. When she found out what had happened, she went straight to the chief and pleaded for us, so I found out afterwards. The chief wouldn't be pressurised – but there was one little chink of light. He said the only thing that would change his mind would be if he was presented with another fox who would do the same sort of tricks.

Well, Brigid didn't have any foxes, let alone tame ones. But she did have one thing – her faith. She prayed to God Almighty to do something to save us from this cruel injustice. And do you know what? As she was driving her horse and chariot full pelt towards the chief's palace – you won't believe this, but I swear to you it's the truth – a fox jumped on to her chariot and sat at her feet. Brigid put on a collar and a lead, and led this fox to an audience with the chief.

'Let it perform in front of the guests,' he said. Well, I would have thought the fox would have run away, but not so. He performed so many tricks that the people laughed even more than they'd laughed with the other fox, and the chief was put into a really good mood. He told them to let me and my family go home.

But who do you think had the last laugh? That wily old fox disappeared into the wild and has never been seen again. Oh yes, that fox had the last laugh all right.

It's funny really, isn't it?

Orthodox Hymn to St Brigid of Kildare

Troparion – Tone 1

O holy Bridget,
thou didst become sublime through thy humility,
and didst fly on the wings of longing for God.
When thou didst arrive in the Eternal City
and appear before the Divine Spouse,
wearing the crown of virginity,
thou didst keep thy promise to remember those
who have recourse to thee.
Thou dost shower grace upon the world,
and dost multiply miracles.
Intercede with Christ our God
that he may save our souls.

Troparion – Tone 4

The holy virgin Bridget, full of divine wisdom,
went with joy along the way of evangelical childhood
and with the grace of God
attained in this way the summit of virtue.
Wherefore she now bestows blessings
upon those who come to her with faith.
O holy virgin, intercede with Christ our God
that he may have mercy on our souls.

Caedmon

11 February
Also suitable for gatherings whose theme is gift discovery,
poetry or creation

CAEDMON MORNING PRAYER

Storyteller
Caedmon was the first to put Bible stories into popular songs in English. His gift was of enormous value in spreading the Faith among the English people who could not read.

Thanksgiving

There may be singing or music making

Reader   Psalm 65

Harp or guitar chords may form background music

Reader   A fragment of Caedmon's first song:
Now must we praise
the Guardian of heaven's realm,
the Creator's might
and his mind's thought;
the glorious works of the Father,
how, of every wonder,
he, the Lord Eternal,
laid the foundation.
He shaped first
for the children of humankind
heaven as their roof, the holy Creator.
Then, the middle earth he,

humankind's Guardian, the Eternal Lord,
afterwards designed
as human ground, the Lord Almighty.
Echoes the inscription on Caedmon's Cross, Whitby

Reader   Genesis 1:1-13

First	All you works of the Lord, bless the Lord.
All	To the Lord be highest praise and glory for ever!
Second	And you angels of the Lord, bless the Lord.
All	To the Lord be highest praise and glory for ever!
First	Heavens of the Lord, bless the Lord.
	And you clouds of the sky, bless the Lord.
	And all you armies of the Lord, bless the Lord.
All	To the Lord be highest glory and praise for ever.
Second	You, sun and moon, bless the Lord.
	And you, stars of heaven, bless the Lord.
	And you, showers and rain, bless the Lord.
All	To the Lord be highest glory and praise for ever.
First	Breezes and winds, bless the Lord.
	Cold and heat, bless the Lord.
All	To the Lord be highest glory and praise for ever.
First	All that grows in the ground, bless the Lord.
	All that swims in the waters, bless the Lord.
	All birds that fly in the air, bless the Lord.
All	To the Lord be highest glory and praise for ever.
First	You, people on earth, bless the Lord.
	You holy ones and humble in heart, bless the Lord.
All	To the Lord be highest glory and praise for ever.

*Selected from the Septuagint version
of the Book of Daniel*

God's Word

Reader Luke 1:46-52

There may be teaching, creative activity and singing

Intercession

Leader O God, who called Caedmon
from the care of your creatures
to sing praises to the Guardian of all creation,
give us grace to heed your call,
that our lives may become one
with the song of all creation.

Leader As love-bearers drew out the songs
that the cowherd dared not sing,

All Bring to flower in your people
the seeds that dormant lie.

Leader We pray for those who have none
to encourage them.

All Bring the seeds of confidence in them to flower.

Leader We pray for those who are trapped
by their circumstances.

All Bring the seeds of freedom in them to flower.

Leader We pray for those who find it difficult to learn.

All Bring the seeds of understanding in them to flower.

Leader We pray for those at the bottom of the social pile.

All Bring the seeds of empowerment in them to flower.

Leader We pray for those who lack food or friendship.

All Bring the seeds of abundant life in them to flower.

Leader We pray for those who are weak
or nearing the end of their earthly journey.

All   Bring the seeds of joy in them to flower.

*There may be meditation on this intercession and
more extended prayer and singing*

Blessing

Leader   God make you to sing with the joy of all creation,
the Guardian to rouse you,
the Saviour to nourish you,
the Spirit to inspire you.

CAEDMON MIDDAY PRAYER

Reader   Let them tell of God's works with songs of joy.
Psalm 107:22

There may be singing

Reader   The first of English poets, he
who nurtured by the Whitby sea,
a poor and simple cowherd seemed.
Yet here the gold of poetry gleamed,
though hidden deep within his soul;
for from the company he stole,
fearful to be found afraid
when they their entertainment made;
the very least among the throng
with little speech nor any song.
Then in the stillness of one night
his soul was filled with heavenly light:
a vision of the world being made
of God's creation all displayed

as in the stable stall he lay
dreaming, he heard an angel pray
and speak to him of God's great world
and how its majesty unfurled.
Then, day by day, to his inspired mind
that had seemed deaf and dumb and blind
there came sweet words so bright and clear.
Then Mother Hilda came to hear
and stayed with all her abbey folk
while Caedmon, poet of Whitby, spoke.
No longer now to steal away
when came his turn the harp to play,
for in his Saxon mother tongue
were all his splendid verses sung,
and improvised, with great delight,
in many a stormy winter's night
when firelight filled the raftered hall
in far-off ancient Streonshalh.
Then folk would learn the poems by heart
or memorise a favourite part,
making them one with Christian praise
in those remote, unlettered days.

Tom Stamp

Reader I cannot speak,
unless you loose my tongue;
I only stammer,
and I speak uncertainly.
But if you touch my mouth,
my Lord,
then I will sing the story
of your wonders!

Teach me to hear that story
through each person;
to cradle a sense of wonder
in their life;
to honour the hard-earned wisdom
of their sufferings;
to waken their joy
that the King of all kings
stoops down
to wash their feet,
and looking up
into their face
says,
'I know – I understand.'

From Celtic Daily Prayer,
The Northumbria Community

Silent or free prayer, music or singing

All May all that is within me,
and all things I touch,
and all people I meet this day,
give highest glory and praise to you!

CAEDMON EVENING PRAYER

There may be singing

Storyteller

It was in the days when Christianity had only
just come to the pagan English people. Christian
communities had been established by the mission

of Aidan of Lindisfarne, but they were run by educated people. The ordinary, uneducated English folk could not understand the church services and knew very little of the Bible. Many were still not Christians.

At that time, in Abbess Hilda's monastic village at Whitby there was a farm labourer who looked after the cows. He could neither read nor write, and he knew nothing of singing. His name was Caedmon.

In those days the locals gathered for their social evenings in a great, fire-lit barn, where they drank mead, feasted and passed round a musical instrument. Each person took a turn to sing or recite something. It was karaoke without the machinery! Caedmon was there. But he was too shy and untalented, he thought, for such a thing, so he slipped out before his turn, and slept in the stable. As he slept he dreamed a visitor came to him, warm and radiant:

Visitor   Caedmon, sing me something.

Caedmon I can't sing. It was the thought of singing in front of all those people that made me escape to here.

Visitor   Don't worry about them. You do have something to sing about – sing it to me.

Caedmon What should I sing about?

Visitor   Sing about the beginning of created things.

Storyteller

In his dream, poetic lines about God the Creator came into Caedmon's head which he had never heard before, and he sang with all his soul.

We only have a fragment, and that only as it was later translated.

There may be background guitar or harp chords or recorded music

Caedmon Now we ought to praise the Guardian of the
kingdom of heaven;
the might of the Creator,
the originality of his thought;
the glories of his created works;
how God existed eternally;
laid the foundations of the universe;
shaped human beings;
gave them sky as their roof;
and then middle earth to live in.
Lord everlasting.
Almighty God!

Storyteller

Strange to tell, when Caedmon awoke, he could still remember the dream, and the words, and the tune – and he could sing them. Overwhelmed, he told his farm manager. His farm manager was convinced, for it was not long before he told someone in the monastery, who told Abbess Hilda, who asked her Bible teachers to invite Caedmon up to the monastery and teach him stories. After telling him a story, they asked Caedmon to see if he could go back and remember it, and compose a poem and a tune and still remember it the next day, and then sing it aloud back to them. To everyone's amazement, Caedmon could do it, and he did it for a different story day after day. So Hilda invited him to live in the monastery as a lay monk and to pursue this new calling. It wasn't long before Caedmon's songs were sung all over the land.

There may be a time of singing songs, reciting poems or telling stories

Reader   1 Peter 4:5-11

Storyteller

Caedmon used his gift all right, and so should we. I reckon he had a gift of humour as well as of poetry, for this is what the historian Bede writes about his last days on this earth:

First   Caedmon, who lived at Whitby monastery, moved into the house for those who were dying. He and his nurse talked and joked in good spirits with each of the other occupants in turn until after midnight. Caedmon asked if they had the Sacrament in the house. 'Why do you need Holy Communion now?' they asked. 'You are not due to die yet, for you talk with us as cheerfully as if you were in good health.' He died with a smile on his face.   *Bede*

Second   Being cheerful keeps you healthy. It is slow death to be gloomy all the time.   *Echoes Proverbs 17:22*

Third   It is the heart that is not yet sure of God that is afraid to laugh in God's presence.

George Macdonald

There may be singing

Intercession

First   Teach us, good Lord,
        to enjoy the fun of your creation,
        not to take ourselves too seriously,
        and to allow the sense of humour –
        which is your gift to us –
        to bubble over as it should.

Second Help us, Lord, to use the gifts you have given us
        without either fearing or flaunting them,
        but to your glory.

Third   We pray for songsters, poets and all those
        who have gifts in the creative arts.
        May they be used for a renewal of faith
        in our time.

Fourth We pray for those at the bottom of the social pile
        who feel the world has passed them by
        and that they have nothing to offer.
        Show them that this is not true.
        May helping messengers come alongside
        who will draw out the best that is within them.

Fifth   We pray for those who live, work, visit or pray
        at Whitby.

Sixth   We thank you for J. R. Tolkien's *Lord of the Rings*,
        with its stories of Middle Earth,
        and we pray that many may be inspired
        by Caedmon's story
        to catch visions of a better world.

There may be free prayer and singing

Leader   May we go with a song in our hearts,
             God's instruments for a renewed creation.

All   Amen.

CAEDMON NIGHT PRAYER

Leader   It was at night that Caedmon's life was changed.

First   Let us honour Caedmon's memory
             by inviting God to open to us
             the treasures of the dark,
             and to come to us in dreams and visions.

             There may be singing

First   In the darkness our fears well up.
             Things unattended to by day rise to the surface;
             low self-image, rage, self-rejection,
             thwarted aspirations.

Second   And in the darkness God's messages can reach us,
             God's messengers appear to us.

Third   In your light we see light.
             Continue your love to those who know you,
             your righteousness to the upright in heart.

                                            Psalm 36:9, 10

Fourth   In a vision I saw a new heaven and a new earth
             . . . The One seated on the throne said, 'I am
             making all things new! Write this down, for
             these words are trustworthy and true . . . I am
             the Beginning and the End.'

                                  Echoes Revelation 21:1, 5, 6

Leader   Caedmon's true calling was at first unrecognised
by himself or others.
Let us pray for all who have not found their calling.

Pause or spoken prayer

Leader   Caedmon had not connected with his creativity.
Let us pray for all who are out of touch
with their creativity.

Pause or spoken prayer

Leader   Caedmon did not know the Source of truth
and power.
Let us pray for those who are cut off from God.

Pause or spoken prayer

Leader   In the night vision Caedmon's soul sang out.
Let us pray that the music of our souls be released.
Release, O Craftsperson of the universe:

First   The music of speech;

Second   The music of thought;

Third   The music of seeing.

Leader   Release, O Guardian of the human race:

First   The music of craft;

Second   The music of laughter;

Third   The music of healing.

A song such as the following is sung

All sing   Glory to you, my God, this night
for all the blessings of the light.
Keep me, O keep me, King of kings
beneath your own almighty wings.

If in the night I sleepless lie,
my mind with peaceful thoughts supply.

Let dreams from you disturb my rest,
and people by their fruit be blest.

Praise God from whom all blessings flow
in heaven above and earth below.
One God, three Persons, we adore,
we praise you now and evermore.

Words by T. Ken and Ray Simpson

Leader   As we settle down with God
let us place our loved ones in the
Everlasting Arms.

Any may name loved ones

Leader   May they, with Caedmon,
come to your eternal glory.
Now may we go to our rest.

All   In the presence of the Creator's flowing power,
in the presence of the Saviour's suffering joy,
in the presence of the Spirit's beauty of vision.

CREATIVE ACTIVITIES

1. Sing or play recorded songs of Bible episodes.
2. Each person brings a poem, story, song or recording and
   say why they have chosen it.

Chad

2 March

CHAD MORNING PRAYER

Storyteller

'A holy man, modest in his ways, learned in the scriptures, zealous in carrying out their teaching' – that is how the Venerable Bede thought of Chad, whom we remember today.

Reader   Faithful God,
from the first fruits of the English people
who turned to Christ,
you called Chad to holy learning and high service
as a missionary monk and bishop.
May we learn from his humility
and loving discipline
to pattern the ways of Christ in our time.

There may be singing

Reader   Psalm 18:1-19

Storyteller

Chad was a boy when Aidan first came to Lindisfarne in 635. He was English and was born somewhere in Northumbria. He and his three brothers were members of the first group of twelve boys chosen by Aidan when he started his first monastery school.

Reader   1 Samuel 3:1-10

Reader We praise you, O God,
we acclaim you as the Lord.
All creation worships you,
the Father everlasting.
To you all angels, all the powers of heaven,
the cherubim and seraphim, sing in endless praise:

All Holy, holy, holy Lord, God of power and might,
heaven and earth are full of your glory.

Reader The glorious company of apostles praise you.
The noble fellowship of prophets praise you.
The white-robed army of martyrs praise you.

All Throughout the world
the holy Church acclaims you:
Father, of majesty unbounded,
the true and only Son, worthy of all praise,
the Holy Spirit, advocate and guide.

Reader You, Christ, are the King of glory,
the eternal Son of the Father.
When you took our flesh to set us free
you humbly chose the Virgin's womb.
You overcame the sting of death
and opened the kingdom of heaven to all believers.
You are seated at God's right hand in glory.
We believe that you will come and be our judge.

All Come then, Lord, and help your people,
bought with the price of your own blood,
and bring us with your saints
to glory everlasting.

Reader Chad was 'learned in the Scriptures'.

2 Timothy 3:10-17

*A young person comes to the centre and, holding a
Bible, kneels and prays the following prayer*

Young person

Blessed Lord, who has caused all holy scriptures
to be written for our learning,
help us so to read, mark, learn
and inwardly digest them,
that we may embrace and ever hold fast
to your Word
and bring forth everlasting fruit.
Echoes a prayer from The Book of Common Prayer

Storyteller

It seems Chad was the youngest, and the brightest,
for he was sent over to Ireland to do further
studies. At this time many young aspiring English
Christians travelled round the cells of various
great Irish teachers. If necessary, the Irish gave
them free board, tuition and even books, such
was their generosity. At one of these communities
Chad met Egbert, another English teenager. Egbert
told Chad that God had told him that he, Egbert,
was never to return to the English, but was to
spend the rest of his life in Ireland, showing his
love for God by going into exile from all he held
most dear at home, and giving his life to serve
Christ in another people. That he did, and he
lived a very long time. Chad, however, did
return to Northumbria.

Reader   Christ, you are the cry of the poor;
you are the caller at the door;
you are the young who seek to find;

you are the other, before or behind.
Keep the door of our hearts ajar
for the one who knocks from near or afar.

There may be singing

Intercession

Leader Chad developed his talents to the full,
but never confused them with the demands of
his ego.
Teach us, good Lord, the difference
between making the best of ourselves
and selling our souls for false gain.

First Chad was a great student and teacher.
We pray for our schools and places of learning
(_____).

Second Chad showed us that a true leader is a servant;
give us and our leaders a serving spirit
(_____).

Third Chad was a great Church leader.
We pray for the cathedral and diocese of Lichfield*
and for the leadership of our churches
(_____).

There may be singing

Leader May you, like Chad, be
lit by the glory of God;
drawn by the light of God;
warmed by the fire of God.
All Amen.

---

* Chad established his headquarters at Lichfield

CHAD MIDDAY PRAYER

Leader   We come into the presence of the creating Father,
we come into the presence of the workaday Son,
we come into the presence of the renewing Spirit,
into the Love of the Three in One.

There may be singing

Reader   If the Lord does not build the house,
the work of the builders is useless.
If the Lord does not build the city,
it is useless for sentries to stand guard.
It is useless to work so hard for a living,
getting up early and going to bed late.
For the Lord provides for those he loves.

Storyteller

Chad was back home when the news came that his elder brother Cedd, who had founded the monastery at Lastingham, in today's Yorkshire, had died of the plague. He was asked to take his place as abbot. Chad was known as an 'admirable teacher', but he valued practical workers as much as academics. An aristocrat named Owine (pronounced oh-weeny), who had given up a successful worldly career, knocked on the door one day wearing the rough clothes of a peasant and carrying only an axe. He asked to join the monastery, but only to do manual work; he was not interested in books. Chad was more than happy to include him.

Reader   Whatever the work you do, do it for God,
with a sense of responsibility towards those you
work for.   *Echoes Ephesians 6:7*

Do not make distinctions between people.
Echoes James 2:9

Leader As we recall the rhythm of work and prayer
at the community at Lastingham,
the noise of hammer and chisel,
the chanting of psalms,
the study and the cooking,
we pray that you will be with us
in the middle of the day.
Be in our working and our praying.
May all we do and think revolve around you
as the earth revolves around the sun.

Reader As the press of work pauses at noon,
may God's rest be upon us.
As the sun rides high at noon,
may the Sun of Righteousness shine upon us.
As the rain refreshes the stained, stale streets,
may the Spirit bring rain upon our dry ground.

Leader We pray for those who work with their minds.

Silence or free prayer

Leader We pray for those who work with their hands.

Silence, free prayer or singing

The Lord's Prayer may be said

Leader Keep us, O God, in your will.
Inspired by the hard work,
the humble heart and the holy life of Chad,
may we, working or resting, give glory to you.

CHAD EVENING PRAYER

Leader   God of Chad and the willing heart,
All   We come to you this evening,
       ready to do your will.

Leader   As Chad kept his rhythm of prayer, service
       and study,
All   Help us keep in rhythm with you.

There may be singing

Storyteller

Chad would go into the church to pray when he
heard wind or thunder. 'Don't you realise,' Chad
explained, quoting Psalm 18, 'that God sends
wind, lightning and thunder to excite earth's
peoples to fear him, to humble their pride and
make them aware that they will be judged?'

*There may be silence followed by the singing of Kyrie
eleison*

Reader   Psalm 18:7-19

Storyteller

Chad was asked by King Oswy to fill the post of
bishop to the Northumbrians, because the man
who had been made bishop, Wilfred, had gone
to the continent and kept delaying his return.
Chad agreed, and was consecrated by three
British bishops in Wessex. After he had spent
three years as Bishop of the Northumbrians, the
new archbishop, Theodore, sent by the Pope to
standardise English Church practices, explained
that Chad's consecration as bishop had not been

done according to the regulations from Rome. Chad said he had never considered himself worthy of the post anyway, and readily resigned. Such was his humility.

The Song of Christ's Glory

Leader Christ Jesus, though you were in the form of God, you did not cling to equality with God.

All You emptied yourself, taking the form of a servant; you were born in human likeness.

Leader Being found in human form, you humbled yourself and became obedient, even to death on a cross.

All Therefore God has highly exalted you and given you a name above every other name.

Leader That at the name of Jesus every knee should bow in heaven and on earth and under the earth.

All And every tongue confess that Jesus Christ is Lord. To the glory of God the Father. For ever and ever. Amen. *Philippians 2:6-11*

Storyteller

Theodore was so impressed with his humility and other qualities that later he reconsecrated him when a vacancy arose in the huge diocese of Mercia (the English Midlands) and appointed him. Theodore had found out that Chad followed the example of Aidan and walked everywhere. He told him this was such a huge diocese that he must sometimes use a horse and physically lifted him up on a horse with his own hands!

Chad travelled far and wide, to the towns and the remote country areas, to homes and to the centres of influence – he wanted no 'no-go areas' for God in his dioceses. He built up a Christian community in Lincolnshire, probably at Barton, which lived by the Rule taught by Aidan at Lindisfarne. He was busy, but he established a hearth of prayer at the heart of his diocese. He built cells near his headquarters at Lichfield, where a group committed to the daily rhythms of prayer serviced the diocese.

Chad was respected for his disciplined prayer, his simplicity and his vivid sense of awe.

There may be singing

Intercession

Leader	God of the storm, God of the stillness,
All	Of squalls of power and of shimmering calm,
Leader	Into life's troughs and into life's billows
All	Come with the reach of your long right arm.
Leader	Chad of the journey, Chad of the prayer,
All	Of the humble heart and the teaching tales,
Leader	Into life's troughs and into life's billows,
All	You bring God's presence that prevails.
Leader	People of faith, Body of Christ,
All	Joined to the saints, joined to our Source,
Leader	In time of temptation, when tossed about,
All	We take heart from Chad's God, we finish our course.
Reader	Luke 14:7-11
Reader	Chad had great humility – King of kings, Source of all power,

you remind us through your servant Chad
that to clutch at position and power is of no use.
As Chad willingly gave up status,
yet eagerly developed his aptitudes to the full,
so may we study and grow into the fullness
of the calling you have for us,
and be content with its dignity,
gladly eschewing that which is not for us.

Reader   Chad was mindful of his last end in all he did.
Help us to keep always before us, O God,
the fleeting nature of this life,
and the eternal community
for which we are destined.
Knowing this, assist us
so we can banish ill will and misuse
of time and talents,
and run the race you have chosen for us
with our eyes fixed on Jesus from beginning to end.

There may be singing

Leader   Go before us, O Lord, in the ups and downs of life,
that we may walk in the inheritance of the saints
in light.
All   Amen.

CHAD NIGHT PRAYER

Leader   In the name of Chad's God of thunder,
in the name of the Saviour from ill,
in the name of the Spirit of mercy,
in the name of the Three we are still.

Reader   Psalm 77:1-15

Leader   Mighty God, you are stronger than the elements.
All   Mighty God, you are stronger than the storm.
Leader   Mighty God, you are stronger than the tyrants.
All   Mighty God, you are stronger than the tomb.

Storyteller

One day a brother heard sweet singing come from the highest point of the winter sun through the roof of the cell where Chad was praying until it filled it. After half an hour he heard the same joyful sounds return with unspeakable sweetness into the sky. As he was wondering what this could mean, the Bishop came to the window and clapped his hands, as was his custom when he wanted people to come to him. He told Owine to bring all the seven brothers, whom he urged to live in love and peace and to follow the Rule taught by Aidan with unwearying constancy, and to follow the example the spiritual fathers before him had set. Then he told them that 'the amiable guest', meaning the plague, would come for him in seven days. 'Commend me to God and prepare yourselves also to be ready to meet your God at any time,' he told them. Seven days later he did indeed die, and one of the brothers saw Chad's deceased elder brother Cedd coming with angels from heaven to greet him.

Reader   I pray you, good Jesus,
               that as you have given me the grace

to drink in with joy
the Word that gives knowledge of you,
so in your goodness you will grant me
to come at length to yourself,
the source of all wisdom,
to stand before your face for ever.

Bede

Reader Philippians 1:18-21

There may be singing

Leader Chad showed us how even the most painful death
can end in glory;
Let us pray for those who are nearing the end
of their earthly journey.

Silence or free prayer

Leader Awesome Lord of earth and heaven,
rule my heart.
My faith, my love, to you be given,
my every part.   *Early Irish Prayer*

Leader Chad cared for so many,
yet constantly retired alone to pray.
Let us pray for those who are on our hearts.

Silence, free prayer or singing

Leader Each day, each night,
in time, in eternity,
we are in your keeping sure.
All We are in your keeping sure.
Leader When storms rage,
All Guard us sleeping.

Leader	When fears loom large,
All	Guard us sleeping.
Leader	When death draws near,
All	Guard us sleeping.
	Amen.

Cedd

Focal Display Feature

Cedd kneeling in prayer surrounded by boulders, cleansing the land.

> *On St Cedd's days we suggest the St Aidan prayer*
> *patterns are used, incorporating the prayer,*
> *readings and storytelling below.*

Prayer

> Thank you for Cedd,
> who was neither corroded by cynicism
> nor cluttered by ecclesiastical bureaucracy,
> but was straightforward, clear, prayerful, confident:
> through friendship, through gathering others,
> through meditation, through teaching others,
> through prayer, through uplifting others.
> He served you willingly. So may we.

Readings Psalm 52; Isaiah 35; Acts 2:1-12

Storyteller

> Cedd and his three brothers were among the first
> twelve English lads recruited by Aidan for the

school he established at Lindisfarne about 635. They learned to read the Bible and the writings of great Christian teachers in Latin, and memorised the psalms and Gospels. Cedd was a bright pupil, and was sent to Ireland for further education. Soon, he was ordained a priest.

The pagan king of Mercia devolved part of his kingdom to his son Peada, who married a Christian Northumbrian princess, became a Christian himself, and invited Cedd and three other priests to evangelise his region (roughly today's Leicestershire and Northamptonshire). Peada said 'I would accept the Faith even without the girl', so Christianity became real and rooted there.

Northumbria's Christ-like King Oswy was keen to win fellow rulers and their peoples to the faith of Christ. His friend, Sigebert, King of the East Saxons, became a Christian and asked Oswy to send him missionaries, too. So Oswy recalled Cedd to Mercia and sent him and another priest to what is now Essex. His work prospered and he was made a bishop, not to a place, but to a people – the East Saxons. He established faith communities at Mersea, Prittlewell, Upminster, Tilbury and perhaps at White Notley and Chadwell Heath. At Bradwell-on-Sea he used stones from an old Roman Fort to build a chapel for a faith community which drew large numbers of ordinary folk who lived by a rhythm of prayer, work and simplicity of life. The chapel still draws many pilgrims to it.

Cedd had the courage to rebuke the East Saxons' king for a wrong he committed, and prophesied his untimely death. This prophecy was fulfilled. During this mission placement, Cedd met the king of the southern part of Northumbria who wanted a monastery where he could pray while he lived and where he could be buried after his death. Cedd was invited to find a place and build it. He chose a place (now known as Lastingham) in the rugged North Yorkshire moors, and set out to fast and pray over it for the forty days of Lent, thus healing the land of evil influences.

Before his death he was made the translator at the Synod held at Hilda's Whitby monastery in 664. The historian Bede likens his role to that of the Holy Spirit at Pentecost.

Cedd died at Lastingham of the plague. His monks from Bradwell came to pray at his grave, and caught the plague themselves. But a little boy who was with them did not, ascribed this to Cedd's intercession for him, and became an instrument of God. According to Egbert, who had befriended Cedd in Ireland, when Cedd's brother Chad died, Cedd was seen to come from heaven with many angels and take Chad back with him.

Prayers During Pilgrimage to Bradwell, Lastingham or Other Churches Founded by Cedd

Pilgrimage Approaching the Chapel

Approaching this apparently isolated Chapel,
once the heart of a bustling community,
I am aware that here
sky touches ground,
land touches sea,
eternity touches time,
heaven touches earth,
and you, Lord, touch me.
Surrounded by
the birds of the air,
the plants of the ground,
the people of the world,
the fish of the sea,
the angels of heaven,
the saints of history,
and you, Lord,
I bring to you
the Community of Creation
of which I am a part.
Amen.   *A pilgrim*

Pilgrimage Within the Chapel

Lord, my heart becomes still
like this chapel
built so long ago
by your servant Cedd.

Like him, may I learn
trust in your loving care,
zeal in sharing your gospel,
courage in confronting evil,
obedience in living your way,
wisdom in overcoming barriers,
devotion in heartfelt prayer.

Thank you for his founding
of this meeting place with you.
Like him, may I always be ready
to move on,
living my life for you.
Amen.   *A pilgrim*

Ciaran of Clonmacnoise

8 February – founded Clonmacnoise Monastery

6 March – born

6 June – conceived

9 September – died

*Also suitable for gatherings whose theme is soul-friendship,
miracles, spiritual initiative, prophecy or dying*

Ciaran lived from about 512 to 545.

*He was one of the great monastic founders who were called
The Twelve Apostles of Ireland.*

CIARAN MORNING PRAYER
Thanksgiving

Leader	We bless you, O God, for holy Ciaran,
	son of a carpenter,
	who blazed with miracles and virtues
	that lit up the Western Isle.
All	Glory to you, O Lord.
Leader	We bless you for Ciaran, born in Connaught,
	conceived on 6 June, born on 6 March,
	died on 9 September;
	fostered by deacon Justus,
	a student eager to learn.
All	Glory to you, O Lord.
Leader	We bless you for Ciaran the soul-friend,
	tender in friendship, wise in understanding.

All   Glory to you, O Lord.

Leader We bless you for Ciaran the chanter of psalms,
with whom we now chant your praise.

*A psalm may be sung as a hymn, or verses from Psalm
80 may be read alternately by males and females or
by those on the two sides of the meeting place*

Reader Psalm 80:8-18

God's Word

First   It was said that Patrick prophesied of Ciaran –
Brigid and Columba too. The king's Druid said
of him in his mother's womb:
'As the sun shines among the stars of heaven,
so he will shine on earth in miracles and marvels
that cannot be told. Lord, you foretold his birth
by prophets, even as Isaac's birth was foretold to
Abraham.'

The following may be read or told as a story

Reader Genesis 18:1-11

There may be meditation

First   Bec Mac De prophesied of Ciaran:
'There, Lord, is a carpenter's son,
in beautiful vestments,
with your choirs, melodies, chariots and songs.'

Reader Revelation 7:9-17

First   Now let us join with that myriad
whom no one can number,

who worship with their faces bowed to the eternal
throne, singing.

All sing or say

All   Holy, holy, holy is the Lord
who was, and is, and is to come.

There may be teaching, sharing or creative activity

Intercession

First   Ciaran was often too poor to pay for things
such as his tuition fees,
and often he would pray, 'May mercy come to me.'
In the spirit of Ciaran
let us pray for all who are too poor
to have a healthy diet.
May mercy come to them.

All   May mercy come to them.

First   Let us pray for all who cannot afford
the education that is right for them.
May mercy come to them.

All   May mercy come to them.

First   Ciaran even knew slavery for a time,
but never inner defeat.
Let us pray for all who are in slavery,
prisons or refugee camps.
May mercy come to them.

All   May mercy come to them.

First   Ciaran caught the plague and was cut down
in the flower of his life.
Let us pray for all young people who have been
cut down through accident, AIDS or violence.

	May mercy come to them.
All	May mercy come to them.
Second	As a result of prophecy Ciaran was led to found
	the great Christian community of Clonmacnoise.
	Let us pray for the flourishing of vocations
	and Christian witness today.

There may be free prayer and singing

Second	At Clonmacnoise Ciaran said:
	'Many souls will go to heaven from here,
	and in this place there will be communion with
	God and God's people for ever.'

Blessing

Leader	May pilgrims to Clonmacnoise find a blessing
	deeper than they know.
	May many souls go to heaven
	in the place you call us to serve.
	May we be in communion with you,
	with Ciaran and with one another for ever.
All	Amen.

CIARAN MIDDAY PRAYER

Storyteller

Unlike most leaders of the early Irish Church, Ciaran came from a poor family. As a boy he had no honey to bring home as did the other boys, so he prayed, and honey seemed to come from nowhere. Later, when he went to study at a Christian centre, he had no money with which to pay his fees so he took a cow. This produced such an abundance of milk that many students' needs, not just his own, were met.

First   Great Provider, take the little we have,
and help us use it to the full.
Multiply it as once you multiplied
the loaves and fishes donated by a boy.

Second   Jesus said we should give to others
and God will give us such a generous helping
that more than we can hold
will be poured into our hands.   *Luke 6:38*

There may be singing

Storyteller

Once some hooligans set a savage dog upon Ciaran. He recited the following psalm and the dog lay down quietly:

First   Some trust in war chariots
and others in their horses,
but we trust in the power of the Lord our God.

All   We trust in the power of the Lord our God.

First   Such people will stumble and fall,
but we will rise and stand firm.

All   We will rise and stand firm.

Echoes Psalm 20:7, 8

First   Lead us from fear to trust.
All   Lead us from despair to hope.
First   Lead us from hate to love.
All   Lead us from war to peace.

Storyteller

Ciaran learned to bless the ordinary things of life, such as the dye his mother used to make his clothes. His blessings had great effect.

Second

Let us bless the ordinary things
in our working lives.
Generous Father, bless the tools of our trade
and the everyday things we take for granted.

A pause for reflection; any may cite examples

There may be singing, sharing or the Lord's Prayer

First
All

This day, O God, bless to me
Each thing my eye sees,
each thing my hand touches,
each thing my head thinks.

CIARAN EVENING PRAYER

There may be singing

Storyteller

When Ciaran was a boy he wanted to chant the psalms in time with his mentor, but he could not, because he had to work in the fields and had no copy of the psalms. So he befriended a stag which brought the Psalm Book that his mentor attached to its antlers, so that Ciaran could recite the psalms straight after his mentor.

A chanter recites one verse of a psalm and everyone repeats it, verse by verse

Chanter	Psalm 107:1-10 or Psalm 119:1-7
All	*Repeat verse by verse*

Lament

Leader	The following prayer has been attributed to Ciaran:

First	O Saviour of the human race,
	O true physician of every disease,
	O heart-pitier and assister of all misery,
	O fount of true purity and true knowledge,
All	Forgive.

Second	O star-like sun,
	O guiding light,
	O home of the planets,
	O fiery-maned and marvellous one,
All	Forgive.

Third	O holy scholar of holy strength,
	O overflowing, loving, silent one,
	O generous and thunderous giver of gifts,
	O rock-like warrior of a hundred hosts,
All	Forgive.
Leader	Forgive us our sins, O Christ,
	for in your light we see light.

There may be silent reflection or music of lament

Forgiveness of sins may be declared

All may say the Lord's Prayer

There may be singing

God's Word

Storyteller

Ciaran's parents sent him to look after the herds as once Jesse sent his son David.

First   1 Samuel 16:4-13

Storyteller

Ciaran went to study under Finnian of Clonard. One day a boy with a squint came to study but he had no book.

On Finnian's advice the boy asked each student if they would give him one, but none would. Ciaran, however, was reading the following passage from St Matthew's Gospel:

Second   Matthew 7:7-12

Storyteller

'Mercy,' said Ciaran, 'that is why I must be reading the words "Do to others as you wish they would do to you". Have my book.' That is not the end of the story. The following saying spread like wildfire 'Ciaran is called Half-Matthew, but soon half Ireland will be his.' So many people were drawn to Christ through Ciaran's generous spirit that he teaches us, through his example, the truth of Jesus' words: 'The measure you give will be the measure you receive.'

Silence followed by singing

Storyteller

Ciaran decided that, having received the best training in scholarship at Clonard, he now needed to receive the best training in prayer, so he decided to go to the Isle of Aran and be discipled by Enda. Before he left, Finnian prayed this blessing over him:

Reader O Ciaran, O little heart,
for your holiness I love you, dear one.
Grace will come to you, my dear one,
an abundance of dignity and wisdom.

Storyteller

At Aran, Ciaran and Enda, that man of prayer, communed together and God granted that both of them saw the same vision. A great and fruitful tree was growing beside a stream in the middle of Ireland. This tree protected the entire island, its fruit crossed the sea, and birds of the world came to carry off some of the fruit.

Enda told Ciaran that he was the tree. 'All of Ireland will be sheltered by the grace that is in you and many people will be nourished by your fasting and prayers. Go in God's name to the centre of Ireland and establish your community on the banks of a river.'

So, step by step, Ciaran was led to establish the faith community at Clonmacnoise. Despite his early death, Clonmacnoise remained a great community for a thousand years, so significant were the foundations laid by this saint.

All sing a hymn of thanksgiving such as 'Now thank we all our God'

Intercession

First   We place ourselves in your hands, dear God.
Give to us that measure of dignity and wisdom
that you have for us.

Second   Give to us your visions for our lands.
Lead us to the places you wish to make fruitful.

Third   Steep us in the ways of prayer,
and give us generous hearts.

*There may be meditation, free prayer or prophesying,
introduced by the reading of Daniel 4:7-9*

First   Rise up, O Father, by your power flowing
show us vision, beauty and joy.

Males   Rise up, O Saviour, by your love flowing
show us vision, beauty and joy.

Females Rise up, O Spirit, by your grace flowing
show us vision, beauty and joy.

Echoes Church of North India

Storyteller

Let us go in peace to love and serve the Lord.

All   In the name of Christ. Amen.

CIARAN NIGHT PRAYER

Storyteller

Ciaran was the son of Beoit and his mother was
Darerca. Glas the poet was his grandfather. His
four brothers and three sisters were all dedicated
to God. And Ciaran was buried at Clonmacnoise.

All   Blessed are you, dear God, for Ciaran
and all his family.

First   Before we lie down to sleep, let us offer to God
our parents, grandparents, forebears and families.

Pause

Second   Let us forgive the wounds any have inflicted
upon us.

Pause

Third   Let us bless the places where they lived.

Pause

All sing   *The following or another song*

Before the ending of the day,
Creator of the worlds, we pray
in loving mercy ever keep
your watch around us while we sleep.

As night enfolds receding day,
our fantasies and fears allay.
Defend us from the tempter's charm,
your peace protect our souls from harm.

O Triune God, Power, Love and Light,
dwell within us through the night.
Renew our hope and with the day,
unveil the Life, the Truth, the Way.

Echoes an eighth-century, or earlier, song,
with words by Jonathan Robinson

First   You are my light and salvation;
whom, then, shall I fear?

Even if my father and mother abandon me, you will take care of me. *Echoes Psalm 27:1, 10*

Second   Precious in your sight is the death of your saints.
Echoes Psalm 116:15

Storyteller

When Ciaran knew he was dying, he asked to be placed on a mound where he could contemplate the wide, open heavens. 'I shudder at the journey I must take to the life beyond,' he told his friends, 'even though I am not aware of breaking God's commands.'

Ciaran had always used a stone as his pillow, but now they took it from him to give him some comfort. 'Don't take it away altogether,' he said, 'let me feel it under my shoulder.' Then he was carried into the little chapel. He raised his hands and blessed the community he loved so much.

Third   Let us pause and bless our dear ones.
Our dear ones, bless, O Lord,
in every place where they are.

Any may name dear ones

Storyteller

After Ciaran had blessed his people, he asked to be left undisturbed in the chapel to await the arrival of his soul-friend, Kevin, who would accompany him as he journeyed from this life.

All sing Faithful vigil ended,
watching, waiting cease;
Master, grant your servant
his discharge in peace.

All the Spirit promised,
all the Father willed,
now these eyes behold it
perfectly fulfilled.

This your great deliverance
sets your people free;
Christ their light uplifted
all the nations see.

Christ, your people's glory!
Watching, doubting cease;
grant to us your servants
our discharge in peace.

Timothy Dudley-Smith

First   Now let us sleep the deep sleep of peace.
Second Sleep, sleep, and away with sorrow,
sleep in the arms of Jesus.
Sleep, sleep in the lap of God,
sleep in the love of all loves.
Third   May we be numbered with your saints
in glory everlasting.

Storyteller

Now we will lie down in peace.
All   Thanks be to God.

CREATIVE ACTIVITIES

1. Display a poster of Clonmacnoise, or pictures of it downloaded from the Internet.
2. Display a chart of some Christian communities today.

Columba

9 June

*Suitable for occasions where the theme is angels (evening prayer),
forgiveness, justice, penitence, prophecy, or nation-building*

COLUMBA MORNING PRAYER

Storyteller

Columba (521–597) was born into one of the
great families of sixth-century northern Ireland.

A brilliant organiser, poet, song-writer and
prophet, he developed the tender simplicity of his
Master; became the leader of a network of monasteries and a strategist for the kingdom of God.

Baptised as Crimthan (the wolf), he entered a
monastery and was given the name Colum (the
dove). After training at Moville monastery, he
transferred to Finnian's famed Clonard monastery,
where he was ordained a priest. He spent some
fifteen years establishing up to three hundred
churches and monasteries throughout his home
region, including Derry – which fed a thousand
visitors a day – and Durrow.

After Columba had secretly copied a beauti-
fully inscribed book of psalms at Clonard, Finnian
took him to the court of Tara's King Diarmait,
whose famous verdict was 'To every cow belongs
her calf'. A slaughter took place in a clan war
that followed. Legend suggests that Columba's
penance for illegally copying the book was to

exile himself from his beloved homeland.* So he sailed to Iona, which his relative Conall, a ruler in Argyll, gave him, and he founded the famous monastery there.

Much of the Highlands of Scotland was evangelised. Brude, a Pictish chief, whose dead child Columba raised to life, was converted. As a result, the Faith spread wider still. Daughter monastic houses were founded. Columba wrote many poems and songs, and his singing could be heard from afar.

In 597, Columba circled and prophesied over Iona before he died and predicted it would return to a mere grazing place, but that one day it would be restored. This is being fulfilled in our time. After Columba's death, Aidan, inspired by Columba's life and discipline, took a mission from Iona south to Lindisfarne, which was to have immeasurable influence in England.

Leader   Let the islands sing God's praise.
                                    From Isaiah 42:12

All   Alleluia!

God's praises may be sung

Reader   Psalm 34:1-14

The following may be sung, or said

---

* It was said that three thousand died in a tribal battle between the tribe of Finnian and the tribe of Columba, and some conclude that Columba's act in 'stealing' the copyright contributed in some way to this. According to a later *Life*, Columba's soul-friend told him to make penance by going into exile – hence his going to Iona.

Leader	O God, you are the Father of all who have believed: from whom all hosts of angels have life and power received.
All	O God, you are the Maker of all created things: the righteous Judge of judges, almighty King of kings.

Leader	High in the heavenly city you reign as God adored: And in the coming glory you shall be sovereign Lord.
All	You shine beyond our knowing, the everlasting Light: unfaltering in loving, immeasurable in might.
Leader	To humble and to poor ones your secrets you unfold: it's you who brings forth all things, all things both new and old.
All	I walk secure and fruitful in every coast or clime: in name of Father, Saviour, and holy Dove sublime.

After Columba

Lament

Reader   Lamentations 3:19-33

A Litany of Turning the Back

Storyteller

Columba turned his back on his beloved Ireland to show he repented for his part in violence to the land, and to win as many converts to Christ's kingdom in a new land as had perished in war in his own. He wrote:

How swift is the speed of my coracle,
its stern turned to Derry.
I grieve at the errand o'er the noble sea,
travelling to Alba of the ravens.
My foot in my good little coracle,
my sad heart still bleeding . . .

In the spirit of Columba we pray:

All   O, that I might turn my back, Lord,
on ill-will, envy and hate;
that I might leave behind regrets and bitter traits.
That I might turn my back, Lord,
on possessiveness and greed;
that I might leave behind
my headstrong foolish ways.
That I might turn my back, Lord,
on misuse of earth and souls;
that I might leave behind my heedless, selfish
days.

Leader   O Christ, hanged on a tree
yet risen in the morning,
scatter the sin from our souls
as the mist from the hills;
begin what we do, inform what we say
and redeem who we are.

All   In you we place our hope, today and for ever.

God's Word

Reader   1 Corinthians 14:1-8

Reader	O, that I might see the ocean's heaving waves
	chanting music to their Father,
	that contrition might come upon my heart,
	that I might bless the Lord who conserves
	all heaven, with its countless bright orders,
	and land, strand and flood.
	That I might search books
	that are good for my soul,
	at times kneeling to beloved Heaven
	and at times singing psalms;
	at times serving the poor
	and at times contemplating the King of heaven,
	the Holy One. *Columba*

All	Holy God, holy and mighty,
	with blest Columba, the saints, angels
	and all creation we chant your praises
	and give you glory through the ages. Amen.

There may be storytelling, creative activity or singing

Intercession

Leader	Lord, Columba's voice echoed across the Isles.
All	May the voice of your servants sound clear
	above the clamour of our times.
Leader	Columba converted new peoples and their leaders.
All	We pray for the conversion of people groups
	and opinion-formers today.
Leader	He established communities of love and learning.
All	Restore community and truth to our places
	of learning.

Leader	He extolled hard physical labour.
All	Bless all who do manual work today.
Leader	Columba rejoiced in creation.
All	Restore joy in creation to our distracted people.
Leader	Columba was angry at injustice.
All	Strengthen us to stand for fairness in our society.
Leader	Prophecy, purity and poetry flourished in his life.
All	Bring these and other virtues to flower in your church.
Leader	Columba's departing to the heavenly country was glorious.
All	Grant us a quiet and glorious end.

Leader	Circle us, Lord.
All	Keep fear without, keep joy within. Keep complaining out, keep peace within. Keep despair without, keep beauty within. Keep deceit without, keep mercy within.

Leader	Circle these whom we now name. *Any may mention names aloud or silently*
	There may be singing

Leader	Dearest Lord, be a bright flame before us, a guiding star above us, a smooth path beneath us, a kindly shepherd behind us.

Columba Midday Prayer

Leader   If I spread out my wings towards the morning
or dwell in the faraway parts of the sea,
even there your hand shall lead and hold me.

Echoes Psalm 139:8, 9

All   Alleluia!

Leader   All seeing God, cleanse our sight
that we may discern your presence in your creation,
your people and your Word.
Give us courage, like Columba,
to let our lives be shaped by holy vision,
that others may come to see you in your glory.

There may be silence

Reader   Let me bless almighty God,
whose power extends over sea and land,
and whose angels watch over all.
Let me study sacred books to calm my soul.
I pray for peace, kneeling at heaven's gates.
Let me do my daily work, gathering seaweed,
catching fish, giving food to the poor.
Let me say my daily prayers,
sometimes chanting, sometimes quiet,
always thanking God.
Delightful it is to live on a peaceful isle,
in a quiet cell, serving the King of kings.

Attributed to St Columba

Leader   Lord, my circumstances are so different,
yet your power extends to here, where I am.
Your angels watch over me.

Fill my mind; grant me peace.
Help me do my daily work, to say my prayers,
whether in bustle or stillness.
May it be my delight to serve you as King
of this day.

Reader Jesus said:
'Forgive others, and you will receive forgiveness.'
Columba taught:
'Forgiveness from the heart towards everyone.'
In the middle of this day
we forgive all who have caused us harm,
and pray for those who need our prayers.

Free or silent prayer

Leader The following prayer,
which Columba prayed for a boy,
we now pray for ourselves:

All May we grow, little by little, day by day,
in goodness and greatness of spirit.
May wisdom, discernment and eloquence
increase in us
that we may serve our communities well.

Reader Confer your greatness on me,
share with me your Spirit,
grace me with such a splendour of mind
that I may rejoice in another's good,
and in this find true joy.

Leader Give us a desire to see others reach their greatness,
give us a word to help another grow.
May petty ways drop from us like scales.
Step by step you lead us.

Feed and renovate us
till we are glad to be givers;
till we rejoice in being brothers;
till we delight in being sisters;
till heaven laughs in delight
at our pleasure in each other.

All Your kingdom come, your will be done,
on earth as it is in heaven.

There may be singing

Leader May we be an island in the sea,
a hill in the valley,
a light in the dark.

All Amen.

COLUMBA EVENING PRAYER

Leader In the name of the sending Father,
in the name of the Son of the call,
in the name of the Dove descending,
in the name of the One in All.

There may be singing

Reader Psalm 18:32-35, 48, 50

Leader Lord, you are my island.
All In your bosom I nest.
Leader You are the calm of the sea.
All In that peace I rest.
Leader You are the waves on the glistening stones.
All Their sound is my hymn.

Leader	You are the song of the birds.
All	Their tune I sing.
Leader	You are the sea breaking on rock.
All	I praise you with the swell.
Leader	You are the ocean that laps my being.
All	In you I dwell.

or

Reader God created good angels and archangels,
the orders of Principalities and Thrones,
of Powers and Virtues,
so that the goodness and majesty of the Trinity
might not be unproductive in all works of bounty,
but might have heavenly beings in which he might
greatly show forth his favours by a word of power.

All Holy, holy, holy is the One who crafts the heavens.

Reader From the summit of the kingdom of heaven,
where angels stand,
from God's radiant brightness,
from the loneliness of his own form
through being proud Lucifer had fallen, whom
he had formed
and the apostate angels also, by the same sad fall
of the author of vain glory and obstinate envy,
the rest continuing in their dominions.

All Holy, holy, holy is the One who crafts the heavens.

Reader At once, when the stars were made,
lights of the firmament,
the angels praised for his wonderful creating
the Lord of this immense mass,
the Craftsman of the heavens,

	with a praiseworthy proclamation,
	fitting and unchanging
	in an excellent symphony,
	they gave thanks to the Lord
	not by any endowment of nature,
	but out of love and choice.
All	Holy, holy, holy is the One who crafts the heavens.

Altus Prosator, attributed to Columba

There may be singing

Reader Joel 2:28-32

Storyteller

One day, Columba asked God for three gifts.

Reader Purity, wisdom and prophecy.

All These gifts, O High King, grant to me.

Reader The lamp of the body is purity,

All And those who have it their God shall see.

Reader Your wisdom bestow as a light for the mind,

All That we may grow compassionate, kind.

Reader The gift of the soul is prophecy.

All Enlarge our vision that we may see.

Reader Luke 9:51-56

There may be silence, teaching, storytelling, sharing or singing

Leader We pray for Scotland to find her well-being in Christ,

to rejoice in her Christian roots,

to release her enemies from judgement,

to become a nation led by God,

a shining mission place among the nations.

Lord, may each of our lands
find their peace and their destiny in your will.
Give us that dynamic which calls out and combines
the moral and spiritual responsibility
of individuals for their immediate sphere of action.
We pray for an uprising of people
who give leadership free from the bondage of fear,
sorry for the blindness of the past,
rising above ambition,
flexible to the direction of your Spirit,
reaching out with generous hearts
to neighbouring peoples.
We pray to you for Iona . . . for Lindisfarne . . .
for faith communities in Columba's Ireland.

There may be free prayer and singing

Leader   May the peace of Columba be yours
in the smooth and in the rough;
may the big-heart of Columba be yours
in your going and returning;
may the God of Columba shield you
wherever you are.

COLUMBA NIGHT PRAYER

Storyteller

On that night when St Columba, by a happy
and blessed death passed from earth to heaven,
while I and others with me were fishing in the
valley of the river Find, we saw the whole vault
of heaven become suddenly illuminated. Towards

the east there appeared something like an immense
pillar of fire, which seemed to illuminate the whole
earth like the summer sun at noon. After that the
column penetrated the heavens, darkness followed,
as if the sun had just set. *Adamnan*

Leader	The sun is setting on the day.
All	Be with us as the sun sets on the day.
Leader	The sun is setting on a life.
All	Be with us as the sun sets on our lives.

Reader O helper of those who toil
and ruler of those who do good,
protect those who are faithful.
Raise up the lowly and cast down the mighty.
Pure life-source of all who live,
Light-giver and Father of lights,
you shine with eternal light.
You do not deny us the strength we need
as we row trembling through the storms of this age.
Christ draw us after you
to the beautiful haven of endless life.
From the envy of foes lead us to the joy of paradise
that we may hymn you for ever you, O Christ,
who lives and reigns for ever. *After Columba*

There may be singing

Reader Psalm 103:1, 2

Reader My dear children, love one another,
let us love one another,
because love comes from God. *1 John 4:7a*

Leader   Our dear ones bless, O God,
and keep, in every place where they are.
These we name before you now:

Any may mention names

There may be free prayer, sharing or singing

Storyteller

These are Columba's last words: Have heartfelt
love among yourselves. If you thus follow the
example of the holy fathers, God, the comforter
of the good, will be your helper. And I, abiding
with him, will intercede for you, and he will not
only give you sufficient to supply the needs of
this present life, but will also give you the good
and eternal rewards which are laid up for those
who keep his commandments.   *Columba*

All   Kindle in us, O God,
the flame of that love which never ceases,
that it may burn in us, giving light to others.
May that light, which shone so brightly
in Columba,
take away the darkness of our hearts,
and bring us to share with him
the light of the eternal city.

Leader   O Christ,
who at this evening hour rested in the tomb
and made it become a bed of hope,
visit this house tonight
that we may pass through the death of sleep
and rise from our beds in hope of life eternal.

All   The Lord give us a peaceful night and a good end.

All sing or say

Alone with none but you, my God,
I journey on my way.
What need I fear, when you are near,
O King of night and day?
More safe am I within your hand
than if a host did round me stand.

My life I yield to your command,
and bow to your control
in peaceful calm, for from your arm
no power can snatch my soul.
Could earthly foes ever appal
a soul that heeds the heavenly call?

(Attributed to Columba)

Leader   Inspire us with your love, O Lord,
that our loving quest for you
may occupy our thoughts;
that your love may take complete possession
of our being.   *Columba*

There may be singing

Leader   May the seven angels of the Holy Spirit
and the two guardian angels
shield us this and every night
till light and dawn shall come.

Carmina Gadelica

All   The peace of Columba be ours in our sleeping
and rising.

Columbanus

21 November outside Ireland

23 November in Ireland

*Suitable for gatherings where the theme is study,
discipline, perseverance or outreach*

COLUMBANUS MORNING PRAYER

Leader 'Let us live by this principle,' says Columbanus, 'that we live as travellers on the road, as pilgrims, as guests of the world singing with grace and power: "When shall I come and appear before the face of my God?"'

There may be singing

Storyteller

In Leinster, about the year 540, Columbanus was born of noble parents. No doubt he learned archery, swimming, riding, and the use of sword and spear. Long were the hours and even days he spent in forest or on farm, learning to catch and cook his own food. It was surely his outdoor training, not his tunics of silk, or Latin learning, that would give him marvellous powers of endurance through a long life of travelling. At the age of ten he had learned the psalms by heart, and to God his life was given.

Time passed, until one day he informed his mother that he must leave home and seek schooling in the adult life of faith, far away on the island of Lough Erne from the saintly Senell. (No doubt Senell was of their clan, and certainly he was one of the Twelve Apostles of Ireland.) There he must certainly go.

Not so, said his mother, who put every obstacle in his way. On the day of his departure she threw herself across the doorway to block his path. With quiet courage the lad stepped over her pleading body. He was to travel the world for God. He would never see her again.

First   O God, as you were there at our beginning,
so you will be at our departing,
and every step of our way.

All   Amen.

There may be singing or music

Reader   Psalm 139:1-10

Storyteller

For six years Columbanus studied in Senell's famed school of scriptures. 'His fine figure, his splendid colour and his noble manliness made him loved by all,' said Jonas, his young biographer. There he wrote a commentary on the psalms he knew so well, and other works, too. But he outgrew the school. A longing grew to join the larger and most learned community at Bangor, under the truly challenging rule of a fellow Pict, Comgall.

Arriving at Bangor, in the north of his land, in about 558, our saint met in Comgall a former soldier who was a soldier still, for Christ; a leader who taught obedience and loyalty to the Great Commander in the struggle against evil. Comgall also taught his monks a love of the land and how to see God's hand in what he has created. Columbanus learned this lesson well, and for the rest of his life he would teach that if you wish to know the Creator, you must get to know the creation.

Reader   Romans 1:18-20

There may be singing or the following proclamation

First   Earth and sun, bless the Lord.
               Winds and rain, bless the Lord.
All   To God be highest praise for ever.
Second   Cold and heat, bless the Lord.
               Crops and cattle, bless the Lord.
All   To God be highest praise for ever.
First   All that grows, bless the Lord.
               All that swims, bless the Lord.
All   To God be highest praise for ever.
Second   All birds that fly, bless the Lord.
               All folk on earth, bless the Lord
All   To God be highest praise for ever.

There may be teaching, creative activity or storytelling as follows

Storyteller

Columbanus was so happy in his calling, with its increasing responsibilities, that he stayed there full thirty years. It is said he was put in charge of the teaching. But those monks lived what they learned. They fought the spiritual war. At times multitudes of demons were seen attacking the outer walls of the monastic village. But the Christians in their cells kept them at bay by a constant barrage of praise and prayer and song.

Comgall, it was said, kindled in peoples' hearts the unquenchable fire of the love of God. Fire cannot be contained, and the fire in Columbanus' heart blazed to reach out to peoples far away. Twice he asked permission to leave Bangor, this vale of angels, and to go to war-torn lands of turmoil. Twice he was refused. But in the end, Comgall agreed that Columbanus could go to the heathen of Europe with the fire of Christ's gospel. He ventured out at fifty years of age, at a time of life when most men prepared to ride into the twilight.

Leader   A prayer of Columbanus:

May we know no other love
except you who are eternal;
a love so great that the many waters of sky,
land and sea will fail to quench it.

Silent or free prayer and singing

Leader   O loving Saviour, reveal yourself to us
so that knowing you we may love you;
loving you we may desire you;
desiring you we may contemplate you –
you alone, by day and by night –
and ever hold you in our thoughts.

Columbanus

COLUMBANUS MIDDAY PRAYER

Storyteller

Our veteran adventurer for Christ sailed down to the south-west coast of Britain, staying for a time in settlements in Cornwall, and then on to Brittany. In both those regions are places to which he gives his name. Columbanus and his team enlisted Breton recruits and ventured into the lands of Gaul ravaged by the pagan Franks. Anarchy, crime and murder ruled. Yet one ruler, Guntrum, seeking expiation for his crimes, gave a home to these godly men. In the Vosges mountains, with Columbanus striding forward with a cross in one hand, a bell in the other, Gall and others chanting psalms behind him, they made a godly home among the wild beasts. At Annegray, these hungry people cleared the ground. They prayed and, just in time, good folk came, perhaps drawn by their singing of God's praise, and brought them food. Soon it became a valley fertile in food for body and soul. Gall made a dictionary – the first for that people. Sick people thronged there. At first Columbanus was not pleased at their intrusion, but soon the penny dropped. He prayed for them and some were healed. So great was the love and patience of these white-robed believers no one could doubt that God was with them. Soon there was a second settlement, at Luxeuil, eight miles away, and then a third.

First   Dear God, they had it hard, but then, so at times do we.

You met their needs
when they were in direst straits.
We are needy, too, though in different ways.
Come to us and help us, we humbly beseech you.

Pause

Second   When sick folk made demands
that seemed unreasonable,
they simply did what you commanded:
they prayed for them that they might be healed.
We bring to you
the people we find demanding,
intrusive, sick. Transform them
and make them whole.

Pause

Third   You, God, made their places fertile,
and multiplied them.
We offer you our places, programmes and projects.
Make them fertile, and multiply them.

Pause

Fourth   Do not consider what you are but what you will be.
What you are lasts for a mere moment;
what you will be is eternal.
Do not be lazy, but acquire in a short time
what you will possess for ever.
Overcome the dislike of exerting yourself now
by thinking of the reward to come.
Why do you chase after vain things?
Remember, life's joys disappear like a dream
in the night.
So wake up.

Columbanus

All	Teach us to serve you as you deserve;
	to work hard, but not to overwork;
	not to put off until tomorrow
	what should be done today;
	to do our work for you, with love in our hearts.
Fifth	Obey your seniors, keep up with your juniors,
	equal your equals, emulate the perfect.
	Don't envy your betters,
	or grieve at those who surpass you,
	or censure those who fall behind,
	but agree with those who urge you on.
	Though weary, don't give up.
	Weep and rejoice at the same time
	out of zeal and hope.
	Advance with determination,
	but always fear for the end.

Columbanus in a letter to a young disciple

Silent reflection or free prayer and singing

Leader	Now, Lord, as Columbanus taught us,
	help us to be up and doing,
	slack to take revenge, careful in word,
	eager in work.
All	In the name of Christ, Amen.

COLUMBANUS EVENING PRAYER

Leader	Listen to these words of Columbanus:
	Jesus has gathered us, is gathering us,
	and will gather us out of all regions, till he should
	make resurrection of our hearts from the earth,

and teach us that we are all of one substance,
and members of one another.

Columbanus's letter to Boniface IV in 613

There may be singing

Reader   Isaiah 30:19-21

Storyteller

Many were the demands on our heroic God-follower. He had to provide guidelines for those who were soul-friends, that they might offer good medicine for the soul. He had to draw up a rule of life, drawing on that of Comgall, but which addressed many problems unheard of in Bangor. He sought out a remote cave in the depths of the forest in order to seek God, and found a wild bear there. He ordered the bear to leave and not to return; nor did it.

And so a rule was formed:

Reader   If we all weigh our actions in the just balance
of true discernment
we shall not be hijacked into crooked ways.
If we walk by the divine light
we shall not go astray either to the right
or to the left
but we shall always keep on the straight way,
chanting with the conquering psalmist,
'O my God, light up my darkness,
for through you I shall be delivered
from temptation.'   *The Rule of Columbanus*

Reader   Psalm 18:25-31

There may be singing

Storyteller

Listen to the words of Columbanus:

Loving Saviour, show yourself to us who seek you, that knowing you we may love you as warmly in return, may love you alone, desire you alone, and contemplate you alone by day and night and keep you always in our thoughts. May affection for you pervade us. May attachment to you possess us. May love of you fill all our senses. May we know no other love except you who are eternal, a love so great that not all the waters of heaven and earth will be able to quench it.

Reader   1 John 4:16-21

There may be singing, teaching, creative activity or storytelling as follows

Storyteller

Young people came to be discipled by Columbanus. Sometimes they left the monasteries and stayed several days with him at the cave. They learned from the way he prophesied when they brought their problems to him; they learned from the way the wild animals played with him and were influenced by his prayers.

When Guntrum died, his nephew, Childebert, inherited two kingdoms, and brought trouble to Columbanus. In sorrow, the monks left Luxeuil and prayed, 'Creator of the world, prepare for us a place where your servants may worship you.' Across France they journeyed, from Bescançon to Nantes, and marvellous were the miracles God worked on their sad way. On the road from Auxerre, a youth, who seemed possessed by a demon, ran twenty miles to catch them up and seek their help. As they camped by the riverside at Orleans, hungry, since the king had forbidden the locals to feed them, a Syrian woman with her blind husband brought them food, and Columbanus laid his hands on the man's eyes, and prayed until his sight began to return. At Tours the guards refused them entrance to St Martin's tomb, but God turned things round and Columbanus spent a whole night in prayer with Martin. Hungry, thirsty, persecuted, on and on they went.

Reader   Hebrews 11:32-38

Storyteller

Wherever they stopped, they prophesied to leaders of State and Church and God worked through them. At Nantes, God used the raging of the sea to stop their boat sailing and to convince the people of the town this godly company must be allowed to stay there awhile, and so its king, Chlotair, welcomed them as a gift from heaven. But Columbanus knew this was not their place of resurrection – the place that would crown their life's calling, where they would be buried and one day resurrected – so once more they travelled until they reached the river Rhine. Rowing hard against the tide, with little food, this is what our intrepid warriors sang:

Male	The tempests howl, the storms dismay,
	but manly strength can win the day.
All	Heave, lads, and let the echoes ring.
Male	For clouds and squalls will soon pass on,
	and victory lie with work well done.
All	Heave, lads, and let the echoes ring.
Male	Hold fast! Survive! And all is well,
	God sent you worse, he'll calm this swell.
All	Heave, lads, and let the echoes ring.
Male	So Satan acts to tire the brain,
	and by temptation souls are slain.
All	Think, lads, of Christ, and echo him.
Male	The king of virtues vowed a prize,
	for him who wins, for him who tries.
	Think, lads, of Christ, and echo him.

There may be music

Intercession

Reader	In the steep common path of our calling –
	whether it be easy or uneasy to our flesh,
	whether it be bright or dark for us to follow –
	may your own perfect guidance be given us.
	Be a shield to us from the ploys of the deceiver,
	and in each hidden thought
	our minds start to weave.
	Be our director and our canvas.
	Even though dogs and thieves try to wrench us
	away from the fold,
	be our Shepherd of glory near us.
	Whatever matter, issue or problem
	threatens to bring us to grief,

hide it from our eyes
and drive it from our hearts for ever.

Carmina Gadelica

There may be free prayer and singing

Reader   Thrice Holy God, eternal Three in One,
All   Make your people holy, make your people one.

Reader   Stir up in us the flame
            that burns out pride and power.
All   Restore in us the love that brings the servant heart
            to flower.
Reader   Thrice Holy God, come as the morning dew.
All   Inflame in us your love which draws all lesser
            loves to you.
Leader   Give us, Lord, the love that does not fail;
            renew in us the flame that burns for ever.
            As we continually gaze on you,
            the Perpetual Light,
            may we shine before you,
            scattering this world's darkness,
            giving light to others.

COLUMBANUS NIGHT PRAYER

A candle is lit with these words

First   I light this candle in memory of Columbanus,
           whose light burned so long and faithfully across
           Europe, and glows still among us
           with all the holy and risen ones.

Second	Christ is the true Light,
	eternal and uncreated,
	from whom we all receive our lesser light.
All	Glory to God for ever.

There may be singing

Storyteller

Columbanus was frail. His struggling company, with his colleague Gall increasingly in charge, made a settlement among Teuton immigrants on the shore of Lake Zurich. There, many turned to Christ. But others, angry at Gall's smashing of their idols, forced them out, and so on they trekked to Bregenz, where they also established the faith anew. They stayed until its rule fell into hostile hands. Invited by Lombardy's king to make a home among his people, Columbanus, old and ill, leaving Gall behind, crossed the perilous Alps.

In this new land he found the faithful torn by heresy, not comprehending the fullness and wonder of Christ. 'Christ is fully divine and fully human,' taught Columbanus, expounding the scriptures to teach the truth held by the universal Church. He found, to his horror, the very citadel of the Church riven by faction and hunger for power. He wrote God-inspired letters to the spiritual father of Rome, whom he addressed as 'the most beautiful head of all the churches in Europe.'

Reader   Psalm 133

Leader	Let us pray for the unity of the Church.
	Lord Jesus Christ, truly human, truly God,
	you unite in yourself humanity and God;
	you prayed for the unity of all who believe.
	May your churches,
	rejoicing in the unity of heaven,
	attain communion around one table.
	Nurture the people through your Church.

Leader	Through her pastors
All	Nourish us.
Leader	Through her teachers
All	Establish us.
Leader	Through her prophets
All	Envision us.
Leader	Through her saints
All	Sanctify us.

There may be silence, free prayer or singing

Storyteller

The Pope sent no answer, and the aged Columbanus sought a final mountain refuge where he and his faithful company might dwell in peace with God and the world. In the lush mountain valley of Bobbio were the remains of an earlier Christian community. There these blessed monks made their home, restoring the ruins, moving great logs with which to build their huts. From this retreat Columbanus could look back on six walled cities, sustained by faith, which he had helped to build. Surely it was no accident that, many years later, young Francis of Assisi would be drawn to Bobbio, to pray in its chapel dedicated to Columbanus who spoke to animals as to God's friends. Was it there that Francis learned to pray, with his arms stretched out, cross-shaped, like the Celtic saints? Was it there that he decided to clothe his friars as Columbanus' monks were clad, to place wooden crosses, like theirs, at the entrance to their friaries, to call his brothers, as did Columbanus, soldiers of Christ? Did Francis there find in Columbanus a soul-friend after his own heart? Is that why his biographer Jonas could write, in his final glimpse of Columbanus: 'His remains are buried there, where they have proved their virtues by the help of Christ'?

Leader   How many, O Christ,
are the virtues of Columbanus.
By your help, may they be proved in us.
You who are our Perpetual Light,
kindle the flames in our hearts,
that they may continually blaze,
always receiving light from you,
always giving light to others,
scattering the darkness of the world.

Echoes a prayer of Columbanus

First   Columbanus urged:
Let us be careful that no image except that of God take shape in the soul.

Leader   Teach us to contemplate you alone,
by day and by night.

Pause

Second	Columbanus, quoting St James, taught:
	Be slow to anger, quick to learn, slow to speak,
	and quick to listen.
Leader	Tonight, Lord,
	let not the sun go down upon our anger.
	We give to you any anger that clings stubbornly
	to us.

Pause

Leader	As Columbanus could look back on so much
	achieved, so many helped,
	so let us look back on this day and on our lives.
	We thank you for all that has been of you.
	We ask your forgiveness
	for all that has not been of you.
First	Support us, Lord,
	all the day long of this troubled life
	until the shadows lengthen and evening comes,
	the busy world is hushed,
	and the fever of life is over.
	Then, Lord, in your mercy
	grant us a safe lodging, a holy rest,
	and peace at the last.
Leader	We place into your hands those for whom you
	wish us to pray.

Any may name people or places in silence or aloud

There may be singing

Leader	On these your dear ones, Lord,
All	May your love descend this night.
Leader	On your Church, Lord,

All	May your love descend this night.
Leader	On your saints, Lord,
All	May your love descend this night.
Leader	On we who sleep, Lord,
All	May your love descend this night.
Leader	May your lives be like a flame that burns through darkest hours, warming and lighting all who come in from the cold.

CREATIVE ACTIVITIES

1. Meditate on what it might mean for you to cut the apron strings and move on, as Columbanus moved on from his mother.

Cuthbert

20 March

*4 September – his remains were placed in a shrine
and the Lindisfarne Gospels, dedicated to God and
St Cuthbert, were unveiled.*

*Also suitable for gatherings where the theme might be
athletes of the Spirit, providence, unity or healing.*

*Some Church denominations transfer St Cuthbert's Day from
20 March to 4 September in order to remove the celebration
from Lent. However, there is much in Cuthbert's life which
helps us to keep Lent with deep meaning, and we commend
the commemoration of his life during Lent.*

CUTHBERT MORNING PRAYER

Storyteller

As a boy, Cuthbert was schooled by Kenswith, one of the first nuns in Northumbria. He was both strong and spiritual, and was a natural leader throughout his life. Once he was with some shepherds on the Lammermuir hills when he saw a vision of a holy person being taken to heaven in a trail of light. Next day he learned that Aidan, the much-loved leader of the Christian mission based at Lindisfarne, had died. This had a great effect upon him and he offered himself for life-service at Melrose monastery, under its prophetic abbot, Boisil. Here Cuthbert excelled in work, prayer, study and outreach. He visited every village and hamlet, however inaccessible, by foot, horse or boat, to explain the Christian faith to people and to bring them to deep and heartfelt conversion. He prepared for this ministry by night-long vigils of prayer and praise, sometimes immersed in the sea throughout!

Leader	Holy God of Cuthbert and the saints
All	You are present with us now.
Leader	God of the hills, God of the outposts
All	You are present with us now.
Leader	God of the streets, God of the people
All	You are present with us now.

There may be singing

Reader	I lift up my eyes to the hills – from where does my help come? My help comes from the Lord, the Maker of heaven and earth.
All	He will not let you stumble – he who watches over you will not sleep.
Reader	The protector of God's people never slumbers or sleeps.
All	The Lord will guard you; he is by your side to protect you. The sun will not hurt you by day, nor the moon by night. The Lord will protect you from all danger; he will keep you safe. He will protect you as you come and go, now and for ever.

Adapted from Psalm 121

Any of these passages may be read

Reader   1 Samuel 3:1-10

My Heart's Desire

Reader   My heart's desire is to serve the King
           to heed his call in everything.
All   My heart's desire is to touch his cloak
           to release his power in ordinary folk.
Reader   My heart's desire is to storm heaven's gate
           till demons flee and storms abate.
All   My heart's desire is that sick are cured
           and that hostile mockers praise the Lord.
Reader   My heart's desire is that Christians are one
           in a church in peace and communion.
All   My heart's desire is to reach the throne
           where God reigns in glory with his own.

Reader   2 Timothy 2:1-10

Storyteller

           Cuthbert was invited to become the steward of
           Ripon monastery, where he excelled in giving
           hospitality. When travellers arrived cold, tired
           and hungry, he would wash and warm their feet,
           and bring them food. Once he was convinced
           that he had entertained an angel without realising
           it, for a visitor suddenly left before eating the meal
           and left no footprints in the snow.

           Cuthbert returned to Melrose where he
           succumbed to the plague, but on learning that
           his monks had prayed for him all night he rose
           from his sick-bed. He recovered, though he
           limped for the rest of his life, and he ministered

to survivors in the plague-ridden villages. On Boisil's death Cuthbert became prior. They spent the last week of Boisil's life studying their beloved John's Gospel together.

Reader   John 10:11-18

There may be silence, teaching, creative arts, sharing, singing

Intercession

Storyteller

When Cuthbert was a boy an infant told him God would call him to be a priest in the Church. Cuthbert grew to have a care for the Church and guarded its unity, its children and its heart for mission. Let us have a time of prayer for the Church and its mission.

First   Let us pray for the children in our homes, churches and neighbourhoods.
May they be introduced to the Holy Spirit, attracted by holy lives,
and respond to divine callings.

Second   From being a winning athlete
Cuthbert became an athlete of the spirit:
Let us pray for Christians in sport,
for all sports people,
that they may see their training as a step towards the eternal race.

Third   Cuthbert never flagged in his faith-sharing, love-sharing journeys to the unreached:

Let us pray for those for whom the Church seems
inaccessible,
that church people may reach out to them
with infectious enthusiasm.

Fourth   Cuthbert warned against schism
and jealously guarded unity:
Let us plead forgiveness for the schisms in the
Church and pray that communion
may be restored.

Fifth   Our soldier of Christ ventured into the battlefields
of the evil powers:
Let us intercede that
human and unseen powers that oppose God
may lose their hold
and that Christ may be enthroned.

There may be singing

Leader   Holy God of Cuthbert and the saints
All   Go before us now.
Leader   God of the hills, God of the outposts
All   Go before us now.
Leader   God of the streets, God of the people
All   Go before us now.
Leader   Grace, mercy and peace be ours for ever.

CUTHBERT MIDDAY PRAYER

Leader   The Spring equinox, one of the two days in the year
when day and night are of equal length owing
to the sun's crossing of the equator, is also St
Cuthbert's Day:

Reader   As the heralds of spring
              golden trumpet
              the arrival of Easter,
              as the dark night of Lent passes
              and the days lengthen,
              so, like Cuthbert,
              bright star of the North,
              we would become
              your Easter people, O Christ,
              shepherds of your sheep,
              peacemakers and hospitality givers,
              open to change and partnership,
              Spirit-led, in solitude and costly service.
                      Kate Mcllhagga, Cuthbert's Folk

Two Readers

          Psalm 23 (*each reads alternate verses*)

Storyteller

          Cuthbert was making his way southward along
          the river Teviot, teaching and baptising the
          country folk, and taking with him a boy he was
          training.

          'Do you think someone has prepared your
          midday meal today?' he asked the boy.

          'I have no family or friends in this district,' the
          boy replied, and he clearly did not expect unknown
          strangers to provide for his needs.

          'Cheer up, the Lord will provide for those
          who trust him,' Cuthbert assured him, quoting
          Jesus' words 'Seek first the kingdom of God and
          all these other things shall be given to you'. After
          building up the boy's faith by quoting such

scriptures, Cuthbert saw an eagle flying overhead and said to the boy: 'This is the eagle the Lord has instructed to provide us with food today.' Shortly after, as they continued to walk, they saw the eagle settle on the river bank.

At Cuthbert's direction the boy ran to it and saw a large fish in its mouth, which he brought to Cuthbert. 'Why did you not give our fisherman his half of it since he was denying himself?' said Cuthbert. So the boy gave half to the eagle. They boiled the other half in the company of some folk with whom they shared it, worshipping the Lord and giving thanks. Then they set out to the mountains, led by God, to teach and baptise the people.   *An anonymous monk of Lindisfarne*

There may be silence, singing or sharing; blessings of the morning, or needs for the future may be named

Leader   Lord, as you called Cuthbert
from the Border hills
to be a shepherd of people and a light to the land,
call us to leave what lies behind us
and to reach out to others
till we, too, touch the gates of heaven.

There may be this or another story about Cuthbert

Storyteller

Cuthbert became famous for his miracles. Through his persistent prayers he restored to health many who were sick; he cured some who were afflicted by unclean spirits, and not only when present – praying, touching, commanding and exorcising –

but also when absent either by prayer alone or even indeed by predicting their cure. Signs and wonders whereby he shone outwardly gave witness to the inward virtues of his mind.

Bede's Life of Cuthbert

Leader	God of springtime,*
	while the sun is crossing over the equator
	may we be crossing over
All	From dark to light,
	from complaining to appreciation,
	from dithering to boldness,
	from stagnation to creativity,
	from coldness to love,
	from ourselves to you.
Leader	In the middle of the day we draw aside
	and listen to Cuthbert's God and ours.

There may be singing, silence or free prayer

Reader	Be with us now Lord, at noon.
	Keep us in the beautiful attitudes,
	joyful, simple and gentle.
Reader	Leaving what is past
All	Let us journey in your light.
Reader	Seeking what is just
All	Let us journey in your truth.
Reader	Forgiving those who harmed us
All	Let us journey in your love.
Leader	May the eternal Creator keep us,
	the beloved Companion beside us,
	the Spirit's smile upon us.

---

* or: 'of autumn' in the Southern Hemisphere.

CUTHBERT EVENING PRAYER

Leader   Cuthbert's Prayer:
Now robed in stillness
in this quiet place,
emptied of all I was,
I bring all that I am
your gift of shepherding
to use and bless.

*Cuthbert's Prayer, St Aidan's Chapel,
Bradford Cathedral*

All may sing 'The Lord's my shepherd' or another song

God's Word

Reader   Ezekiel 34:11-16

First   King of heaven, inspire us by Cuthbert's example
to win the godless, heal the sick, guard unity,
and reach out in love to others until we,
like him, touch the gates of heaven.

Second   Like Cuthbert,
bright star of the North,
we would become
your Easter people, O Christ,
shepherds of your sheep,
peacemakers and hospitality givers,
open to change and partnership,
Spirit-led, in solitude and costly service.

Kate McIlhagga, Cuthbert's Folk

Storyteller

None of those present would presume to hide from him the secrets of their hearts, but they all made open confession of their sins because they realised that these things could never be hidden from him; and they cleansed themselves from the sins they had confessed by fruits of repentance. He used especially to make for those places that were far away in steep and rugged mountains, which others dreaded to visit and whose poverty and ignorance kept other teachers away. Giving himself up gladly to this devoted labour, he instructed them with such devotion that he would often leave the monastery for a week, and sometimes for up to a month.   *Bede*

Reader   Matthew 18:12-14

Thanksgiving

Leader   Most glorious Giver of Life,
All   May coasts and islands praise you.
Leader   May town and country praise you.
All   May healers and artists praise you.
Leader   Darkness and light praise you.
All   Stars and moon praise you.
Leader   The guillemot and the gulls praise you.
All   The ducks and the sea otters praise you.
Leader   The Gospels and the relics praise you.
All   Cuthbert and the risen ones of Lindisfarne praise you.
Leader   May all creation praise you
All   and give you glory for ever.

There may be singing

Storyteller

Following the imposition of Roman regulations at the Council of Whitby there were certain brothers at the Lindisfarne monastery who preferred to conform to their old usage rather than to the monastic rule. Nevertheless Cuthbert overcame these by his modest virtue and his patience, and by daily effort he gradually converted them into a better state of mind. In fact, very often during debates in the chapter concerning the rule, when he was assailed by the bitter insults of his opponents he would rise up suddenly and with calm mind and countenance would go out, thus dissolving the chapter; but nonetheless, on the following day, as if he had suffered no repulse the day before, he would give the same instruction as before to the brothers . . . For he was a man remarkable for the strength of his patience and unsurpassed in bravely bearing every burden, whether of mind or body.

Bede's Life of Cuthbert

Leader   May the serenity of Christ and kindly Cuthbert be ours;
the serenity of Christ, King of tenderness,
be upon each corner of our homes,
each corner of our minds,
each thing our eyes take in,
each person our ears listen to,
and upon our inmost spirit.

First   Cuthbert gave himself to God
while sporting around as a child:
God who created me
nimble and light of limb,
in three elements free,
to run, to ride, to swim:
not when the sense is dim,
but now from the heart of joy
I would remember him:
take the thanks of a boy.

H. C. Beeching

Second   Cuthbert's tender hands warmed cold feet
and anointed sick bodies:
Father, take my hands.
May your compassion always flow through them.
May they offer tender touch
to people who are deprived of touch or tenderness.
May they offer human warmth
to people who are cold or dispirited.
May they offer practical care
to people who are weary and overworked.

Third   Cuthbert helped the monks of Lindisfarne, who
miserably complained at the difficult conditions
following the Synod of Whitby,
to make the transition from criticism to joy:
God of renewal, lead us
from complaining to appreciation,
from stagnation to creativity,
from coldness to love,
from ourselves to you.

There may be silent or free prayer and singing

Leader   God be our light in the dark,
our shelter in the storm,
and our companion evermore.

All   Amen.

CUTHBERT NIGHT PRAYER

Storyteller

Cuthbert's call to serve God began as he sat under the night sky, guarding the sheep on the Lammermuir hills. His life drew to a close also under the night sky, for although his little hermitage on the Farne Isle had high, stone walls, its roof was open to the heavens.

Leader   In the darkness we can see the splendour
of the universe –
blankets of stars, the solitary glowings
of the planets.
In the darkness the wise three found the star
that led them to you.
In the darkness of dreams
you speak to your people.
In the darkness of fading life
your eternal light draws near.

All   O God of life, darken not to us your light.
O God of life, close not to us your joy.
O God of life, crown to us your goodness.

A candle is lit

225

Leader   Christ is the light that is drawing near –
All   A light that no darkness will quench.
             There may be silence

Reader   Psalm 27:1-4

             There may be singing

Storyteller

Cuthbert kept throughout the same countenance, the same spirit. At all hours he was happy and joyful, neither wearing a sad expression at the remembrance of a sin nor being elated by the loud praises of those who marvelled at his manner of life.

Leader   Father,
             you called Cuthbert out of the darkness of night
             to be the Fire of the North.
             Call us out of the darkness of unbelief
             that the torch of faith may burn brightly in us,
             as it did in him.

A chant such as 'Kindle a flame to lighten the dark and take all fear away' (Iona Community) may be sung

Storyteller

These were Cuthbert's last words to his brothers: 'Always keep God's peace and love among you, and when you have to seek guidance about your affairs, take great care to be of one mind. Live in mutual goodwill also with Christ's other servants, and do not despise Christians who come to you for hospitality, but see that you welcome them, give them accommodation, and send them on their way with friendship and kindness. Never think you are superior to other people who share your faith and way of life.'

Reader Romans 12:9-13

Storyteller

Though infirm, Cuthbert had remained alone in his last months on earth apart from visits of his brothers at Lindisfarne when the weather allowed. One of Lindisfarne's monks observed that he put his trust wholly in God, satisfied with the converse and ministry of angels.

Leader 'Satisfied with the converse of angels'.

First I lie down this night with the nine angels
from the crown of my head to the souls of my feet.
Carmina Gadelica

Second I lie down this night under the protection
of the archangel Michael.
Third I lie down this night under the healing
of the archangel Raphael.
Fourth I lie down this night under the promise of the
archangel Gabriel.
All I lie down with a guardian angel to my right
and my left.

Leader May God and Cuthbert and the angels watch over our loved ones too, especially these we name before you now:
Any may mention names

*'God who madest earth and heaven' or another
song may be sung*

Leader   Father, this night may we cross over with Cuthbert
All   From complaining to appreciation,
          from despair to joy,
          from dark to light,
          from death to life.

CUTHBERT AND THE SHINING PEOPLE

Suitable for family or all-age occasions.

A picture of the night sky may be projected or displayed.

*If you know anything about stars, discuss.
Let someone explain what a comet is*

Storyteller

When Cuthbert left school he got an unusual job.
Unusual for us, that is. He had to take his turn
looking after the sheep on the hills at night. These
were part of his family's big farm. The sheep
were a long way from any houses, and thieves
might steal them or wild animals attack them.

Cuthbert lay on his back, looking up into the
twinkling stars. In the distance was the Milky
Way. He knew that this was really thousands and
thousands of stars but, so far away, they looked
like a stream of little dots of light. Then he saw
something else, something that he had never
seen before. It was brighter and moving faster
than all the other stars. Was it a comet? It came
nearer. No. These bright lights looked like shining

beings each side of – of what? In a flash, Cuthbert felt sure he knew. A special person, someone very close to God, was being taken to heaven. He was sure now, and as he gazed in wonder he felt a glow inside himself. He knew that he wanted to be like that special person, close to God.

The next morning he told his family all about the shining beings in the sky. Amazed, they informed him that Aidan, so beloved by them all as the bringer of gospel light to their kingdom, had died down the coast at Bamburgh. Then they knew that Cuthbert had seen angels carrying Aidan's soul to God.

Cuthbert would never be the same again. He knew what he must do. He told his parents: 'I saw something else that night, besides Aidan. I saw that I must change my life. Aidan has left a big gap. I will try and help fill it. I will go to the Christian brothers and learn from them about the Bible and prayer and the spiritual battle, and how to serve God. Instead of being a shepherd to the sheep, I must become a shepherd to the people, because people are like sheep, they are always getting lost and hurt and they need shepherds too.'

That was how Cuthbert stopped being a shepherd of the sheep, and became a shepherd of the people.

Night lights may now be lit

Everyone thinks about the story while quiet dreamy music is played, then read the following:

Reader   Listen to this poem by Angus, aged six:

> My eyes like to see
> the lovely stars in the sky
> shining like diamonds and crystals,
> and the sun above my head
> and the moon shining and shining.
>
> Eyes are shiny, too,
> and the golden water shines.
>
> My eyes like to see candles
> and the light in the sky.
>
> God will give me a new heart
> that shines with happiness inside me.
>
> *Angus*

Reader   Thank you for stars that shine in the night.
Thank you for people that shine so bright.
Thank you for things that shine inside me.
May they help me know what I should be.

> *All may sing a song such as 'O star of wonder' (the chorus of 'We three kings')*
>
> *Discuss what feelings or callings anyone thinks they have*
>
> *There may be refreshments or a meal*

CUTHBERT AND BOISIL CREATIVE ACTIVITY

Set your hearts on spiritual gifts, especially the gift of prophecy.   1 Corinthians 14:1

Storyteller

Cuthbert decided to join a monastery. He had heard of the prophetic leadership of Boisil, Abbot of Melrose, so he rode to Melrose with his boy servant. As Cuthbert dismounted and gave his sword and spear to his servant to take away, Boisil was watching. Foreseeing in spirit how great the man whom he saw was going to be, he uttered this one sentence to those who were with him: 'Mark this. Here is a servant of the Lord.' Bede comments that in saying this Boisil was echoing Jesus' words on first seeing Nathaniel: 'Here is truly an Israelite in whom there is no deceit!' (John 1:47).

Years later, Cuthbert returned to Melrose monastery, where he fell victim to the plague, though he was to recover. Boisil prophesied: 'You will not get the plague again, nor will you die at the present time; however, I will die of this plague, so let me use the seven days left to me to teach you.' They spent each of those days studying John's Gospel.

In fact, Boisil had predicted the plague to his abbot Eata three years before it appeared, and did not hide the fact that he himself would be carried off by it; but he declared that the abbot himself would not die of this but rather of dysentery, and events proved his prophecy was true.

Cuthbert used to tell people 'I have known many who far exceed me in their prophetic powers. Foremost amongst these is Boisil who trained me up, and foretold accurately all the things which were to happen to me. Of all these things only one remains to be fulfilled.' This was the prophecy that Cuthbert would become a bishop. It may be Cuthbert would have refused the pressures on him to become a bishop had it not been for Boisil's prophecy. After his death, Boisil appeared in prophetic dreams which helped shape the future of the kingdom.

David

Patron Saint of Wales

9 February (Teilo)*

1 March

26 September (Cadoc)

6 November

Also for gatherings where the theme is authority, blessing, water, healing, protection or 'little things'

DAVID MORNING PRAYER

Leader We come into the presence of David's God
and ours

All The Creator of the elements,
the Christ of the washings,
the Spirit of the well-springs.

There may be singing

Leader Great God, who called your servant David
to be an apostle and parent in God
to the people of Wales:
fire us with his faith, clothe us in his joy,
and bring forth fresh fruit in our lives and lands.

Reader Psalm 23

---

* Teilo and Cadoc are Welsh saints associated with David, and these are their saints' days. See Vol. 2 of *The Celtic Prayer Book – Saints of the Isles: a year of feasts.*

Reader	David, grandson of the military hero Coroticus,
	David the child, lovely to behold, son of Non,
	David, schooled in Old Menevia,
	taught by monks the Latin psalms,
	David of the blessed life,
	of the monastery of Menevia,
	David the Waterman,
	who often lived on bread and water only,
All	We honour your life, we cherish your faith,
	we serve your Lord.

Reader	Proverbs 4:10-27
Leader	Let us reflect in silence on ways we have fallen short.

Leader	Lord, David worked with unflagging zeal,
All	Forgive us for our flickering flame.
Leader	Lord, David witnessed with unfaltering faith,
All	Forgive us for our faltering steps.
Leader	Lord, David served with unstinting generosity,
All	Forgive us for our fickle friendship.

There may be silence or music of lament

Leader	Loving Father who has redeemed us
	and who reigns serenely as sun and sea,
	forgive our past and present sins,
	remedy in heaven our faults
	that today we may welcome Christ with joy.

There may be singing

Reader	1 Thessalonians 2:12

Storyteller

The boy David was sent to be taught by the aged
Abba Paul, the fosterer of righteousness. Here he

learned to master saving knowledge and the evil powers. Once the ailing Paul, suffering from failing sight, asked each of his pupils to lay hands on his eyes and pray for a cure. None could avail, until shy David's touch was used by God to heal.

All   Open our eyes, that we may see,
open the eyes of the blind.

Storyteller

Paul advised Non to send his growing son to the college of the great faith community founded by Ninian at Candida Casa, which we know as Whithorn. Before this, God spoke to his father in a dream. While hunting he came upon a stag, a fish, and a hive of bees. He was to send the hive, and portions of the stag meat and the fish to the monastery. The honeycomb symbolised wisdom, for as the honey lies embedded in the wax, so his son would perceive the spiritual meaning embedded in words of the Bible. The fish symbolised his lifestyle; for as fish live in water so this son would reject addictive food and drink, instead living in God, and eating only basics such as bread and water. The stag represented the power he would have over Satan, who is often depicted as the ancient serpent. As a stag, after it has fed itself off the snakes it has killed, longs for a water spring to reinvigorate its youth, so Non's son, after overcoming humanity's ancient enemy, the devil, would choose a spring of life with tears often flowing.

Leader	May we draw wisdom from your Word
All	As honey is drawn from the comb.
Leader	May we live in you
All	As fish live in water.
Leader	May we conquer the demons
All	And draw life from eternal springs.

Groups may think of examples of wisdom drawn from God's Word, living in God as fish live in water, conquering evil and finding sources of fresh life

There may be singing

Storyteller

David's training at Whithorn was partly on the job. He spent some time at Glasserton, the cave where Ninian kept his vigils, and where many pilgrims pray today. He went on missionary journeys and learned the universal lessons of faith and prayer; and he helped to compose a liturgy for Ireland's Second Order of Saints.*

Reader	Holy Spirit, you protect the seed-thoughts of my mind;
	through the Cross you redeem my deepest desires;
	your grace protects me from those who wish me ill;
	your seas protect me from enemies afar.
All	Father and Son, you protect me
	from all that harms.

---

* An ancient Irish *Catalogue* lists three Orders of Saints in the early centuries. The First Order were mainly Spirit-filled bishops in Patrick's time. The Second Order were mainly presbyters in the period following that. The Third Order were mainly hermits.

Reader	Great God, you protect me through Peter,
	the Keeper of Heaven's Gate;
	you protect me through the great angels,
	who over-arch us all;
	you protect me through Michael and Gabriel,
	beautiful spiritual companions.
All	Father and Son, you protect me from all that harms;

Reader	You protect me through the Virgin,
	gentle and pure;
	you protect me through John of noble gaze,
	first among apostles;
	you protect me through your prophets
	of constant prayer;
	you protect me through your massed teams
	of saints.
All	Father and Son, you protect me from all that harms.
Reader	Great God,
	through your eternal unity of Three Persons
	you protect me as I journey to the freedom
	of heaven's land,
	you protect me in order to place me in a wealth
	of light.
All	Father and Son, you protect me from all that harms.

*Echoes a lorica ('armour prayer') attributed to the
Welsh bard Gruffudd ab yr Ynd, 1280*

Intercession

First	Teach me, O God, how to live,
	how to serve you with all my being from youth.
Second	For the daily conflict, give vigour,
	that I may be more than a conqueror in the strife.

Third	Teach me how to employ heart and head and hand for your glory, and not to be idle.
Fourth	Teach me to find in humblest service highest joy, always prepared to do your bidding cheerfully.
First	Teach me, O God, how to live.

Echoes a prayer of Ellen Burman

Leader	As birds soar high and carefree
All	May we soar with you.
Leader	As deer run straight and graceful
All	May we run with you.
Leader	As waters flow so clearly
All	May we flow with you.

There may be free prayer and singing

Leader	Bless to us, O God, our souls and bodies. Bless to us, O God, our belief and our condition.
All	Bless to us, O God, our heart and our speech, and bless to us, O God, the work of our hands.

Carmina Gadelica

Leader	As it began to be in the time of David, so may it be again for us. Everywhere may voices be raised to heaven in prayer, everywhere may virtues be restored to the heart of the Church, everywhere may supplies be shared with the needy.

DAVID MIDDAY PRAYER

Storyteller

David returned south and set out to plant faith communities among the pagan invaders from the east: in Somerset and Lincolnshire, in Derbyshire and Herefordshire, in Monmouthshire and Radnorshire. They say he taught the people four rules: pray; watch; work; abstain from strong drink.

First Mark 14:38

There may be singing

Second Ephesians 5:15-18

Storyteller

David said 'Do the little things you have heard and seen me do.'

Reader	In the little things I do,
All	Be present, Lord.
Reader	In the little things I speak,
All	Be present, Lord.
Reader	In the little moments I fill,
All	Be present, Lord.
Reader	In my working and in my going,
All	Be present, Lord.

Leader Teach us, our God and King,
to care by noticing the little things,
to love by cherishing the little things,
to serve by serving in little things,
to pray by offering the little things.
These we offer to you now.

There may be free prayer or a pause

Reader   Psalm 121

Storyteller

Soon, loved by so many, David was made a bishop
and founded his great monastic centre at what is
now St David's. There, instead of employing animals to pull the ploughs, the brothers placed the
yoke upon their own shoulders, dug the ground
tirelessly, carried hoes, and saws for cutting, and
provided with their own efforts for all the needs
of the community. They had all things in common,
no one should even say 'this is my book'. Their
clothing was basic, mainly skins. David upheld
St Paul's rule: 'If a person will not work, he will
not eat.'

Leader   Let us pray for our own work
and that of the world.

*There may be silent prayer, free prayer, or the Lord's
Prayer or singing*

All   Lord our God,
we would be true in all the work we do.
All that is done, we do it unto you.
We would be true in watch of day or night;
be vigilant and watch with only you in sight.
We would be true in all the words we pray;
be heartfelt, caring, in all the words we say.

Leader   May the God of David and our God watch over us,
pouring generously upon us through the day.

David Evening Prayer

Storyteller

David daily poured forth fountains of tears, blazed with a double flame of divine love, consecrated the Lord's Body, conversed with angels, and cooled his flesh in a cold bath.

Leader   Teach us to offer our daily round to you, O Lord, and to praise you with all our being.

Reader   Psalm 16

There may be singing

Reader   Ecclesiasticus 15:1-6

Leader   Hail, glorious Lord!
May church and chancel praise you.

All   May valley floor and mountainside praise you.
May the well-springs praise you.
May night and day praise you.
May silk and fruit-tree praise you.

Leader   Abraham, founder of the Faith, praised you.

All   May birds and bees praise you.
May after-grass and fresh shoots praise you.

Leader   Aaron and Moses praised you.

All   May male and female praise you.
May the seven days and the stars praise you.
May the air and the upper atmosphere praise you.
May books and letters praise you.
May fishes in the river praise you.
May thought and action praise you.
May sand and soil praise you.

Leader	May all the good that has been done praise you.
All	I praise you, Lord of glory!
	Hail, glorious Lord!

'May all things praise you',
adapted from Llyfr Du Caerfyrddin

| Reader | John 10:1-5, 11-18. |

Storyteller

David brought the best out of others, as when he encouraged the timid Cynnyd to share fully in the conversation. He was generous towards those whose work seemed more successful: he offered accommodation to his soul-friend, Justinian, for his many new recruits.

David had some beautiful relationships, such as that with young brother Aidan. Once he sensed in his spirit that a man with an axe was about to kill Aidan in the woods, and rushed towards him with only one boot on. He arrived to find the would-be murderer with his hand held aloft with the axe, frozen in that position. Aidan left him holding the axe and ran towards David, who saw innumerable angels around the lad as he ran. When Aidan was back in Ireland, he sensed in his spirit that someone would try to poison David at Easter, and managed to get a message to him in time.

Intercession

| Leader | Lord, as fish live in water, may we live in your love. |
| All | Bathe us in your cleansing rivers. |

Soak us in your healing waters.
Drench us in your powerful downfalls.
Cool us in your bracing baths.
Refresh us in your sparkling streams.
Master us in your mighty seas.
Calm us by your quiet pools.

There may be free prayer

A hymn may be sung

Storyteller

Modomnoc came to study under David at his Pembrokeshire monastery. One of his duties during his many years there was beekeeping, an essential part of the monastery's provision. The time came when God called him back to Ireland, and David sent him on his way with God's blessings, but unfortunately the entire swarm of bees followed him and settled on his boat. Beekeepers know the effort required to get a swarm of bees back into their hive. Modomnoc succeeded in doing this, and a day or two later, he repeated his farewells and set out again for the boat. The same thing happened all over again and Modomnoc once again painstakingly returned the bees.

Modomnoc went back to David, and suggested that he hang around until the bees were tired and sleepy, and then he would quietly slip away. His return afforded another opportunity for all the brothers to pray over him and invite God's blessings on him and his new ministry in Ireland. This time, as David prayed, he realised that God intended the bees to be part of the blessing he was to give to Ireland. So David prayed for the bees in the words of the blessing below. David's twelfth-century biographer observed that the blessing had been fulfilled completely – that bees sent back from Ireland had dwindled to nothing in Wales but that the bees in Ireland, which previously had no reputation for bees, had flourished beyond measure.

David's Blessing on the Bees

May the land to which you are journeying
abound with your offspring.
May you for ever leave our land
and your offspring never increase here.
But may they never fail to increase
in the land to which you go.

There may be singing

Leader   May the places to which you shall journey
abound with spiritual fruit.

David Night Prayer

Storyteller

David was called to speak at a large open-air Church synod that had gone pear-shaped. Nobody was listening to the Church leaders. They had lost their authority in the hearts of the people. The crowd was so big that they had to pile clothing together to create a mound from which the speakers could be seen and heard. But speaker after speaker failed to get the ear of the people, and the leaders panicked, lest the people return disillusioned with the organised Church. Then old Paul, under whom David had studied, urged that they bring David to the synod, for he 'conversed with angels, was a man to be loved', and had stature. Eventually David agreed to come. As he reached the outskirts of the crowd, David heard the wailing of mourners. They wanted to hurry him on to the platform, but David insisted on going to the bereaved mother whose son lay dead. He comforted her and spent more time praying over the son, who revived. She instantly dedicated him to serve God under David. David gave this young man the Gospel Book which he carried in front of David. All eyes followed them, word spread fast, and there was a clamour for David to speak. For years afterwards, people swore that the mound of clothes grew bigger as David spoke. For he spoke with authority and not as others had done.

Leader   Give to us the authority that belongs to us.
          May it grow through prayer and service.

All   As waters spring from the earth,
          signs of your generous giving,
          may we draw deeply from you,
          the Wellspring of life.

There may be singing

Males   May the virtue of our daily work
          hallow our nightly prayer.

Females   May the seven days and the stars praise you.

Males   May our work and our rest praise you.

Females   May our watching and our sleeping praise you.

Reader   Psalm 4

Storyteller

David and his disciples were called Water People,
for folk said they lived on little more than water
and leeks, and as fish live in water, so they lived
in God.

Leader   As fish live in water,
All   May we live in you.
Leader   As rivers flow in land,
All   May we flow in you.
Leader   As evening rests the day,
All   May we rest in you.
Leader   Let us lay before God the concerns of our hearts
in silence or aloud.

*There may be silence or free prayer accompanied or
followed by harp music, or followed by singing*

Reader   1 Thessalonians 2:6-12

Storyteller

David's final words to the Christian people of
Wales were: 'Be happy and keep your faith . . .
Always be of one mind.' It was said that at his
death 'kings mourned him as a judge, the older
people as a brother, the younger as a father'.

Leader   Thank you for David, Lord,
for his love flowing out through his tears,
for his faith flowing out through his prayers,
for his work, continued by his peers.
Kindle the flame in us through the years.

Storyteller

After David's death, Wales continued to honour his memory. The monasteries influenced the pattern of life for centuries. Gerald, in his *Description of Wales*, states that 'the Welsh churches enjoy far greater tranquillity than elsewhere. For not only is protection assured for animals to pasture in churchyards, but also in boundaries far beyond'.

The twentieth-century poet Gwenallt (1899–1968) from Eples portrayed David as 'strolling from county to county like God's gypsy, with the Gospel and the Altar in his caravan . . . he brought the Church to our homes, and took bread from the pantry and bad wine from the cellar, and stood behind the table like a tramp so as not to hide the wonder of the Sacrifice from us.'*

First	We will lie down in the wisdom of the teachers.
Second	We will lie down in the nurture of the mothers.
Third	We will lie down in the simplicity of the hermits.
Fourth	We will lie down in the generosity of the givers.
Fifth	We will lie down in the warmth of the welcomers.
Sixth	We will lie down in the upbuilding of the fathers.
Leader	Father, the day is gone.
All	Guard us sleeping.
Leader	Our energy is spent.
All	Guard us sleeping.
Leader	Our lives are open before you.
All	Guard us sleeping.

---

* (Gomer Press)

| Leader | May the saints and the Saviour watch over us that as we go to our sleep there be no injury in our hearts, only mercy towards all. |
| All | May we, and every soul, return in rest to God as the waters return to the sea. |

CREATIVE ACTIVITIES

1. Grow leeks.
2. Wear daffodils.
3. Decorate places with flowers, a fifth element in Welsh tradition. (In addition to the universally recognised elements of earth, air, fire and water, the Welsh celebrated a fifth, the flowers.)
4. Provide a bowl of water so that each person may splash their face.

Fursey

16 January

*Also for gatherings where the theme is visions,
fire or lament*

Storyteller

Fursey travelled Ireland with the Good News of Christ, attracted large crowds, and founded a monastery at Killfursa (now named Killarsagh). In 633 he arrived in East Anglia with a few others to convert the pagan Angles to Christianity. The king gave Fursey a base, at Burgh Castle, near today's Great Yarmouth.

During an illness he received powerful visions. He heard a voice say 'The saints shall advance from one virtue to another and the God of gods shall be seen among us.' In another vision he saw four fires that threatened to consume the world. Ever afterwards he confronted people with the choice between life or death with an intensity that made him sweat. Fursey's visions were written down but are now lost. After a time as a hermit in the Fens, Fursey travelled to France and established a monastery at Lagny-sur-Marne. After his death in 650 his body was taken to Peronne monastery which became a large shrine where many miracles were witnessed.

There may be singing

Reader   Psalm 84

Proclamation

Leader	The saints shall advance from one virtue to another.
All	The God of gods shall be seen among us.
Leader	We shall be changed from glory to glory.
All	The God of gods shall be seen among us.
Leader	The fire of God shall purge the wastelands.
All	The God of gods shall be seen among us.
Leader	Destroyers and demons will have to flee.
All	The God of gods shall be seen among us.
Leader	The kingdoms of this world shall become the kingdoms of our God.
All	The God of gods shall be seen among us.

Reader   Job 33:15-30

Leader	The arms of God be around our shoulders.
All	The light of the Holy Spirit be in our minds.
Leader	The sign of Christ's Cross be upon our foreheads.
All	The sound of the Spirit be in our ears.
Leader	The fragrance of the Spirit be in our nostrils.
All	The vision of heaven's company be in our eyes.
Leader	The conversation of heaven's company be on our lips.
All	The work of God's Church be in our hands.
Leader	The welfare of God and neighbour be in our feet.
All	Our hearts be a home for God.

Old Irish, attributed to St Fursey

Reader   Revelation 20:11–21:4 or Matthew 13:36-43

There may be the following or another creative activity

Lament of the Four Fires

*Real or imitation fires may be lit
in the four corners of the building,
or pictures of fires may be projected on to a screen*

Storyteller

Once Fursey had a near-death experience. He was out of his body and at a great height, and an angel told him to look back at earth. He saw some kind of dark valley beneath him and four fires in the air. He was told these fires would consume the world. Each fire had a name. The first was Falsehood, representing the times when we are false to our promises to God and to good. The second was Greed, representing the times when we put the love of gain above the love of God. The third was Discord, representing the times when we thoughtlessly upset our neighbours in little things. The fourth was Injustice, representing the times when we misuse our position and rob the needy through neglect or dishonesty. The fires converged and threatened to devour him. He cried out. The angels told him that though the fire was terrible, it would burn each person according to their deserts. Then two angels divided the fires and made a protected space for him even though devils tried to stir up hostile fires against God's people.

Four prayer leaders come, each with a banner depicting one of the fires, or with a torch of living flame. They move to four different areas and hold their banner or torch high.

Everyone chooses which topic they wish to pray about and gathers round the prayer leader

Following the opening words by each prayer leader and the response, there is a time of silent reflection followed by free or silent prayer on the theme

First Prayer Leader

From all that is false and evil,

All   Holy God, deliver us.

Second Prayer Leader

From greed and envy,

All   Holy God, deliver us.

Third Prayer Leader

From discord and strife,

All   Holy God, deliver us.

Fourth Prayer Leader

From misuse of others.

All   Holy Lord, deliver us.

This may be followed by silence, sharing, teaching and singing

Intercession

Storyteller

Once when Fursey was ill, he was told in a vision to continue his ministry of bringing God's Word to people, and to continue to watch and pray without wearying, because death was certain but the time of death was uncertain.

Leader God of the journey, whose holy scholar, Fursey,
impelled by the visions you entrusted to him,
gave his life as a pilgrim for love of you,
spare us your anger,
and help us to heed and speed your Word,
through Jesus Christ our Lord.

Leader Lord, make us ready like Fursey
to be pilgrims for love of you,
to go wherever you open the doors.

Males Open the doors of devotion to sorrow
and restitution.

Females Open the doors of devotion
to the worship of heaven.

Males Open the doors of devotion to beautiful deeds.

Females Open the doors of devotion to truth and justice.

There may be singing

Leader Perspiring in the power of prophetic passion,
Fursey touched the deep places of God
in empty souls and brought heart-change.
May we go out from this place
impassioned to touch the deep places of the world.

All So help us, God! Amen!

Joseph of Arimathea
and Glastonbury Saints

31 July

*Suitable for gatherings at Glastonbury and on English and
British national occasions. Glastonbury has been thought of as
England's Jerusalem, as in Blake's poem,* Jerusalem,
in the preface to Milton, *which begins
'And did those feet in ancient time'*

Leader The light of Christ has come into the world.
All The light of Christ has come into the world.

Leader May the Holy Thorn of Glastonbury,
sprung from Arimathean Joseph's staff,
in winter's dark and summer's light
proclaim the birth of Christ – the true Sun.

There may be singing

Leader Britain's Jerusalem, and towns and villages
everywhere,
clothe yourself in the garments of Christ.

Reader Psalm 122

All may repeat this phrase after every second verse

All Peace be within you, Jerusalem.

Reader Isaiah 62:1-5. This is the Word of the Lord (*at close*).
All May our lands receive afresh the beams of light,
the heartfelt sharings, of Christ, the true Sun.

Leader   We weep for the sins that have driven you
from your dwelling place:
for pride and prejudice,
for domination and division,
for belittling young or old, women or men –
your children all,
for abuse of your creation,
for worshipping what you created
instead of you alone,
for not welcoming the stranger and the needy.

There may be silence, or an activity that expresses sorrow

Reader   John 19:38-42. This is the Word of Christ (*at close*).

All   May our islands receive afresh the beams of light,
the heartfelt sharings, of Christ, the true Sun.

There may be singing

Reader   Acts 8:1b-4

Leader   After Jerusalem's Christians were scattered,
the entomber of Christ,
the noble commander Joseph,
the enlightener of Britain,
planted here the Tree of Salvation.
Gildas the Wise, first writer of the Britons,
recounted for us in Tiberias's last year
the coming of the Light.
In these islands, stiff with pagan coldness,
the Sun's rays shone.

Reader   With Aristobulus, first Bishop of Britain,
fanning the bright flame of Joseph's kindling,
Fagan and Dyfan, for King Lucius the Glorious,
restored here the church built by Christ's apostles'
hands.

Leader   Set in the jewel of Avalon,
a church of wattles was made by holy hands
and dedicated by command of Christ
to the dearest Mother of God,
that in these northern lands this first of churches
should honour her who brought humanity's
fullness to birth.

There may be singing

Reader   We give thanks for Glastonbury, cradle of faith,
which drew to it, so 'tis said,
Patrick and holy Irish hermits.
Brigid and her winsome faith,
David and his fiery zeal,
Columba and his mighty prayers,
which draws to it still a multitude –
saints, sinners, strangers – seekers all.

All   May the Christ of the cosmos
also be to this multitude the Christ of the womb,
the workshop and the wounds.
May this Christ of the resurrection
live in our bodies
now and for ever.

Leader   We pray for the withering of gods that fail us.
We pray that these seven jewels may shine

from Britain's Jerusalem and from the place
where we live:

First	Penitence.
Second	Praise.
Third	Holiness.
Fourth	Hospitality.
Fifth	Forgiveness.
Sixth	Justice.
Seventh	Healing.

At longer gatherings each of these jewels may be expressed through creative activities such as pictures, mime, clay, writing, music or prayer corners

There may be teaching, discussion or singing

First   Here may the earth be cherished,
the Faith be cradled,
energies be released for God.

Second   Here may seekers be drawn to the eternally Real,
and wanderers find their home in Christ.

Leader   From the thorn of Glastonbury
may the goodness of creation blossom.
From the thorn of past pride
may loving friendships bloom.
From the thorn of unquiet spirits
may angelic harmonies burst forth.
May Mary's Son live among us,
and the Sacred Three encircle us always.

All   In the name of the Lord of the elements,
in the name of earth's Risen Son,
in the name of the transforming Spirit,
eternally Three in One.

Illtyd

6 November

*Suitable for gatherings where the theme is hermits,
agriculture, reclaiming the land, wisdom or dying*

ILLTYD MORNING PRAYER

First   They called Illtyd 'The most famous teacher of the Britons'. He was schooled and ordained by Bishop Germanus; he was a master in the Old and New Testaments, in languages, mathematics and philosophy, and born with strong powers of intuition – he was a seer in our land.

Second   The prophet Amos spoke of there being times of famine – not of food, but of hearing the words of God: 'The time is surely coming, says the Lord GOD, when I will send a famine on the land; not a famine of bread, or a thirst for water, but of hearing the words of the LORD.' (Amos 8:11)

    One such famine was at the time of Samuel's birth. Our own land, too, has often had such famines. But as God raised up Samuel, so God raised up Illtyd, and still calls out the seer that lies hidden in us all.

Third   Illtyd prophesied over the child Samson: 'He will be the leader of us all, many will greatly benefit from his ministry both this side of the

Channel and the other side. He will be the greatest founder of churches since the first apostles.'

There may be singing

Reader Psalm 119:97-104

Storyteller

Two great saints, Samson and David, were pupils in the famous monastery of Illtyd, who may be regarded as the founder of the Welsh Church though holy hermits prepared the way. Illtyd was a very well-educated soldier who came to Wales from Brittany and, according to one medieval record, fought in the army of King Arthur. But it was while serving the king of Glamorgan that he became a Christian.

One day Illtyd took a party of knights hunting, and became separated from them. They stumbled upon the hut of the hermit Cadoc and treated him disgracefully, shouting obscenities at him. When Illtyd arrived he was shocked by his men's behaviour, and riveted by Cadoc's, for he refused to retaliate and smiled on them. Illtyd dismissed his men and fell on his knees, asking Cadoc to forgive their behaviour. Cadoc lifted Illtyd up and warmly embraced him.

That night, as Illtyd lay awake, his heart was filled with love for the old hermit. The life of such a man, who was victorious in the battle with Satan, seemed so much finer than that of a soldier whose only battles were with other soldiers. When he had fallen asleep he dreamed that an angel spoke to him these words: 'Until now you have been a knight serving mortal kings. From now on you are to be in the service of the King of kings.'

At dawn Illtyd crept out of the royal palace, leaving behind his sword and his armour and set out, clothed only in a rough woollen cloak, to be a soldier of Christ. In his mind, he would spend the rest of his life as a hermit.

A song such as 'Down by the riverside' may be sung

Reader   Ephesians 6:10-18

Intercession

Leader   Teach me, King of kings,
            to fight with all of my being
            for the things that are good and true and peaceable
            as a faithful servant and soldier
            of our Lord Jesus Christ.

            Unlock the treasures of wisdom to me,
            but first give me a heart for humble learning.

            Help me to know right from wrong,
            truth from falsehood.
            Help me to sense what is appropriate,
            to avoid false choices,
            to learn those things that contribute to the greater
            wholeness of myself and of the world.
            Eternal God,
            the light of the minds that know you,
            the joy of the hearts that love you,

and the strength of the wills that serve you,
grant us so to know you
that we may truly love you,
and so to love you that we may fully serve you,
whom to serve is perfect freedom.   *Augustine*

There may be free prayer and singing

Leader   May we be drawn by the light of God,
stilled in the peace of God,
wise in the truth of God.
All   Amen.

ILLTYD MIDDAY PRAYER

Storyteller

After Illtyd was converted he left his soldier's
career and his family and asked the holy Cadoc
to accept him as a monk. That night as he
prayed a voice said, 'When you get up tomorrow
go straight to the wooded valley to the west
where you will find the place you are to make
your home. This is God's will for you, for this
place is convenient, fertile and suitable for
human dwelling.' Illtyd arrived to find a valley
watered by springs from which brooks flowed
into the river.

There may be silence and singing

Storyteller

Illtyd had been living the life of a hermit for
some three months when a stag burst in, quickly

followed by a pack of hounds from the king's hunt. When the king realised it was Illtyd, he erupted in fury and accused Illtyd of betraying him. Illtyd, like Cadoc, simply smiled and invited them into the hut for a meal. Astonishingly, the stag which the hounds had been pursuing lay down outside, together with the hounds! At the end of the meal it was the king's turn to have his heart changed, and he asked Illtyd's forgiveness. Then the king asked if he could send his son to Illtyd to be educated. This marked the beginning of a miracle in Christian education. Soon Illtyd's place in the valley by the sea became the largest school in the whole of Britain, a school for Christ, and Illtyd became known as the wisest teacher in Britain.

Reader　　Psalm 23

Leader　　You are here, Lord, in this place.
First　　You are here, Lord, in our work.
Second　　You are here, Lord, in the resources of this earth.

Storyteller

They called the whole community to prayer and walked to the shore at low tide, when the sea used to withdraw a mile or two. Illtyd marked a line near the shore with his staff and in the name of God forbade the water to pass that mark again. The result was that they were able to cultivate much land, reclaimed from the sea, which produced abundant crops.

On appropriate occasions everyone may silently meditate and identify in their minds a place or situation that needs to be reclaimed. They then walk to an actual or a simulated place that needs to be reclaimed; one person places a staff there, all raise their right hand in prayer and silently or aloud pray that these places may be reclaimed

They then complete the Midday Prayer in that place or upon their return

Reader   Jesus said: 'The law of God is like a landowner who invited some people to look after his fertile land as his tenants. But they were greedy and beat up his representatives. So eventually he sent his only son to them. They killed him and took all that belonged to him. So the landowner had to take away the estate from these tenants and offer it to others.'   *Echoes Matthew 21:33-41*

Reader   Jesus said: 'The kingdom of God is like a seed someone planted in their garden. It grew and became a tree so large that many birds perched in its branches.'   *From Luke 13:18, 19*

Leader   We place ourselves, the land, and all who work it into the hand of our God. May the wealth and work of the world be available to all and for the exploitation of none.

There may be singing

Leader   Now let us go in peace to cherish the earth, to serve the planet, and to love our God.

ILLTYD EVENING PRAYER

Storyteller

The *Life* of Samson described Illtyd as the wisest and most learned of all the Britons in the knowledge of Scripture, and in every branch of philosophy. Illtyd was also famed as a God-inspired steward of the earth. He invented a much improved method of ploughing. 'Seed multiplied and toil met with abundant reward,' says an ancient account.

There may be singing

God's Word

Reader   Deuteronomy 8:1-10

Storyteller

Illtyd was a great teacher. His method was to combine spirit, mind and body in a harmony. He divided students into twenty-four groups, each responsible for one hour's worship and adoration, so that ceaseless praise would flow to God. The intellectual side of his teaching involved instruction in the 'seven sciences', the best knowledge the times could offer. Physical well-being was fostered by clearing the land, digging and ploughing. Great future leaders such as Samson, Gildas, David and Paul Aurelian were drawn there to study.

Reader   2 Timothy 3:14-4:2

Storyteller

Illtyd used to withdraw at regular intervals to a cave by the river Ewenny to seek God alone. He slept on a cold stone and lived on barley loaves and fish.

Sometimes he made retreat at Llanhamlach, five kilometres to the east of Brecon, where the horse that brought his provisions was accompanied by a stag who inspired the horse to go at a gallop!

Leader   Retreat is necessary in order to advance.
Let us retreat a little and wait silently on God.

There is silence

There may be sharing and singing

Storyteller

A new king came to power who saw Illtyd as a threat. He decided to destroy Illtyd's work. The king's henchmen, who secretly honoured Illtyd, warned him that he was to be murdered.

Illtyd took this as God guiding him to go back to being an anonymous hermit. So he secretly trekked to a cave further along the coast, and grew a beard and long hair so that no one would recognise him.

There is a story that, hearing of a famine in what is now Brittany, Illtyd loaded a boat with much needed seed corn. He met up with his former pupil, Samson, over whom he had prophesied that he would be 'the greatest founder of churches since the first apostles'.

Intercession

Leader You who are the everlasting Essence of things
beyond space and time and yet within them,
you who transcend and pervade all things,
reveal yourself to us who feel after and seek you
in the shadows of ignorance.

John Scotus Eriugena 813

Help us to live content with small means;
to study hard, think quietly, talk gently, act frankly;
to listen to stars and birds, babes and sages,
with open heart;
to bear all cheerfully;
do all bravely;
await occasions, hurry never;
in a word, to let the spiritual, unbidden
and unconscious grow up through the common.
Dear God, make this our symphony.

Echoes words of William Ellery Channing*

Grant me, Lord,
the serenity of knowing that I do your will,
and contentment with my lot.
Grant me the courage to change what I can change,
the grace to accept what I cannot change,
and the wisdom to know the difference.

Traditional

Free prayer and singing

---

* p.108 of *Earth Prayers from Around the World*, ed. Elizabeth Roberts
(HarperCollins, San Francisco, 1991)

Leader   Send us out to nurture the seeds of your kingdom,
to see with your eyes,
to serve with your hands,
to live with you for ever.

ILLTYD NIGHT PRAYER

Storyteller

Illtyd had been back in his secret cave for some
time when a monk took a wrong turning and
passed near Illtyd's cave. The monk was travelling
to a new monastery David had founded and
carried a brass bell which was a gift for him. Illtyd
heard the bell, came out, and struck it three times.
The monk did not recognise his former leader
but, strangely, the bell stopped ringing. The
monk told David about this on his arrival. 'God
has told us where our dear Illtyd is hiding,' said
David, and sent the monk to invite him to join
him. Illtyd declined the invitation to go back
into a large community, but three of David's
monks went to support him and care for him
until he died.

Reader   Psalm 63:1-8

Storyteller

When Illtyd was terminally ill he asked two
brothers to be with him. Even then it was Illtyd
who gave a prophetic lead. He focused on the

inner spirit of each of them. 'God will carry me to heaven, in your presence, just before midnight,' he told them. 'You will see my departing soul look like an eagle with two gold wings. God has also shown me how each of you are to depart this life. You will also see an eagle, but weighed down with wings of lead. This is because although you have led a life in religion, you have greatly coveted material things. Greed pulls you down to earth. That is why you have not the firmness of gold in the wings that carry you upwards. Nevertheless, God will take these things from you and receive you.'

Reader   Matthew 6:19-21

Males   This night, O Victor over death,
raise me from the death of greed,
raise me from the death of deceit,
raise me from the death of despair.

Females   This night, O Victor over death,
wake me to the eternal 'Yes',
wake me to the rays of Hope,
wake me to the light of Dawn.

Leader   We lie down in peace,
knowing our sins are forgiven.
All   We lie down in peace, knowing death has no fear.
Leader   We lie down in peace,
knowing no powers can harm us.
All   We lie down in peace, knowing angels are near.

There may be singing

Leader   Our loved ones bless, O God, and keep,
               wherever they are.

               Any may name loved ones aloud or in silence

               *There may be other petitions followed by silent,
               prepared or free prayer*

Leader   You fell asleep in mortal flesh, O Christ,
               but on the third day you rose again.
               Now you watch over us as we sleep,
               you restore our souls and preserve our life.
               We walk in the inheritance of Illtyd
               and of the saints in light.
               Now in love of you we will take our rest.
All   In love of you, we will take our rest.

John the Loved

6 May

3 September

27 December

*Suitable for gatherings where the theme is love,
soul-friendship, or the Bible*

JOHN THE LOVED MORNING PRAYER

Storyteller

Although scholars debate whether or not the Apostle John and John the Evangelist are the same person, the Church honours on this day John, 'the disciple whom Jesus loved'. John, an intimate companion of Jesus, portrayed Jesus in his Gospel as the eternal Word of God who became a human being. Tradition gave John the name *paranymphos* ('friend of the bridegroom'). Through Mary, John became like Jesus' foster brother to succeeding generations of believers. In the *Carmina Gadelica*, the prayers and poems of the Western Isles of Scotland collected in the nineteenth century by Alexander Carmichael, John is sometimes referred to as 'John of love', 'foster son of Mary' or 'foster brother of Christ'.

Leader   Hear the words of the Blessed John:
'In the beginning was the Word, and the Word was with God, and the Word was God . . .

and the Word became flesh and lived among us.'
(John 1:1, 2, 14)

All Glory to Christ who has come to live among us.

There may be singing

Reader Psalm 84

Leader We muse on the eternal Light,
All And all people are lit up.
Leader We muse on the eternal Logos,
All And all creation is lit up.
Leader We muse on the eternal Lamb,
All And eternity's tenderness is lit up.
Leader We muse on the beloved disciple at the Last Supper,
All And God's sacrament is lit up.
Leader We muse on mother and foster son at the Cross,
All And Christ's Church is lit up.
Leader We muse on the radiance of the eastern Light,
All And pray that it becomes the transforming glory of the west.

Reader Exodus 33:7-11

Reader John of love portrayed the intimacy of communion in Jesus' life with his eternal divine Father, with his mother, and with friends.
The following love song was taken by early Christians as an allegory of such a spiritual communion.

Reader Song of Songs 2:8-17

Reader Spiritual brother to Jesus,

All	You are our brother, too.
Leader	Guardian to Mary,
All	You are our guardian, too.
Reader	Father of the Church,
All	You are our father, too.
Leader	Like Mary, you stayed close to her son.
All	Jesus, keep us close to you.
Leader	Like her, you stayed faithful at the Cross.
All	Jesus, keep us faithful too.
Leader	You were the first apostle to believe that Christ rose from death.
All	Jesus, help us to believe too.

Storyteller

The Church honours the one who proclaims Jesus as the Word made flesh, the one who is 'the disciple whom Jesus loved', and who was a spiritual parent to churches in the Celtic world of Asia.

John and the Gospel that bears his name were much loved in the churches of Columba and Aidan. The Celtic vision derives much of its insight from John's Gospel, whose emblem is an eagle. An eagle was believed to be the only bird that could gaze directly into the sun's light without being blinded. It is an image of the contemplative, who gazes into the face of God.

Early Celtic Christians loved the Gospel of John, which portrays John as a soul-friend to Jesus, and they regarded John as their spiritual father.

Reader   John 14:18-23

Leader	Jesus said: I am the light of the world –
All	Your light drives out the dark.
Leader	I am the way, the truth, the life –
All	Your way has brought true hope.
Leader	I am the resurrection and the life –
All	You broke the power of death.
Leader	I am the bread of life –
All	You feed and fill the hungry.
Leader	I am the true vine –
All	Your life becomes our life.
Leader	I am the good shepherd –
All	You guide us and lead us on.

Mark Slater

There may be teaching, creative activity or singing

Intercession

One or more of these or other prayers may be said

Leader	In the origin of life was the Word of God
All	Who came to live among us.
Leader	In the darkness of the cosmos was the Light of God
All	Who came and shone among us.
Reader	John records great acts of Jesus which are signs of his abiding power in human life. Jesus transformed water into wine.
All	Transform our everyday lives.
Reader	Jesus healed an official's son.
All	Heal our wounded souls.
Reader	Jesus fed hungry thousands.
All	Feed our parched souls.
Reader	Jesus restored sight to a person blind from birth.

All	Open our eyes to your presence.
Reader	Jesus raised Lazarus from death.
All	Raise us up to new life with you.

Reader Grant to me, O Lord,
that tender love, that deathless vision,
that flowing life
that marked John the loved disciple,
until the Logos, the Lamb, and I,
your loved one,
flow together as one.

There may be free prayer and singing

Leader May we who know the Life of the world
share his life with others.

All May we who know the Light of the world
give light to others.
In the fellowship of John with the Holy Three.

JOHN THE LOVED MIDDAY PRAYER

Storyteller

John leans on the bosom of the Lord,
which is the sacrament of contemplation.
John Scotus Eriugena

There may be silence

First Lord of my heart,
give me vision to inspire me
that, working or resting,
I may always think of you.

Second	Lord of my heart,
	give me light to guide me
	that, at home or abroad,
	I may always walk in your way.
Third	Lord of my heart,
	give me wisdom to direct me
	that, thinking or acting,
	I may always discern right from wrong.
Fourth	Heart of my own heart,
	whatever befall me,
	rule over my thoughts and feelings,
	my words and actions. *Early Irish*
Reader	John 13:12-17
Leader	You washed the feet of those
	you could not rely upon,
All	Teach us to wash the feet of the world.
Leader	You loved the world so much
	that you gave your life for it,
All	Teach us to wash the feet of the world.
Leader	You call your friends to serve others,
All	Teach us to wash the feet of the world.
Leader	In the heat and burden of the day,
All	Teach us to wash the feet of the world.
Leader	Let us bring to mind the weary and wounded
	of this world and invite Jesus,
	through his friends, and our prayers,
	to wash their feet.

Any may mention names

Leader	Jesus, John allowed you to wash his feet,

All	Help us to receive your grace through the giving of others.
Leader	The life blood of your son washes us from sin,
All	Have mercy on us, and make us clean.
Leader	If we walk in the light as Christ is in the light,
All	We have fellowship with one another and the blood of Christ cleanses us from all sin.

There may be singing or the Lord's Prayer

Leader May you remain in the love of Christ
as the branch remains in the vine.
May the Father's glory be revealed in you
by your bearing much fruit.

JOHN THE LOVED EVENING PRAYER

Storyteller

John became one of Jesus' most intimate circle of three. At the final Passover meal which Jesus shared with his team the evening before his arrest, he told them he no longer regarded them as followers, but as friends. As John leant across him, Jesus confided in him. John and two others stayed with Jesus during three hours of foreboding (Mark 14:33). After more than two hours in agony, nailed to a wooden cross-beam, Jesus gasped out his dying wishes for the two people who were dearest to him. He asked his mother, 'take John to be your son', and he asked John, 'take her to be your mother'.

Ever afterwards people would be able to wander

into places of Christian worship and see portrayed on the altar, either side of the crucified Jesus, his mother and his adopted brother. The arms of Jesus outstretched in welcome seem to say: 'Come to me and you come also into my family.'

Leader   Open our eyes to your presence.
Open our ears to your call.
Open our hearts to your love.
Until you are our All in all.

There may be singing

God's Word

Reader   Psalm 97

All   May we see you in the glowing of fire
and in the flowing of water.
May we see you in the glory of a sunset
and in the beauty of fellowship.
May we see you in the care of another
and in the fruit of long toil.

Reader   Isaiah 6:1-8

There may be silence or music

Leader   John our brother, you saw with your eyes and touched the Word of Life, revealed in human flesh.
All   In fellowship with you we see the Word of Life.
Leader   You saw the true Light that shines on
in the darkness.
All   In fellowship with you we see the Light of Life.

Leader	You saw him lay down his life,
	God's gift to human kind.
All	In fellowship with you we see the Donor of Life.
Leader	You saw the empty tomb, the risen Christ of glory.
All	In fellowship with you we see the Eternal Life.
Leader	You saw the community of love,
	birthed by the Holy Spirit.
All	In fellowship with you we see the Church's Life.

Reader   1 John 1:1-7

Storyteller

Tradition says that John suffered under the persecution of the Roman Emperor Domitian. He barely escaped being plunged in a cauldron of boiling water, and he suffered exile on the Isle of Patmos. John survived these trials and lived into old age at Ephesus, where he penned his three New Testament letters. Jerome records how, when John was dying, his friends asked him if he had any last message for them. 'Little children, love one another,' he repeated once again, as he had repeated in his letters. They asked him if that was all he had to say. 'It is enough,' he said, 'for it is the Lord's command.' Love was the essence of John's friendship.

There may be teaching, creative activity or singing

Intercession

There may be free prayer and singing

Reader   Jesus said: I give you a new command:
              Love one another.

As I have loved you, so you must love one another.
No one has greater love than to lay down his life
for another.

All   Jesus, we love you.
Restore us to our first love.
That we may lay down our lives for one another.

Leader   We pray for our brothers and sisters
as Jesus prayed on the night before he died,
that they may be one with you
and one with one another.
We pray for those who live on the surface,
not daring to go deeper.
We pray for the whole human family
for whom you were willing to be betrayed.
We pray for Christian Churches
that they may become one flock.
We pray for those who are persecuted.

There may be singing

Reader   Bless to me, O God,
each thing my eye sees,
each sound my ear hears,
each aroma my nose smells,
each flavour my mouth tastes.
Bless to me, O God,
each ray of light,
each thing I pursue,
each pull I resist.
May the Three who seek me
heal me and make me whole.

JOHN THE LOVED NIGHT PRAYER

Leader	John of love, you took Mary into your home so that she could sleep in peace.
All	We will sleep in the peace of God's family.
Leader	The One who was in you was greater than the One who was in the world.
All	We will sleep in the peace of God's family.
Leader	To your dying day you called your children to live in love.
All	We will sleep in the peace of God's family.
Leader	Glory to the Father who wrought us, glory to the Son who sought us, glory to the Spirit who taught us.
First	Who are they at the foot of my bed?
Second	John and the loveliest Mary.
First	And who is that who watches over them and who draws near to me?
Second	The One of their love, the all-bright King of the sun, the Son of God, without beginning and without end.

A candle may be lit. There may be silence or chanting

Storyteller

In his old age John met with other Church leaders to compile meditations on the life of Jesus which would help Christians advance along their journey of faith. In these pages (which we know as John's Gospel) he reveals intimate moments in Jesus' friendships. He records Jesus' friend Mary anointing his feet with costly perfume, and drying them with her hair (John 12:3). John, more than any other Gospel writer, delights in the fragrance of intimacy expressed with all the senses.

John recalls Jesus saying to his apostles 'I do not call you servants any longer, because the servant does not know what the master is doing; but I have called you friends' (John 15:15).

Reader God is love, and those who abide in love abide in God, and God abides in them. Love has been perfected among us in this: that we may have boldness on the day of judgement, because as he is, so are we in this world. There is no fear in love, but perfect love casts out fear . . .'

John 4:16-18

Leader In your love we will take our rest.
To your love, we will commend our kin.
Enfold in your love, dear Christ, those we name before you.

Any may mention names

There may be singing

Leader God with us lying down.
All God with us rising up.

All Bless, O Jesus, your family who lives on this globe,
the brothers and sisters of John,
bound to our Lord in love.
Leader May the Being of Life bless,
may the Christ of love bless,
may the Spirit holy bless
each and every one.
All Each and every one.

CREATIVE ACTIVITIES

1. Massage another person's feet in the spirit of Christ who washed his disciples' feet.

2. Visualise Christ holding your feet and looking you in the eyes. What do you say to him? What might he say to you?

John the Forerunner

7 January – as baptiser

24 June – birth

29 August – death

23 September – conception

*Suitable for gathering where the theme is courage,
justice or baptism*

JOHN THE FORERUNNER
MORNING PRAYER

Storyteller

There was a man sent by God, whose name was John. He came as a witness to the Light. He calls us to know the Light, who lights up every human being.

All

Light of the world, in grace and beauty,
mirror of God's eternal face,
transparent flame of love's free duty,
you bring salvation to our race.
Now, as we see the longest daylight,
we raise our voice in hymns of praise.
Worthy are you of endless blessing,
sun of our night, light of our days.

There may be singing

Storyteller

John was a prophet whose work earlier prophets and poets had foretold. They told of a person who

would make a way for God's feet to touch the
earth; it would be a way of right living, making
the world worthy to receive God.

First	Restore us again, O God our Saviour,
	and put away our false ways.
	Show us your unfailing love, O God,
	and grant us your salvation.
All	Righteousness shall go before our God
	and make a way for his steps.
First	Will you not revive us again
	that your people may rejoice in you?
	Show us your unfailing love, O God,
	and grant us your salvation.
All	Righteousness shall go before our God
	and make a way for his steps.
Second	I will listen to what the Lord God will say.
	He promises peace to his people,
	but let them not return to their folly.
	Surely his salvation is near those
	who reverence him
	that his glory may dwell in our land.
All	Righteousness shall go before our God
	and make a way for his steps.
First	Love and faithfulness meet together,
	righteousness and peace kiss each other.
	Faithfulness springs from the earth
	and righteousness looks down from heaven.
All	Righteousness shall go before our God
	and make a way for his steps.
Reader	Isaiah 40:1-11

Storyteller

This is the song John's father sang when he was told God would give them such a son:

The Song of Zechariah

Reader   We bless you, Lord God of Israel,
coming to ransom your people.

All   Raising up saving power
in the family of your servant David,
as you said by the mouths of your prophets
in days of old.

Reader   You set us free from oppression,
free from the hands of our foes.
This is your bond of love with our forebears,
your covenant, binding for ever.

All   Your oath to our father Abraham
assuring us that, freed from fear,
delivered from all oppression,
we will serve you in goodness and love
to the end of our days.

Reader   This child will be called your prophet.
He will walk in your presence
and prepare the way you will come,
announcing your people's salvation
with pardon for all their sins.

All   Through the love in the heart of our God
the Rising Sun will come to us,
shining on those in the dark
who lie in the shadow of death,
and guiding our steps into peace.

Echoes Luke 1:68-79

There may be singing

Storyteller

John was a cousin of Jesus Christ, and was born not long before him of elderly parents. This is how it happened.

Reader   The child that is born to us today is greater than any prophet: this is he of whom the Saviour said, 'Among those born of women there is no man greater than John the Baptist.'

Leader   Give us, O God,
something of the spirit of your servant
John the Baptist –
his moral courage,
his contentment with simplicity,
his refusal to be fettered by this world,
his faithfulness in witness to the end.

From Brendan O'Malley, A Pilgrim's Manual

There may be teaching, creative activity and singing

Reader   Father God, thank you for making John
a forerunner who prepared a way for you.

All   Help us to prepare a way for you.

Reader   Where there is falsehood,

All   Help us prepare a way for you.

Reader   Where there is violence,

All   Help us prepare a way for you.

Reader   Where there is misuse of others,

All   Help us prepare a way for you.

Reader   Where there is despair,

All   Help us prepare a way for you.

Reader   Where there is hatred,

All   Help us prepare a way for you.

or

Reader	Where crooks exploit asylum seekers for money,
All	Turn their hearts to you.
Reader	Where governments exploit voters through fear or favour,
All	Turn their hearts to you.
Reader	Where hooligans exploit peaceable citizens for kicks,
All	Turn their hearts to you.
Reader	Where monopoly financiers exploit nature for short-term gain,
All	Turn their hearts to you.

Reader	Mighty God, thank you for sending John to learn your ways in the silent deserts.
All	Teach us the silence of humility. Teach us the silence of wisdom. Teach us the silence of faith, and then send us out.

Silence

There may be singing

Leader	God send us out
All	To prepare ways of holiness, to point others to Christ, to live in the Spirit's power.

JOHN THE FORERUNNER MIDDAY PRAYER

Storyteller

When John's mother Elizabeth heard Mary's news, the child in her womb leapt for joy and she was filled with the Holy Spirit.   *Echoes Luke 1:41*

Reader   Prepare the way of God Almighty.
Make straight the paths for God.
The down-and-out shall be raised up;
the high and mighty shall be humbled.
What is crooked shall be straightened out,
and the rough diamonds shall be made smooth.
All people shall see the wholeness
God comes to bring.   *Echoes Luke 3:4-6*

There may be silence, singing or The Lord's Prayer

Storyteller

John took vows as a Nazirite. This required him to live a very disciplined life. He went into the wilderness area, and lived on the food he could get in the wild such as honey and locusts. It was a tough life. Maybe he stayed with one or more of the many religious communities in the area, but it seems he never joined one.

After being schooled in the disciplines of prayer and godliness, the spirit of prophecy came upon him, and he emerged as a communicator. Crowds flocked to hear him. He told them that their society was like a rotten tree which needed to be cut down with an axe. A new beginning was necessary. God was calling forth a creative minority who would pay their taxes, respect other people, and honour God. This would pave the way for the coming of the long-awaited Messiah, for whom John felt unworthy even to perform the lowliest service.

Reader   Luke 3:1-17

Intercession

Leader	In the middle of the day we mourn with John for the things that mar God's ways, and we heed God's urgent warning: the axe is about to cut down the bad trees.
Leader	We mourn for the misuse of this planet.
All	The axe is about to cut down the bad trees.
Leader	We mourn for the grasping of that which belongs to others.
All	The axe is about to cut down the bad trees.
Leader	We mourn for dominating those weaker than ourselves.
All	The axe is about to cut down the bad trees.

There may be music of lament and meditation

Leader	Spirit of God, we thank you that you were present in our birth, we thank you that you are present in our work, we thank you that you are present in our world, convicting it of what is wrong, showing it what is right.
All	We offer to you all that we are, all that we do, and all that we shall ever be.

There may be singing in the Spirit, free prayer,
or sharing

Leader	Let us go
All	With purity in our hearts, truth in our heads, honesty on our lips, courage in our spirits and mercy in our being.

JOHN THE FORERUNNER
EVENING PRAYER

Leader   In the stillness of the womb
you brought a prophet to birth.
Still you are calling: prepare a way for your God.

There may be singing

Reader   Psalm 80:1-3, 14-19

Reader   Let the summits of heaven praise you
with roaming lightning,
O most loving Jesus, O righteous King of kings.
Blest for ever, ruling in right government,
is John, forerunner of the Lord, who,
ever since he was in his mother's womb,
was filled with God's grace instead of strong drink.
Elizabeth and Zechariah begot a great man,
John the Baptist, the forerunner of the Lord.
The flame of God's love shall dwell too,
in my heart
like a golden jewel placed in a silver dish.

After Columba

Reader   Malachi 4

First   God our Father, you chose John
to announce the kingdom of Christ to all.
All   Guide us in the way of Christ.
Second   Even in his mother's womb,
you chose John to prepare the way for your Son.
All   Give us faith to know Christ better
and make him better known.
Third   You inspired John to recognise the Lamb of God.

All	Through us, inspire the world to recognise the One of Suffering Love.
Fourth	You disposed your prophet to give Christ pre-eminence.
All	Give us humility to build up Christ in others.
Fifth	You called John to die for you.
All	Give us his zeal for truth.
Sixth	Remember the dead, O God, who have been faithful to you.
All	Bring them to new life, cleansed from all stain of sin.

There may be singing

Storyteller

One day Jesus came to John for baptism.

Reader   Mark 1:9-13

Storyteller

Josephus, the Jewish historian, said of John: 'He was a good man who bade the Jews practise virtue, be just to one another, pious towards God and come together by means of baptism.' John baptised, that is immersed, many people in the river Jordan. They publicly repented of their sins. John was not interested in outward rites but in a real change of heart.

For a time John took his campaign to Samaria and baptised many there. He returned to the territory ruled by Herod Antipas, to whom the Roman colonisers permitted certain powers. Herod disliked the mass movement and was hostile. His illicit second wife, Herodias, was even more hostile, for John had denounced Herod's betrayal of his first wife. So they put John in prison. This is how he came to be beheaded.

Reader   Jesus began to speak about John the Baptist to the crowds . . . You saw much more than a prophet . . . John is greater than any one who has ever lived. But the person who is least in the kingdom of God is greater than John.

Luke 7:26, 28 or Acts 13:23-25

There may be singing

Intercession

Leader	May babies in the womb praise you.
All	May mothers and fathers praise you.
Leader	May silent ones in deserts praise you.
All	May holy ones at prayer praise you.
Leader	May those who speak truth praise you.
All	May prophets and writers praise you.
Leader	May those who stand for justice praise you.
All	May those who challenge tyrants praise you.
Leader	May churches and seekers praise you.
All	Glorious God, may all that has breath praise you.

There may be teaching, creative activity or singing

Prayers from the morning or midday may be used

Leader   Holy God, holy and mighty, you can bring
a holy child to birth in a barren womb,
you can bring a new thing to birth in a barren land;
bring to birth in us that new thing that is your will.

A blessing

JOHN THE FORERUNNER NIGHT PRAYER

Leader   The bright sun has faded.
The Forerunner points us to the Sun that never sets.
A voice cries out 'Prepare the way of God'.

All   We will prepare a way.

There may be silence

Leader   These are some things Jesus said about John:

Reader   Luke 16:16; Matthew 9:14-17; 11:11-15

Reader   We are members one of another.
Never let the sun set on your anger.
Give no opportunity to the devil.

All   Before we lie down to sleep
we leave behind our anger.
In our hearts we give back
what we have wrongly taken.

Leader   Where there are imperious ways,

All   Creator, give us your Father heart.

Leader   Where there is hatred,

All   Saviour, grant us forgiveness.

Leader   Where there is anything false,

All   Holy Spirit, make it true.

Leader   Now bind us in truth and mercy
as we offer our hands to you.

If desired, those present may join hands

All   We pray to almighty God to forgive us our sins
and to keep us in life eternal.

There may be sharing or singing

Reader	Psalm 31:1-5
Leader	Hide us under the shadow of your wings.
	Protect the babies in the womb.
	Protect prisoners of conscience.
	Protect those we name before you now.

Any may mention names

There may be singing

Leader	In the stillness of the womb a new life was born.
All	Into your hands I commend my spirit.
Leader	Keep me as the apple of your eye.
All	Into your hands I commend my spirit.
Leader	Awake, may we watch with Christ.
	Asleep, may we rest in peace.
All	Into your hands I commend my spirit.

Kevin of Glendalough

3 June

*Suitable for gatherings where the themes are animals,
athletes of the Spirit, pilgrimage, prayer,
soul-friendship, dying or the Cross*

KEVIN MORNING PRAYER

Storyteller

Kevin was born to a noble sixth-century Irish family in Leinster. They say his mother did not experience labour pains. Perhaps that is why at his baptism Cronan the priest named him Coemgen, or Kevin, which means 'beautiful, shining birth'. 'For,' said he, 'this is the name God fashioned in heaven which shall always cling to this child.' His mother took him to the Fort of the White Fountain and there the women fostered him. From the age of seven Kevin was schooled by monks until he was ordained. Then he withdrew to a place of solitude near the Upper Lake at Glendalough. They say that thirty years previously Saint Patrick had prophesied that a person would come to this glen and build a great monastic city for the refreshment of residents and pilgrims. So it came to be.

Reader

Fair-skinned and holy athlete of Christ who, in the valley of the two broad lakes, made a home for God, today we praise your God and ours for the wonder of God's Presence with you and with us.

There may be singing

God's Word

Reader	Psalm 23
Reader	High-borne eagles and nesting birds
All	Give ear to the friend of God.
Reader	Speckled trout and mountain deer
All	Hear God's praises chanted.
Reader	Snarling wolf and savage boar
All	Lie down at sainted feet.
Reader	Serpents of fear and fierce desire
All	Uncoil and concede defeat.
Reader	Isaiah 11:6-9

The following may be enacted as a procession

Leader	We will journey into wild places with God.
All	With you we shall neither faint nor fear.
Leader	The wild creatures shall become God's friends
All	With you we shall neither faint nor fear.
Leader	Their Creator also created me.
All	With you we shall neither faint nor fear.
Leader	Give glory to the God of heaven and earth.
All	Give glory to God who is in this place.
Reader	Mark 1:9-13

There may be teaching, creative activity, singing or storytelling as follows

Storytelling

Storyteller

It seemed warm at the Fort of the White Fountain, however great the frost and snow outside. Cattle and wild animals came there to find grass, and a white cow would come whenever the babe fed at his mother's breasts. Kevin learned early about fasting, for during fast days he only sucked his mother's breasts once a day. Thus it was that, when he arrived at Glendalough and had only herbs and nuts and water of the forest for his food and drink, he was not diminished. His clothes were the skins of wild animals. His pillow was a stone, his bed a sheet of rock. Daily, and sometimes by night, he would stand in the lake up to his waist, chanting psalms and saying his prayers. Each day he would scramble up to a cave fifty feet above the lake for long vigils of prayer and the sacrament of Christ. This is known still today as Kevin's Bed.

Intercession

There may be a silent prayer vigil, with people lying or standing with arms in the shape of a cross, or there may be a time of reciting praises of God from the psalms or songbooks

There may be free prayer and singing

Leader	The Father be with you.
All	And with you.
Leader	The Saviour be with you.

All	And with you.
Leader	The Spirit be with you.
All	And with you.
Leader	May Kevin, the saints and the Saviour watch over you.
All	May they bless the earth that is beneath us, the sky that is above us, the day that lies before us, your image deep within us.

KEVIN MIDDAY PRAYER

Storyteller

In the lake the hermit stands in prayer. In the heat of the day we will pause, immersed in you.

All

Bathe us in your presence.

There may be silence

Storyteller

Once the cows of a farmer named Dimma grazed not far from Kevin's solitary hollow, and one of them would come all day and lick his feet, returning home with the rest of the cows. More milk came from her than from any other cow. Dimma was so astonished that he asked his cowherd to observe where the cow went, and that is how he discovered Kevin, weak through lack of nourishment. Dimma was overjoyed to learn of this holy man's presence on his land. He and his children cleared a way through the forest, and persuaded Kevin that they should build a church where they could worship with him. And so the neighbourhood was blessed.

All   Peace be to each thing that breathes.
Peace to each creature.
Peace to each person.
Peace to the land and the sea.

Storyteller

Once Kevin said: All the wild creatures on the mountains are my house-mates, gentle and familiar with me.

Leader   Loving God,
who creates all the creatures on the earth,
help me to respect each living thing
as your handiwork
and to live my life in kindness and consideration
for the animals whose bodies may feed me,
whose skins may clothe me,
and whose lives give me companionship and care.
                    *Mary C. Earle and Sylvia Maddox**

Reader   Psalm 63:1-5

Storyteller

Every Lent Kevin would keep vigil in a wattled hut. There he lay on the flagstone with his arms stretched out in the shape of his Saviour's Cross, and with the palms of his hands open to heaven. So long and still did he lie there that a blackbird made the hollow of his hand its nest and laid an egg. It was said that gentle Kevin, steely of will, stayed thus until the egg was hatched.

---

* *Praying with the Celtic Saints*
(St Mary's Press, Christian Brothers Publications, Minnesota)

Leader   Kevin stretched out his arms in the shape
of the Cross.

Jesus said:
'And I, when I am lifted up [on the Cross] from the
earth, will draw all people to myself' John 12:32.
    Lord Jesus, at this hour you hung on the Cross,
stretching out your arms in love to all.
    May all the peoples of the world be drawn to
your uplifted love, especially the people we name
before you now.

Any may mention names

*Alternatively those present may move to a space
where they can pray, standing or lying, with their
arms stretched out in the shape of the Cross.*

There may be silence and singing

Leader	Your kingdom come.
All	Your will be done one earth, as it is in heaven.
Leader	For yours is the kingdom, the power and the glory.
All	For ever and ever. Amen.
Leader	Let us go in peace to love and serve our Lord.
All	Amen.

KEVIN EVENING PRAYER

Leader   Ancient legend says that Kevin and his folk used
to sing 'St Patrick's Breastplate' and that St Patrick
blessed them from heaven when they ceased
singing.
    Let us now sing 'The Breastplate'.

Thanksgiving

All sing   This day God gives me
strength of high heaven,
sun and moon shining,
flame in my heart,
flashing of lightning,
wind in its swiftness,
deeps of the ocean,
firmness of earth.

This day God sends me
strength as my steersman,
might to uphold me,
wisdom as guide.
Your eyes are watchful,
your ears are listening,
your lips are speaking,
friend at my side.

God's way is my way,
God's shield is round me,
God's host defends me,
saving from ill;
angels of heaven
drive from me always
all that would harm me;
stand by me still.

Rising, I thank you,
mighty and strong one,
King of creation,
giver of rest,
firmly confessing

threeness of Persons,
oneness of Godhead,
Trinity blest.

'St Patrick's Breastplate', eighth-century
Irish translation by James Quinn; tune: Bunessan

God's Word

Reader   Psalm 121

Leader   We give you thanks for Kevin's call to Glendalough.
All   All you pilgrims, praise our God.
Leader   We give you thanks for Kevin's prevailing prayers.
All   All you pilgrims, praise our God.
Leader   We give you thanks for Kevin's friendship of souls.
All   All you pilgrims, praise our God.

Storyteller

After the farmer's family helped Kevin to move, other Christians joined him. They formed a little village, with their own meagre crops and cattle. Often they knew not where their next meal would come from, yet in this tough situation two things shine out: God sustained them through his creatures, and even when they had nothing to spare they were generous to the poor who came to them. What was happening echoed what God foresaw for his people when, speaking through the prophet Hosea, he likened them to a woman who had gone astray.

Reader   Hosea 2:14-18

Storyteller

Once Kevin was looking after his sheep when a crowd of starving people asked for money with which to buy food. Kevin had neither money nor food. The beggars began to leave. Suddenly Kevin had a thought. He asked them to wait, and started to kill some sheep, so that they could feed on them. Some time later, when they did their next count of their sheep, they found they had the same number as they had before. Perhaps we are surprised, but didn't Jesus promise that things like this would happen?

Reader   Matthew 6:2-4

There may be singing, teaching, creative activity or the following storytelling

Kevin and His Foster Child

Storyteller

Kevin became sought after as a soul-friend. The local ruler brought his seven-year-old son to be fostered by Kevin. He was fearful, for all his other sons had died after evil women had cursed them. The women did come to curse the boy at Kevin's place. So, in the name of Christ, mighty Protector and Saviour of all, Kevin cursed the evil soothsayers, who died – and with them died the threat.

Now another hurdle faced the saint. They had no milk for the child. As Kevin prayed he saw a doe with her fawn, and asked that God would tame it. The doe gently came and left some of her milk in a hollow stone – enough for the boy as well as for her fawn. Day after day the friendly fawn came to nourish these two young creatures beloved of God.

On other occasions Kevin protected a hunted boar and healed pilgrims who were attacked on their way to Glendalough.

Intercession

Leader   As we remember Kevin,
may the building stones of our lives by remortared;
may our dreams be restocked with sacred meaning;
may our journeys lead to peace.

All   Bless to us, O God,
each thing our eyes see,
each thing our hands touch,
each thing our minds think,
each word we speak,
each step we take,
until we reach our home.

There may be a time of singing, informal prayer, blessings, music or silence

Leader   May the Three in One be with us,
one God who mothers us all.
In the depths of the waves,
in the steeps of life's climbs,
may God's motherly arms uphold us.

KEVIN NIGHT PRAYER

Storyteller

One day Kevin set out to visit his soul-friend, Ciaran, the magnetic young leader of the community at Clonmacnoise, on the banks of the Shannon river. But before he arrived Ciaran, struck down with the plague, died, and his bier was placed in a little chapel until Kevin could take his funeral. When Kevin arrived he asked all the brothers to leave the chapel, so that he could be alone with his deceased friend. But, waiting outside, they distinctly heard conversation. Ciaran's spirit had re-entered his body so that these soul-friends could commune. Ciaran asked that as a sign of lasting friendship they should exchange their garments. Ciaran's body was filled with heat and he looked radiant. Kevin believed that, through this sign, God had established a lasting fraternity between the two communities.

All sing

Faithful vigil ended,
watching, waiting cease.
Master, grant your servant
his discharge in peace.

All the Spirit promised,
all the Father willed,
now these eyes behold it
perfectly fulfilled.

This, your great deliverance,
sets your people free;

Christ their light uplifted
all the nations see.

Christ, your people's glory!
Watching, doubting cease;
grant to us your servants
our discharge in peace.
Timothy Dudley-Smith

Reader   Psalm 63:1-8

Storyteller
Kevin returned to Glendalough.

Leader   You are beautiful in the stillness of lakes,
in the rustling of leaves,
in sleep on the bed of earth.

Leader   Still is the earth.
All   Make still my body.
Leader   Still is the night.
All   Make still my mind.
Leader   Still are the spheres.
All   Make still my soul.

Storyteller
Kevin's bed remains a symbol to pilgrims of a way
of being with God.

Leader   Grant me, sweet Christ, the grace to find,
Son of the living God,
the place where you alone suffice,
where you are in the sod.

All I ask is enough on which to live
from the King of fairest face,
and to lie in peace, alone
and on your face to gaze.

All We, too, are pilgrims with a dream,
in touch with sacred things.
Seal us now and encircle our lives,
and those for whom we pray.

Any may name needy people or places

There may be singing

Leader Kevin's bed was a hard place,
but he slept at peace with you.
All May we sleep at peace with you.
Leader The hard places of our lives –
we offer these to you.
All May we sleep at peace with you.
Leader With the earth as our bed and the skies as our roof,
All May we sleep at peace with you.

Leader Sleep in the lap of Jesus,
the angels encircling you,
the Three of Kindly Love enfolding you.

Mary

1 January – her role in God's plan

2 February – when she presented Christ in the temple

*25 March – when God's messenger told her
she would conceive Jesus*

31 May – when she visited her cousin Elizabeth

15 August – her entry into heaven

8 September – her birth

8 December – her conception

*Suitable for gatherings where the themes are birth, homemaking,
purity, soul-friendship, spiritual gifts or resurrection*

*Churches in Celtic lands felt a deep bond with Mary,
mother of the Son of God*

MARY MORNING PRAYER

Her Birth and Her Conceiving of Jesus

Leader	Mary, chosen gateway,
	through you there came to earth
	the Son of God to aid us, to give us eternal worth.
All	Now you live in glory, Mother of much grace,
	Jewel of the heavens, light shining from your face.
All sing	How blest are you who are poor,
	the kingdom of God is yours.

Taizé chant

God's Word

Reader   Psalm 147

All may sing or say
> Lord have mercy, Lord have mercy.

Reader   Zephaniah 3:14-18

Proclamation

Reader   The shield of the Son of God covers her face.
His star is a bright revealing light to her.
The darkness of night is to her
as the brightness of day.
The day to her gaze is always a joy,
while the Mary of grace is in every place
with the seven beatitudes encompassing her.

Carmina Gadelica

All   Give us, like Mary,
openness to your Word,
awareness of your presence,
obedience to your will,
faithfulness in sharing your suffering,
joy in sharing resurrection with you.

Reader   Luke 1:26-45

All sing   *(To the tune of 'Amazing Grace')*
My soul proclaims the Lord my God,
my spirit sings God's praise!
Who looks on me, who lifts me up,
whose gladness fills my days.

All nations now will share my joy,
your gifts you have outpoured.
Your little ones you have made great;
I magnify the Lord.

Your mercy is for evermore!
Your name I praise aloud!
Your strong right arm puts down the proud
and raises up the bowed.

You fill the hungry with good things,
the rich you send away.
The promise made to Abraham
you fulfil every day.

Magnificat, magnificat,
Magnificat, praise God!
Magnificat, magnificat,
Magnificat, praise God.

R. J. Simpson

There may be teaching or creative activity and singing

Intercession

Leader Your messenger revealed your purpose to Mary
and she conceived by the Holy Spirit.

All Holy Spirit, conceive in us whatever you will,
and we will carry it with joy.

Reader High King of the universe,
by choosing to be born as a child
you teach us to reverence every human life;
may we never despise, degrade or destroy it.
Rather, help us sustain and preserve it.

Leader	As it was in the stillness of the morning,
All	So may it be in the clamour of the day.
Leader	As it was in the hidden vitality of the womb,
All	So may it be in the hidden life of our home.

There may be singing

Leader The shield of the Three be over you,
the shield of Mary
and the whole company of heaven,
to guard you at your back,
to preserve you at your front,
from the crown of your head
to the soles of your feet,
so that an island shall you be in the sea,
a hill shall you be on the land,
a well shall you be in the desert,
a light shall you be in the dark.

All Amen.

MARY MIDDAY PRAYER

Home-Making

All The Virgin was beheld approaching;
Christ so young on her breast,
angels bowing lowly before them,
and the King of life was saying, 'Tis meet.

The Virgin of locks most glorious,
the Jesus more gleaming-white than snow,
seraphs melodious singing their praise,
and the King of life was saying, 'Tis meet.

O Mary, Mother of wondrous power,
grant us the succour of thy strength,
bless the provision, bless the board,
bless the ear, the corn, the food.

The Virgin of mien most glorious,
the Jesus more gleaming-white than snow,
she like the moon in the hills arising,
he like the sun on the mountain-crests.

Carmina Gadelica

There may be silence and singing

Reader Luke 2:41-52

All Mary nurtures the Son of tenderness,
God, supreme ruler of every nation:
her father, her strengthener, her brother.

Mary nurtures a Son on whom dignity rests –
none can violate his boundaries –
whose words are beauty, who is neither young
nor grows old.

The unwise can never perceive
how Mary is related to God:
her Son, her Father, her Lord.

But I know, though I be but frail and earthly,
how Mary is bonded in the Spirit to the Trinity:
her Son and brother in the flesh,
her Father, her Lord, blessed Almighty.

translated by Paul Quinn
Early or Middle Welsh

Reader   Honour your father and mother
as the Lord your God has commanded you,
so that you may have long life and prosper in
the land that the Lord your God gives you.
Deuteronomy 5:16

All   May our sons grow up strong and straight
like young trees.
May our girls have the beauty of inner serenity.
May our farms and industries overflow.
May the voice of complaining
cease from our streets.
Happy are the people from whom such blessings
flow, who put their trust in God.   *From Psalm 144*

There may be singing

Leader   May our homes be gladdened
by the love of parents, the laughter of children,
the wisdom of elders, the memory of forebears.
No word or thought to darken the day,
no memory or hurt to trammel the night,
songs, smiles and stories to open the doors of joy.
We pray for people who have no decent house
to live in,
for those who provide foster homes,
for parents to keep their marriage vows,
for parents to think deeply about their child's
character and calling.

There may be silent or free prayer

Leader   Homemaker God, wherever we are, help us to be
homemakers, like Mary, for you.

All   Amen.

MARY EVENING PRAYER
Spiritual Mother

Storyteller

In this service we will trace how Mary moved on from being a mother in a private home at Nazareth to being a mother in the worldwide family of her son.

There may be singing

Reader John 2:1-11

Storyteller

Mary knew that Jesus could turn tasteless emptiness into tasteful plenty. At a wedding in a friend's village or in any place else.

Reader As Jesus was speaking, a woman in the crowd raised her voice and said, 'Happy the womb that bore you and the breasts you sucked!' But he replied, 'Still happier those who hear the word of God and keep it!' *Adapted from Luke 11:27*

Storyteller

Jesus was teaching, and Mary got the point, that a person who does God's will becomes true family to Jesus. Mary, by doing God's will above all else, became not just a blood mother, but a spiritual mother. As she said 'Yes' to God with all her being, so may we.

All I give you assent with all my being.
I give you affection with all my senses.
I give you worship with all of my mind.

I give you joy with all of my frame.
I bow my knees before you.
I still my heart before you.
I am yours,
and I will be yours, every day of my life.

There may be singing or music

Reader   John 19:25-27

Storyteller

Mary learned to let go of her son. But as she did so, she received another son. She became spiritual mother to John.

Reader   Acts 1:12, 13; 2:1, 2

Storyteller

Mary was with them in an upper room as they were all filled with the Holy Spirit and as the Christian Church, Jesus' worldwide family, was born. Something like a tongue of fire alighted on each one of them.

A woman distributes red cardboard cut-outs of a tongue of flame. On one side is written a fruit or a gift of the Holy Spirit (some examples are given in Galatians 5:22, 23 and 1 Corinthians 12:8-10). Then a man gives to the woman a similar tongue on which is written the words 'bearing God'

Storyteller

What gift of the Spirit was Mary given? Was it the gift of spiritual mothering? Listen to what is written:

Mary   This is the gift of receiving – receiving all manifestations of new life that the Great Birther wishes to give. Only those who are pure through and through can be such receivers. This is the gift of waiting: even through long periods of uncertainty. Only those who have trust can be such waiters. This is the gift of bearing. Love bears all things. Only those who love can be bearers. This is the gift of accompanying, and being fully present to the others. Only those who are freed from self-concern can be an accompanier. This is the gift of tending, to practical and to deepest needs, without ever possessing. Only those who are secure in God can be tenders.

There may be a time of listening, journal writing or sharing in pairs followed by singing.

Intercession

Leader   May the prayers of this woman, clothed in light, bring Jesus to a waiting world, and so fill its void.

All   Inspired by her love, help us to be God-bearers in the world.

There may be free or prepared prayers and singing

Leader   The love that Mary gave her son

All   May we give to the world.

MARY NIGHT PRAYER
Resurrection

Leader   Glory to the Birther, who used a mother's womb.
Glory to the Son, who lay in a mother's lap.
Glory to the Spirit who transformed
a mother's life.

There may be singing

Reader   Psalm 113

Poet   To come into your presence,
Virgin of the lowly,
to come into your presence,
mother of Jesus Christ.

To come into your presence,
dwelling of meekness,
to come into your presence,
home of peace.

To come into your presence,
beauteous one of smiles,
to come into your presence,
beauteous one of women.
Carmina Gadelica

Leader   You lead the procession of holy and risen ones,
the first fruits of a new creation.

Reader   1 Corinthians 15:35-44

Leader   With you we shall reign with Christ.
With you we shall share eternal joys.

First	Teach us to live like a seed
	that is buried in bare, wintry earth,
	that we may rise to ever new life.
Second	We pray for those whose heart, like Mary's,
	is pierced with a sword.
	For those whose loved ones
	have been cruelly snatched away.

Any may mention names

Second	Give us and them the grace of acceptance,
	that by embracing suffering love they may come
	to the deepest place of compassion
	where body and soul are transformed.
All	For in you
	truth is stronger than falsehood,
	light is stronger than darkness,
	love is stronger than hate,
	and life is stronger than death.
Leader	Let us name those we wish to pray for.

Any may mention names

Leader	You, Christ, are the King of glory,
	the eternal Son of the Father.
	When you took our flesh to set us free,
	you humbly chose the Virgin's womb.
	You overcame the sting of death
	and opened the kingdom of heaven to all believers.
	You are seated at God's right hand in glory.
	We believe that you will come and be our judge.

All	Come then, Lord, and help your people,
	bought with the price of your own blood,
	and bring us with your saints
	to glory everlasting. *Te Deum*

There may be singing

Leader	Jesus, lie down with us.
All	Spirit, lie down with us.
Leader	Father, lie down with us.

Leader	King of the universe, you gave a humble virgin
	the honour of being the mother of your son,
	and crowned her with the glory of heaven.
	Now may we sleep in the assurance of sins forgiven,
	and in the promise of the resurrection of the body.
All	To the glory of God. Amen.

Martin of Tours

4 July – his ordination

11 November – his death (in the West)

12 November – his death (in the East)

Suitable for gatherings where the theme is child labour, lepers, church planting, outreach, simplicity, or service

MARTIN MORNING PRAYER

There may be singing

Storyteller

I'd like today to tell you the story of one of the most significant Christians in the early Church. His name was Martin, and he was born in the year 316. His father was a tough professional Roman soldier, and a very keen pagan: none of this Christian stuff for him. He even named his little boy Martin, after the pagan god of war, Mars. But parents can't always make choices for their children. The Christian faith was spreading, and when he was ten, young Martin wandered into a Christian meeting. He was fascinated. He couldn't go right in, as he wasn't baptised, but he could see in and hear the songs and the stories and the bishop's address. He came back again and again, and then asked whether he could be prepared for baptism. The wise elders said, 'Not yet', but they did put him on to a list of those who were interested. So all through his early teens he was listening, learning and growing keener. When he heard about the very early monks of the desert he decided that, as soon as he came of age at seventeen, he would be off to join them.

Then his father took a hand. He was really fed up with all this religion, and he wanted to have a real macho son. The Roman army needed soldiers so much that the emperor had brought the minimum age down to sixteen. Martin's father arranged for him to be kidnapped and forcibly enrolled in the army. So the army was his fate for the next twenty-five years, the usual length of a soldier's service. On Remembrance Day, 11 November, when we think about so many young folk who went to fight against their will, it seems right to think of yet another – Martin.

First   We pray to you, O God, for young people
who are forced into service of any kind
against their will:
Those who fight in wars
or work in trades they do not believe in;
those who, in order to keep others happy,
violate their own aptitudes or ideals.

There may be music or mime

God's Word

Second   Psalm 137:1-6

Storyteller

Martin did not die, but for the moment, there was for him no baptism, no desert, no life among believing Christian brothers. All the same, in the army he tried hard to continue to be Christian. He gave away as much of his pay as he could to the poor. As the son of an officer he became an officer and had a servant, but his custom was that one day the servant cleaned his boots and the next day he cleaned the servant's. That couldn't have gone down too well in the officers' mess.

Third   Daniel 1:1-17

The following may be read or another song sung

Reader or singers

When my life seems all duty and dust
in the midst of the day when we droop,
when routine things turn to rust,
and people from valour do stoop,
then the Wild Goose* comes to my aid –
his wings pass o'er and give shade,
make the day's scorching heat soon fade
and I know in God's image I'm made
and that nothing of this world can degrade.
Nothing of this world can degrade.

Andrew Dick †

The following may be mimed

Storyteller

The best-known story about Martin belongs to this early time in the army. One severe winter's day he noticed a beggar without clothing who was ignored by everybody. Martin had little else

---

* The Wild Goose is a Celtic symbol of God's Holy Spirit.

† The tune is in *The Celtic Hymn Book*, to be published in 2005 by Kevin Mayhew Ltd

to give, so he drew his sword, slashed his military cloak into two parts, and gave one to the beggar. That night Martin had a vision of Christ dressed in the half-cloak he had given to the beggar, and he heard Jesus say, 'Martin, who is not yet a baptised Christian, gave me this robe.'

Fourth   Matthew 25:31-40

There may be a mime. Square cloths are placed over some of those present

There may be teaching and singing

Intercession

After each of the following petitions there may be a pause or free prayer

First   God of the call,
we thank you for Martin the soldier.
Let us pray for all those in armed services.

Second   We thank you for Martin the solitary.
Let us pray for hermits and contemplatives
and those who feel nudged in this direction . . .

Third   We thank you for Martin the servant.
Let us pray for a revival of the ideal of service
in public and private life.

Fourth   We thank you for Martin the soul-winner.
Let us pray for those who have lost their way,
and for the rekindling of the tender reaching out
of the soul-winner.

Fifth   We thank you for Martin the spiritual parent.
Let us pray for parents, priests and other leaders.

Leader   Inspired by Martin's example,
              give us Christ-like disciplines,
              stillness of heart, compassion for the people,
              and an eye for building others up.

              There may be singing

All   The grace of our Lord Jesus Christ,
              the love of God and the fellowship
              of the Holy Spirit be with us all, evermore.

MARTIN MIDDAY PRAYER

Storyteller

              Eventually Martin reached the age of forty-one
              and was free of the army. His mind was still on
              the early monks of the desert, but he experimented.
              He made friends with the bishop of the big city
              of Poitiers, and for a little while lived with a
              group of priests and deacons in his house. Then
              he tried roughing it with one companion on a
              tiny island, where they lived on roots and what-
              ever they could scratch from the land.

              Then the same kind bishop gave him a ruined
              villa at a place called Liguge, and here he lived a
              hard but happy life with a group of brothers.

              He began to be famous in the local area as a
              healer, especially of those who were believed to
              be possessed by demons.

First   For two years Martin lived on little more than
              roots.

For several years his friend and mentor, Hilary,
was exiled for being true to himself and God.

O Lord, when we find it hard
to bear the heat and burden of the day,
help us to stick it out; meet our daily needs
and steer us along the right path.

Second Once Martin was attacked by thieves. One of
them asked him, 'Are you not afraid?' Martin
replied that he was a Christian and had never felt
so safe, but he grieved for the state of his attacker.
He explained Christ's way to the robber, who
believed and asked Martin to pray for him.

Third Psalm 121

All Lead us from fear to trust.
Lead us from despair to hope.
Lead us from hate to love.
Lead us from war to peace.
Deep peace of the son of peace,
fill our hearts, our workplace, our world.

Silence, free prayer or singing

First Jesus said: Unless you deny yourselves,
pick up your cross and follow me,
you cannot be my disciples.

Second Be with us, now, Lord in the middle of the day,
and be with all whom we shall meet.
Keep us in the beautiful attitudes,
simple, joyful and gentle.

Third   May the Three of limitless love
             pour upon us tenderly and graciously,
             hour by hour.
All   Amen.

MARTIN EVENING PRAYER

There may be singing

Storyteller

It was Martin's reputation which brought that happy phase of his life to an end. In those days, when there was a vacancy for a bishop, the local people used to get together and elect one, and their choice was supposed to be confirmed by the other bishops of that area. A vacancy occurred in the important city of Tours. The people of Tours knew who they wanted: Martin. So a crowd of them set out for Liguge, and the unsuspecting Martin was kidnapped for the second time in his life and brought to Tours. But it didn't please the local bishops. They were gentlemen: wealthy, well-educated, cultured. Martin's clothes were wrong, his hairstyle was wrong: they were not going to accept this wild and woolly man. But then a strange thing happened. The presiding bishop was playing for time; he ordered the service to begin with the readings, and one of the readers read the wrong lesson. He read, apparently by accident, part of Psalm 8.

Reader   Psalm 8:1-3

Storyteller

'Out of the mouths of babes and infants . . . '
That settled it. The babes and infants were felt to
be the ordinary people; God had spoken through
them, and Martin became bishop of Tours.

Now Martin was not an administrator and he
was not a scholar; he was above all a pastor, and
he wanted to be out among the people. For a
little while he lived in the bishop's palace in the
city. Then he shook everyone by moving out to a
field. It was within walking distance of the city,
so that he could still be there as the bishop, but
he wanted to live in a little wooden hut. Of
course others joined him, and there, in that
meadow, at the foot of a sheltering cliff, there
grew up a colony of hermits, all under Martin's
direction. Don't think of a highly organised
monastery: it was too early for that. Think of an
experiment in Christian living, in which those
who had been rich shared equally with those who
had been poor.

There may be discussion

God's Word

Reader   Deuteronomy 15:7, 8, 10, 11

*The following may be sung twice to the tune of
'Amazing Grace'*

All sing   Magnificat, magnificat, praise God my soul,
praise God.

The proud are downed, the poor raised up,
magnificat, my soul.

Reader   1 Thessalonians 5:1-11

There may be singing, teaching or creative activity

Intercession

Reader   Lord, we thank you for Martin – soldier, servant
and soul-winner. Inspired by his example we pray:
give to us discipline for Christ,
give to us the heart of stillness
that desires to enjoy you alone,
give to us compassion towards others
for Christ's sake,
give to us an eye for building others up.

Storyteller

The coat of arms of Martin of Tours contains a
wild goose and a sheet of flame: for Christians
these are two symbols of the Holy Spirit. In the
cathedral at Tours those who wish to pray are
invited to light a candle and pray the following
prayer:

A person comes centre with a candle and lights it:

Candlelighter Lord,
this candle that I have lit –
may it be Light from you to lighten my way
through difficulties and decisions.
May it be Fire from you
to burn up my selfishness, my pride

and all that is impure within me.
May it be Flame from you to warm my heart
and teach me love.
Lord, I cannot stay long in your house.
This candle is a little bit of myself
that I offer to you.
Help me to continue my prayer
in all that I do this day.

There may be silence and singing

Leader Go forth strong in Christ as Martin was strong.
Strong to overcome the weakness of our nature.
Strong to uphold the ways of simplicity and
truth in Christ's Church.
Strong to reach out in burning love to others.

All Amen.

MARTIN NIGHT PRAYER

Reader Psalm 112:1-9

Storyteller

Martin himself lived to the age of eighty-one.
He still had to go into the city, to take the principal part in the Church's liturgy; he was expected
to be the main preacher. But he cared about those
in the more distant parts of his diocese and, every
year in the late autumn and early winter, he would
tour his parishes, walking, praying and seeing to
the needs of his people.

Everyone could see that this bishop was different from others. Martin took the imitation of

Christ so literally. He prayed, he fasted, he cared for the poor; he had no possessions, he healed the sick, he taught, he served. And he inspired a great following, though he did not know of the far-flung places where men would seek to be monks after his pattern. One of those far-flung places was Lindisfarne. Somehow news of Martin spread through France, across the Channel, to Canterbury, up to the north-west at Whithorn, and over into Ireland. Martin was the first bishop who was also a monk, but many followed, among them St Aidan. At a time when monasticism was a living, growing, dynamic force within the Christian Church, Martin showed that far from being something separate it was in fact the central structure of the Church: not a breakaway movement of the distant deserts but an instrument of the Spirit which could bring the faith to the places where people lived and worked.

So Martin is yet another of those whom we look upon as our ancestors. He would have been astonished. And now we thank God for him, and for all those who have built up for us, and handed down to us, a rich inheritance.

Reader   In his old age Martin offered this prayer to God:
Wholly given to you,
I will fulfil whatever duties you assign to me,
and serve under your banner for as long
as you prescribe.
Though release is sweet to an old man
after long years of toil,
my mind is a victor over the years.

First   Teach us, good Lord, to serve you with all our being
to the last breath of our lives.
Teach us not to question why
but to embrace each day's duties with childlike trust.

All sing   Faithful vigil ended,
watching, waiting cease;
Master, grant your servant
his discharge in peace.

All the Spirit promised,
all the Father willed,
now these eyes behold it
perfectly fulfilled.

This your great deliverance
sets your people free;
Christ their light uplifted
all the nations see.

Christ, your people's glory!
Watching, doubting cease;
grant to us your servants
our discharge in peace.
            Timothy Dudley-Smith

Second   Martin, faithful pastor, faithful in prayer,
may we be faithful in our prayers
for those who need them.
Our dear ones bless, O God,
in every place where they are,
especially those we name before you now.

Any may mention names

There may be singing

Reader	I lie down this night with God.
All	And God will lie down with me.
Reader	I lie down this night with Christ.
All	And Christ will lie down with me.
Reader	I lie down this night with the Spirit.
All	And the Spirit will lie down with me.
Reader	God and Christ and the Spirit,
All	Lying down with me.
Reader	With Martin and the saints in glory we make the sign of the Cross of Christ. +
All	May your Cross be between us and all things harmful. And your Cross light up for us the company of heaven.
Reader	May your cloud of witnesses who shine so brightly enfold us as we sleep.
All	The saints of God to will us, the peace of God to still us, the love of God to fill us, tonight and always.

The storyteller's words are
by Kate Tristram with permission

CREATIVE ACTIVITIES

1. In Germany, St Martin songs are sung while someone rides a horse and re-enacts Martin's giving of half his coat to a beggar.

2. Make biscuits in the shape of a coat, cut these in half and distribute them. Or biscuits may be in the shape of a goose, recalling the legend that Martin hid from those who wished to make him bishop, but the noise of the geese betrayed his presence.

Mungo (Kentigern)

Suitable for gatherings where the theme includes animals,
the sanctity of life, prayer or nation building

MUNGO MORNING PRAYER

Storyteller

The story of Mungo and of his courageous mother is the story of great difficulties overcome with even greater faith.

Leader The angel of the Lord encompasses those
who reverence God,
who will deliver them.

There may be singing

God's Word

Leader I keep the Lord always before me;
because God is at my side, I shall not be moved.
All I keep the Lord always before me.
Leader Those who choose another god
multiply their sorrows;
God is the One I have chosen.
All I keep the Lord always before me.
Leader Therefore my heart is glad, and my soul rejoices;
my body also rests secure.
All I keep the Lord always before me.

Leader	For you do not give me up to the dead,
	or let your faithful one see the pit.
All	I keep the Lord always before me.
Leader	You show me the path of life.
	In your presence there is fullness of joy.
All	I keep the Lord always before me.

Echoes Psalm 16

Storyteller

Mungo was very nearly never born. His grand-father, Loth, the arrogant ruler of the region to which he gives his name, Lothian, in Scotland, had tried to force a marriage upon his mother, Tannoc. She felt called to serve Christ as a virgin and refused. Loth threw her out in a rage. The Prince whose love she had spurned rode after her and raped her on his way home. When her father heard that she was pregnant, he ordered his staff to take her to the summit of Traprain Law and push her over the edge – an alternative to stoning. Somehow she survived the fall. Perhaps the wind ballooned her large dress into a kind of parachute. God seemed to be with her, but Loth's officials would have none of that. They took her a few miles to the eastern coast, put her in a little boat without sail or oars, and pushed her out to die in the wild, vast ocean. God's winds, however, blew her northwards, up into the Firth of Forth, until her little boat was beached at some fields near Culross. The locals had become Christians, and they took her to their priest, a monk named Serf, who had a little community there.

Serf took this poor woman into the care of the community and in due course a baby boy was born. What name should they give him? She, with an audacious flair, and perhaps a touch of humour, named him Big Chief – Kentigern in her tongue. But when Serf gently took the infant into his arms, he said 'My beloved' – 'Mungo' in his tongue. And the pet name Mungo has stuck ever since.

There may be singing or music

Reader Zechariah 13:7-9

Leader The compassing of God be on you.
All The compassing of the God of life.
Leader The compassing of Christ be upon you.
All The compassing of the Christ of love.
Leader The compassing of the Spirit be upon you.
All The compassing of the Spirit of grace.
Leader The compassing of the Three be upon you.
All The compassing of the Three preserve you.
The compassing of the Three preserve us all evermore.   *Carmina Gadelica*

Reader Hebrews 11:39-12 or Mark 13:9-11

There may be teaching or discussion

Storyteller

One day at Culross some robins started to peck scraps of food on the ground and some village boys threw stones at them. One stone hit a robin head-on and it lay there, apparently dead. Mungo took it into his hands, stroked it, and asked Jesus to make it better. It soon revived and flew off. The story of that robin was told and retold ever after, and the robin flew into Glasgow's coat of arms where it perches to this day on top of an oak tree.

A song such as 'All things bright and beautiful' may be sung

Intercession

Leader   We thank you for Mungo's mother Tannoc,
who cherished the child born of rape
as God's precious gift.

All   Blessed God, may every child be cherished.

Leader   We thank you for the robin,
restored through Mungo's prayers.

All   Blessed God, may every creature be cherished.

There may be prayer for unborn babies and for the wild birds and animals followed by singing

Leader   The King of life encompass you.
The loving Christ encompass you.
The Holy Spirit encompass you.
And give you the crown eternal.

MUNGO MIDDAY PRAYER

Leader   In the middle of the day, open our eyes,
as you opened Mungo's, to the flying birds.
Open our ears to their song,
and to the song you plant in our own hearts.

Storyteller

When he was fifteen, Mungo left Serf's fosterage and trained for ten years under Fergus in Stirling, until Fergus died. They buried him in a Christian cemetery consecrated by Ninian years before. There Mungo built up a Christian community so joyful that it came to be known as Glesgu, meaning the 'happy family'. And that is how Glasgow got its name.

Reader Psalm 127:1, 2

Leader We remember the dying old man,
whom Mungo anointed for eternal life,
All Blessed God, may every dying person be cherished.
Leader For founding the Dear Family of Christians
now known as Glasgow,
All Blessed God, may our church and city be cherished.

There may be singing

Storyteller

Mungo, from his base at Cathures, became a firm friend of Rhydderch, the Christian King of Strathclyde, whose headquarters were fifteen miles down river at Dunbarton. But Morcant, the local ruler and patron of the Druid altar at Craigmaddie Moor, was a bitter enemy of them both. His mercenaries looted the local crops, which they stored in Morcant's barn. That winter real hunger struck Mungo's people. He walked to Craigmaddie Moor and confronted Morcant, telling him that the people needed food. 'You Christians teach that God will provide for those who serve him. Well, I don't serve him and I have plenty; you serve him and have nothing, so your teaching must be false,' Morcant mocked him.

Mungo returned to Cathures empty handed, but he was not defeated. He gathered the people to pray. Their prayers were answered in this way: The rain came down in deluge after deluge. The rivers flooded their banks, and Morcant's barn took off towards the river Clyde like an ark on a wild cruise. On the banks of the Molindar it went hard aground beside Mungo's church!

Next morning, Mungo gathered his flock to thank God and eat a good breakfast. Morcant did not find it at all funny!

Reader   The Selkirk Grace before a meal:

Some have meat and cannot eat,
some cannot eat that want it:
But we have meat and we can eat,
sae let the Lord be thankit!

Robert Burns

There may be music or singing

Reader   Matthew 7:7-11

Leader   As we thank God for the way he met the needs
of Mungo's hungry community,
and for the power of prayer,
let us pray for the people we know of
who are hungry, homeless or harassed.

Silent or free prayer, or the Lord's Prayer and singing

Leader	Be with us now, Lord, for the rest of the day.
	Mindful of Mungo's example, keep us faithful, caring and true.
All	In the name of Christ.
	Amen!

MUNGO EVENING PRAYER

Storyteller

Following the example of Ninian and Serf, he dressed in the roughest hair cloth, used a simple, ungilded staff, and spent Lent alone in a desert place. The spiritual poise he gained there attracted many people to him.

A pagan revival took place in the North. The Christians were left without shepherds, so Rhydderch, the Christian King of Strathclyde, insisted that Mungo be consecrated a bishop even though he was only twenty-five. After some seventeen years as overseer in the North, hostile forces drove the Christians out. Mungo had to head south, walking via Cumbria and stopping at meeting places on the way to rally the faithful and win new converts to Christ.

First   Psalm 18:2, 3

Second   The name of the Lord is a strong tower;
All   The righteous run to it and are safe.

Reader   Proverbs 18:10

There may be singing

Storyteller

Mungo sought out David, the great Christian leader of the western Britons, at his great monastery at what is now St David's, in Wales. They embraced each other with tears like long lost brothers. Mungo stayed with David and while he was there he reached out to befriend the poor and the powerful alike.

First

Help us, Lord,
to reach out to poor and rich alike,
making no distinctions,
letting the love in our hearts
overcome fear and apathy alike.

A person comes to the centre and teaches everyone to reach out their right hand as a way of taking authority in Christ's name to reach out to people

He or she teaches everyone to first face north, then east, then south, then west, visualising the people who are present in these four quarters

All repeat (R) each line after the leader

Leader

Touch them, Lord. *(R)*
Melt them, Lord. *(R)*
Open their hearts, Lord. *(R)*
Stimulate friendships, Lord. *(R)*
Heal misunderstandings. *(R)*

Then repeat for each area

Storyteller

The local ruler said that Mungo could choose anywhere in his kingdom to establish a monastic community. Many old friends from the north joined him as he searched for the right place. Yet it was a wild boar that God used to befriend them and lead them to the right place. Once there, Mungo prayed over the boar who then left them in peace.

The company set to work clearing the ground and erecting buildings until a hostile pagan ruler, who claimed they had strayed into his territory, demanded that they demolish everything and leave. All seemed lost until this man was suddenly smitten with blindness. Desperate, he returned to Mungo and begged him to pray for his cure. Mungo prayed, laid hands on the man's eyes and signed them with the Cross. Sight was restored and the ruler was baptised. Thereafter he became a generous benefactor of the burgeoning community.

This is an example of how we can overcome evil with good.

Reader   Romans 12:17-21

There may be singing

Storyteller

In 573, Strathclyde's Christian King Rhydderch won a victory and was reinstated. He sent for Mungo to return. God spoke to Mungo with prophesies of innumerable people to be won for the Lord. He wept, but in obedience, he left.

Intercession

Leader   There are innumerable people
to be won to God now,
and our obedience is still the key.
So let us pray for the people who know not
our God,
and let us give God the worship of our obedience:

May your church, filled with the Holy Spirit,
unite the world in a fellowship of peoples
where mercy and justice,
truth and freedom may flourish;
where we honour one another
and acknowledge you as the source
of our common good.

*There may be free prayer for children, for birds, for
mothers, for the persecuted*

There may be singing

Leader   May we act justly,
love kindness
and walk humbly with our God.
May hope be ours in every step,
may healing flow from our every word.
May our hearts become bright
with the light of God,
the peace of God possess us,
the love of God caress us,
the grace of God bless us.

MUNGO NIGHT PRAYER

Storyteller

Mungo returned with over six hundred monks to King Rhydderch at his castle at Hoddam. The ageing king placed his sword in Mungo's hands and surrendered his kingdom to Christ the King of Heaven, and Mungo helped to bring into being a Christian nation.

Reader   Psalm 8

There may be a song which enthrones Christ

Storyteller

After eight years at Hoddam, Mungo returned to his beloved church family at Glasgow. He met with Columba to plan for the evangelisation of the pagan kingdoms to the north and south, and journeyed to Rome to help forward this grand strategy. It seems likely this led Rome to send a delegation to Iona and a mission team to Kent.

Reader   Matthew 5:13-16

Leader   May our inner life give flavour to the world
and our actions shed light.
As the sun sets on our half of the globe
and rises on another,
we bring to you the peoples of the world
who know you not.

There may be silence and singing

Leader   Now we bring to you our concerns this night.

Any may mention names or say prayers
There may be singing

Storyteller

Throughout his life Mungo continued two practices: baptising people at Epiphany time, and having a daily warm bath – a custom which his father had learned from the days of the Roman Empire. One day in a vision he was told that his life had been one long martyrdom, and that he would be allowed to leave it in an easy way. His friends lifted him for the last time into a warm bath. After some time in it, seemingly free from all pain, he lifted his hands to heaven, bowed his head, and slid effortlessly into the sleep of death which for him was eternal life.

Leader   Now let us sleep the deep sleep of peace.

Reader   Sleep, sleep, and away with sorrow,
sleep in the arms of Jesus.
Sleep, sleep in the lap of God.
Sleep in the love of all loves.

All   May we be numbered with Mungo and your saints in glory everlasting.

Ninian of Whithorn

26 August

16 September

Suitable for gatherings where the themes include church planting, circling, miracles

NINIAN MORNING PRAYER

Leader	The people who walked in darkness have seen a great light. Light has come into the world through Christ our High King. Light has come into dark places through his saints.
All	The light of Christ has come into the world.
Leader	You led your people through Moses by a pillar of fire. You led your people through Ninian to a place of shining brightness.
All	The light of Christ has come into the world.
Leader	May we who walk in the light of Christ's presence acclaim him, that he may banish all darkness from our lives and our land today.
All	The light of Christ has come into the world.

There may be singing

Storyteller

Ninian came from the demoralised runt of Christianity that survived after the Romans, along with much of their civilisation and much of the Christian Church, had departed from Britain at the beginning of the fifth century. Instead of going with the tide of retreat, he rekindled the flame of faith, made contacts with the Church in Europe and touched base with the life-changing community at Tours, founded by Martin, which was changing many lives. Inspired by this community, he returned to his native region with stone masons and built a village of God at what is now Whithorn in Galloway. This became a beacon throughout Britain and Ireland. It was known as the White House, the same word used in the Gospels to describe the shining white of Jesus' clothes at his mountain-top transfiguration. Thus we may think of his faith community not only as a white house, but also as a large household shining with Christ's light.

Leader   God of light,
who led Ninian to witness to you
in a land ignorant of your ways,
to establish a community that shone in the dark,
and to pray with courage for miracles,
establish the work of our hands
that with courage we may bring healing and light
into the dark places of our time.

Reader   Psalm 56
Response after verses 4, 7, 11, and 13:

All   I walk in the light that shines on the living.

Reader   2 Chronicles 5

Almighty God, Creator

Leader   Almighty God, Creator,
         greyness has enveloped our world.

All   As we lift our hearts to you may your glory
         make all things clear.

Leader   Almighty God, Creator,
         you seem absent from your world.

All   Sun of suns,
         in everything we touch and everyone we meet,
         light up your presence.

Leader   Almighty God, Creator, awake for us your presence
         in cloud and grey and storm,

All   Till our trivial tasks become sacraments
         in the temple of your love.

There may be music

Reader   2 Peter 1:10-19

There may be singing

Storyteller

The first wave of Christianity in Britain came to the southern part occupied by the Romans, and this had largely fallen away. The Cymric tribes of the west, and of Strathclyde and Galloway, had never fully integrated into the Roman Empire, and they defended their culture against the invading Anglo-Saxons (as well as against the Gaels from Ireland) for much longer than did the people left behind in Roman Britain. Ninian became an apostle of Christ, not only in his own Galloway, but amongst the Picts beyond the river Tay with their pagan Druid ways.

Intercession

Leader   We pray for modern Ninians who will establish
communities of light in slum places,
sanctuaries of prayer in unvisited places,
links of faith and love with the Continent,
our spiritual home.

*There may be free or prepared prayer on these themes
and singing*

Storyteller

Ninian is the first Christian who is recorded as
using the Caim Circling prayer. When he had to
leave his fledgling community, he feared lest
bandits would rob and steal. So he gathered all
the cattle into one place and made a circle in the
earth around them with his staff, praying protection for all inside the circle and that hostile
people would be kept out of the circle. Bandits
did indeed come, but when they reached the
circle they were overtaken by seizures and their
leader seemed about to die. Ninian returned to
find them shivering in the bushes, not knowing
what to do with their leader. He explained there
was no longer any need to steal in the land since
pilgrim centres like theirs would feed any hungry
person. He prayed for their leader, who was
restored to full health. The bandits began to
praise God.

Leader   Circle us, O God,
keep harm without, keep good within.

Any may say a circle prayer:

Any Circle _____ O God,
keep _____ without,
keep _____ within.

There may be singing

Leader May the countenance of the Father of glory,
the countenance of the Sun of suns,
the countenance of the radiant Spirit,
pour pure white light abundantly upon us,
hour by hour.

NINIAN MIDDAY PRAYER

Storyteller

Young men developed into disciples through
experience of the kingdom of God totally lived.
Discipline sometimes had to be exercised. One
young man who had committed a serious offence
ran away rather than face his discipline, taking
with him Ninian's staff. He took to sea in a boat
which began to leak. This brought him to his
knees in penitence and prayer. He struck the
leaking side of the boat with Ninian's staff, the
leak stopped and he was saved. He returned to
Ninian a changed person, imbued with awe at the
signs and wonders God can work, and remained a
pillar of support to Ninian thereafter.

Leader Lord, help us to stay with our duties
even when they are daunting or dull.
All In the middle of the day
keep us in Christ's disciplines of hard work,
responsible service and perseverance.

First	Unless the Lord builds the house, those who build it labour in vain. *Psalm 127:1*
Second	Whatever the work you do, do it wholeheartedly, as if you were doing it for God, for you know that God will reward each person for the good they do. *Echoes Ephesians 6:7*
Third	My brothers and sisters, whenever you face trials of any kind, consider it nothing but joy, because you know that the testing of your faith produces endurance. *James 1:2*

There may be silence, singing and free prayer

Leader	Lord, Ninian was the guileless one,
All	Take from us all guile.
Leader	Ninian was the tireless one,
All	Take from us all sloth.
Leader	Ninian was the fearless one, take from us all cowardice.
All	Ninian was the radiant one, take from us all that clouds the soul.
Leader	Let us go forward into this day, strengthened by Ninian's example, armed with the truth of Scripture and the power of the Spirit, praying at all times, overcoming evil with good.
All	For yours is the kingdom, the power and the glory, for ever and ever. Amen.

NINIAN EVENING PRAYER

Before this begins a papier mâché cave may be made and placed in a central position. Pens, pieces of paper and Blu-Tack are made available

Leader   We come into the presence of the affirming Father.
We come into the presence of the enabling Son.
We come into the presence of the succouring Spirit.
We come into the presence of the Three in One.

There may be singing

Storyteller

Although Ninian had a following among his own people, he was bitterly opposed by the local ruler Tuduvallus, whose power was threatened, albeit by a kingdom not of this world. Ninian entered into spiritual warfare. The ruler, struck down with a disease that cost him his sight, became penitent and asked Ninian to forgive him. Echoing Jesus' action with the man whose sins he forgave (Mark 2:10), Ninian forgave him, but also laid hands upon him and healed him. From then on the ruler warmly supported Ninian's evangelisation programme.

Leader   In Ninian there was nothing of fear, all was love;
forgive us for the places in our lives
where fear has driven out love.
Lord have mercy.

All   Lord have mercy.

There may be silence or free prayer on this theme

Leader   In Ninian, truth and warmth shone forth; forgive us for the places in our lives that are false or frozen.

	Christ have mercy.
All	Christ have mercy.

There may be silence or free prayer on this theme

Leader	In Ninian was a radiant face and a fruitful frame; forgive us for the places in our lives which are tarnished and unfruitful. Lord have mercy.
All	Lord have mercy.

Reader	Psalm 36:1-9

Leader	Father, who through Ninian caused the light of the Good News to shine in the Western Shores, lead us by its brightness to become children of a new birth, growing into your image from glory to glory.

Reader	Jeremiah 1:4-9

This Catechism attributed to Ninian may be said:

Leader	What is best in this world?
All	To do the will of our Maker.
Leader	What is his will?
All	That we should live according to the laws of his creation.
Leader	How do we know those laws?
All	By study – studying the scriptures with devotion.
Leader	What tool has our Maker provided for this study?
All	The intellect which can probe everything.
Leader	And what is the fruit of study?
All	To perceive the eternal Word of God

reflected in every plant and insect,
every bird and animal,
and every man and woman.

Reader   Matthew 9:35-38

Storyteller

Ninian established parishes throughout the region, and ordained presbyters. Now spiritual warfare had to be fought in the Church. One unmarried Church member who was found to be pregnant accused her presbyter of rape; he denied it. How would Ninian handle this? He was given faith to call forth a rare spiritual gift. At a meeting of the whole Church, after he laid hands in prayer on all those who had been baptised, the woman held up her day-old baby and shouted out her accusations against the presbyter. Ninian fixed his eyes on the infant, and commanded it to speak out if the presbyter was its father. The baby stretched out his little fingers towards another man who was the real culprit, and sounds came from his mouth which everyone understood to mean: 'He is my father'.

There may be singing

Intercession

Storyteller

A thirty-minute walk from the community buildings at Whithorn brings one to a cave on the shore to which the hermit in Ninian loved to retreat. There this prayer warrior spent long hours in vigil. Today many pilgrims still come to pray, and prayers are carved or hung on the

stones and rocks around the cave. This evening
we, too, will gather around Ninian's prayer cave.

Leader   Let us pray for the rekindling of faith,
for the building up of places of prayer,
for the turning of the tide.

*Each person takes a stone from the a pile of stones
at the cave, and holds it in their hand as they pray
along the lines suggested by the leader. If and when
anyone is ready, they scratch a prayer on the stone,
or write it on a piece of paper and place the stone or
paper in the cave*

*The leader may read these out or invite each to read
out their own prayer. Everyone says 'Amen' after
each prayer*

*There may be singing and sharing of scripture verses,
pictures or words from God*

Leader   May the eternal Father ground you
in the rock of truth.
May the saving Christ free you from all that harms.
May the flowing Spirit spring up
as the fountain of wisdom in your hearts.

NINIAN NIGHT PRAYER

Leader   We are told that all was love,
there was nothing of fear
in this enpurpled radiant one,
and that Ninian died full of years,
with his powers undiminished.

There may be silence or music

Reader	Psalm 139:1-12
Leader	This night, O Lord,
All	May all be love.
Leader	Where there is fear
All	May all be love.
Leader	Where there is hostility
All	May all be love.
Leader	Where there is regret
All	May all be love.
Leader	As we sleep
All	May all be love.

There may be singing

Leader	This night, as we thank you for Ninian reaching out to the Picts,
	we bring to you the people who do not know you.
All	Bring them into the circle of your love
Leader	We pray especially for _____.
Leader	This night we bring to you also our dear ones.
All	Bring them into the circle of your love.
Leader	Let us name these, silently or aloud.

Any may mention names

Leader	We pray for all whom we have named.
All	Bring them into the circle of your love.
Reader	1 Peter 5:8-11

There may be silence, sharing or singing

Leader	Lord of Ninian,
All	Tonight we sleep with you.
Leader	Lord of the years,
All	Tonight we sleep with you.
Leader	Lord of our past,
All	Tonight we sleep with you.
Leader	Lord of our future,
All	Tonight we sleep with you.
Leader	Lord of our resurrection,
All	Tonight we sleep with you.
Leader	In glory we shall see the Lord.
All	May we walk with the saints in the glory of the Triune God through the ages of ages, Amen.

Leader	The radiance of the Father
All	Bathe our being tonight.
Leader	The radiance of the Son
All	Bathe our being tonight.
Leader	The radiance of the Spirit
All	Bathe our being tonight.
Leader	May the almighty and merciful Lord be with us.
All	Awake, may we watch with Christ. And asleep, may we rest in peace.

Oswald

5 August – death

8 October – enshrined

Suitable for gatherings where the themes include nation-building, government, service, prayer, humility

OSWALD MORNING PRAYER

Leader   Let us worship the King of kings,
and honour Oswald,
the first to model Christ-like rule
to the English people.

There may be singing

Reader   Psalm 72:1-8
After every second verse all say the following response:

All   May our rulers be like gentle rain on parched fields.

Leader   In the light of Oswald's example of selfless service, let us confess our failure to use our opportunities to serve the common good and to bring Christ to others. In the light of Oswald's boldness in action and diligence in daily life, let us confess our cowardice and our lukewarmness in prayer:

All   Have mercy on us, O God,
forgive our foolish ways.
Turn our hearts again, redeem our nights and days.

There may be silence or a Kyrie eleison may be sung

Reader	Joshua 1:1-9
First	Young Oswald on Iona, learning ways of God.
	Young Oswald on Iona,
	under yoke of work and Word.
Second	King Oswald in Northumbria,
	reflecting ways of God.
	King Oswald in Northumbria,
	winning subjects to his Lord.
First	Onward Christian soldiers,
	from training grounds of prayer,
	with shield of faith march into
	new lands to cleanse and clear.
Second	Onward Christian soldiers,
	slay feuding, fear and strife;
	bring to lands long-blighted
	Christ's truth and love and life.
First	Onward Christian soldiers,
	prepare Christ's folk a home;
	with tongue of fire assist them
	as through the land they roam.
Second	Onward Christian soldiers,
	have mercy on the poor;
	and give to Christ's proclaimers an ever-open door.
All	Onward Christian soldiers,
	teach folk to live and die:
	Confident in heaven, reborn eternally.
Reader	1 Timothy 2:1-7

There may be singing, teaching, the following reading about Oswald or a creative activity

When the two kings of northern and southern Northumbria were slain, one of whom was his elder brother, Oswald sought to defeat the invading tyrant and reclaim the throne. In exile he had been discipled as a Christian at Columba's Christian community on the island of Iona in north-west Britain. Now he came with an army, small in number but strengthened by its faith in Christ, to confront his opponent, who had far greater forces, at a place near the wall built by the Roman Emperor Hadrian.

Before the battle began they planted a wooden cross in the ground. Oswald himself held it with both hands while the soldiers filled in the hole. Then he raised his voice and shouted: 'Let us all kneel and pray for the almighty, ever-living and true God to defend us in his mercy from the proud and fierce enemy, for he knows ours is a just cause for the preservation of our people.'

Victory followed. That field of battle was named Heavenfield, and is still so named. Innumerable miracles of healing followed, transmitted through fragments or moss from the wooden cross.

Echoes Bede's Ecclesiastical History, *Book 3, Chapter 3. See Adomnan's* Life of Columba, *Book 1, Chapter 1, for an alternative account*

The Heavenfield cross-planting and prayer may be mimed

There may be marching, and songs
Ribbon crosses may be pinned on all those present

Intercession

Leader High King of heaven, who raised up Oswald to plant the healing tree of Christ's passion in his kingdom, redeem our land from the curse of disobedience and bring it into the wholeness of your just and gentle rule.

Four people may each hold up an Intercession Pole with the following colours: Red (First) Green (Second) Grey (Third) Orange (Fourth). Any of the following prayers may be said, followed by informal intercession – or painting or clay modelling on the theme.

First We bring to you the lands of hate and conflict;

All May these be seen as heaven's field (_____).

Second We bring to you the lands of crop and dairy (_____);

All May these be seen as heaven's field.

Third We bring to you the lands of town and commerce (_____);

All May these be seen as heaven's field.

Fourth We bring to you the lands of home and leisure (_____);

All May these be seen as heaven's field.

There may be silence, free prayer or singing

Leader God bless our land.
May its door be open to your kingly presence,
may its gates be closed
to corrupt and uncaring ways.
God bless you as you leave here,
and make you saintly all your days.

OSWALD MIDDAY PRAYER

Leader   Holy God, you have been our dwelling place through the years,
dwell with us now in the middle of the day.

First   Psalm 90:1-4
Second   Psalm 90:12-17

Storyteller

Oswald was a man of prayer who rose early every morning to pray with the palms of his hands open to receive from God. He was the first English ruler to appoint an officer to look after the needs of the poor. At an Easter Day banquet, when he, Aidan and other guests were enjoying rich food on silver plates, his officer for the poor announced that many hungry people were begging outside. Oswald ordered that their own food be taken to them, and that even the silver plates be broken up and the silver distributed to them. Aidan was deeply moved.

Leader   Together, in the spirit of Oswald, let us seek justice, serve the poor, respect all, and build the future. We are a royal priesthood: as Oswald raised his hands to bless and give to the poor, so let us raise our hands to bless the needy.

Hands may be raised

All   With these hands we bless the hungry,
the forgotten and the lost.

Any may mention names for blessing

There may be silent or free prayer

Reader   Matthew 25:34-40

Leader   High King of heaven and earth,
from whom all authority flows,
may the diverse authorities of our times
acknowledge you as the Source of life,
emulate you as the Servant King,
and fear you as the Judge of truth.

All   Our Father in heaven . . .

There may be singing

All   Lead us from greed to care,
lead us from falsehood to truth,
lead us from fear to trust,
lead us from hate to love.

OSWALD EVENING PRAYER

Storyteller

Oswald's reign was short but God-inspired, bold, energetic and civilising. Kingdoms speaking four different languages, British, Pictish, Irish and Anglo-Saxon, were linked together for the first time under his influence. He provided breathing space for perhaps the most significant mission to the English people ever to get under way.

Reader   High King of heaven and earth,
from whom all authority flows,
may the diverse authorities of our times,
with Oswald,
acknowledge you as the Source of life,

emulate you as the Servant King,
and fear you as the Judge of truth.

There may be singing

Reader   Psalm 45:1-9 or 1-17

All   Glory to the High King,
glory to his Son,
glory to the Spirit,
ever Three in One.

Reader   Deuteronomy 17:14-19

Storyteller

Oswald's personal influence continued after his death. The *Life* of Oswald caught the imagination of peoples of Europe who were looking for models of God-inspired leaders, and many churches in the European Union are dedicated to him. In German-speaking lands, legends and romantic stories were written about him, rather like those about Arthur in Britain and France, and these became vehicles of high ideals of love and chivalry. Fiction such as the twelfth-century Regensburg poems, portrayed Oswald as wanting his future bride to be both intimate and equal in all respects, and climbing always to a higher plane. These stories retained attributes of the real Oswald such as his reliance on God's help when confronting enemies, his charity to the poor, and his zeal to win pagan youth to Christ. This evening we will reflect these ideals in our prayers.

There may be singing

Reader   Matthew 20:25-28

There may be teaching, a creative activity or singing

Intercession

Leader   Almighty Father, whose will is to restore all things
in your beloved Son, the King of all,
govern the hearts and minds of those in authority
and bring the families of the nations,
divided and torn apart by the ravages of sin,
to be subject to his just and gentle rule.

From the Alternative Service Book (1980)

Where selfish ambition distorts leadership,
bring about good government.
May our political leaders be quiet in spirit,
clear in judgement,
and mindful of the needs of those
who have least power.
May they keep your laws,
be patient in setback,
and bold to take good measures.

First   We pray for churches dedicated to St Oswald
(_____).

Second   We pray for our local and national Government,
the European Parliament, the United Nations
(_____).

Third   We pray for young people to be recaptured
by high ideals of love, faithfulness
and chivalry (_____).

There may be singing

Leader   May heaven's King go with you;
may Christ's Cross grow in you;
may the Spirit's fire glow in you
till the final victory dawns.

OSWALD NIGHT PRAYER

Storyteller

There was once a popular saying: 'May God have mercy on their souls, as Oswald said when he fell to the earth.' At the close of St Oswald's Day, let us seek the mercy of God for all.

Reader   Psalm 80:1, 2, 4-6

Response after verses 2 and 6:

All   Bring us back, O God!
Show us your mercy, and we will be saved.

All may say

Lord have mercy, Christ have mercy, Lord have mercy.

or sing

Lord have mercy (*x 8*); Christ have mercy (*x 8*).

Leader   Let us pray for God's mercy on those who are on our hearts.

Any may mention names

There may be singing

Reader   Jesus said: I am with you always.
                                          Matthew 28:20

Reader   St Paul wrote: I am convinced that nothing in this
               world or the next can separate us from the love
               of God which is ours through Christ Jesus.
                                          Echoes Romans 8:38, 39

Storyteller
               Before Oswald fought the battle which won back
               his kingdom, he had a vision in the night. In this
               St Columba assured him that God would be
               with him. Years after Oswald's death a dying boy,
               along with some of the monks in a monastery at
               Bardney, had a vision in the night. St Oswald
               assured him that God would take him peacefully
               to the bliss of heaven, and that no more monks
               would die of plague. Let us consecrate our sleep
               to the God of the night visions.

Reader   O Christ, Son of the living God,
               may your saints and angels
               guard us in our sleep.
               May they watch over us as we rest,
               and hover around our beds.
               Let them reveal to us in our dreams
               visions of your glorious truth.
               May no nightmares darken our dreams,
               may no fears or worries
               delay our willing, prompt repose.

Leader   I lie down this night with God
All   And God will lie down with me.

Leader	I lie down this night with Christ
All	And Christ will lie down with me.
Leader	I lie down this night with the Spirit
All	And the Spirit will lie down with me.
Leader	God and Christ and the Spirit
All	Lying down with me.
Leader	I make the sign of the Cross of Christ. +
All	My Christ, my Shield, my Saviour;
	each day, each night, in light, in dark,
	my Treasure, my dear One,
	my eternal home.

CREATIVE ACTIVITIES

1. Practise using hands in the prayers. Palms are turned upwards in praise as Oswald's often were. Hands are raised in royal blessing.

2. Oswald died amid the slaughter of the battlefield, praying 'God save these souls'. Re-enact this, lying down as if about to die, and write prayers for the souls of others.

3. A junior dresses up in crown, sceptre and orb. A silver dish is brought to him or her, full of goodies. Each person present takes one and gives it to someone more needy than themselves.

Patrick

17 March – death

24 March – finding of his relics by Malachy

10 June – placed in a shrine

*Suitable for gatherings where the theme includes Ireland,
the Trinity, slavery, words of knowledge,
prayer, lament, art or spiritual warfare*

PATRICK MORNING PRAYER

Leader	The sun rises daily because you, O Lord, command it.
All	Its splendour will not last, created gods all perish.
Leader	Christ the true Sun nothing can destroy.
All	The Splendour of God, he shall reign for ever.

There may be a hymn or orchestral music

Storyteller

Patrick, who is loved in many lands far from Ireland, was born somewhere on Britain's north-west coast. It is quite possible he went to school with Ninian at Carlisle, though Dumbarton also claims him as its son. He was probably born about 390, although some argue it was some decades later.

Patrick's father was Calpornius, a Roman alderman who had a wealthy estate with male and female slaves. Although his grandfather was a Christian priest, it seems that Patrick and his parents were only nominal Christians. At the age of sixteen he was captured by pirates and sold as a slave in Ireland. He was denied the polished education he might otherwise have had, and instead tended his master's sheep on the hills of County Antrim. Later, in what we might call his 'Diaries', he bemoaned his wasted teenage years:

Patrick At the time I was about sixteen years old, and I did not know the true God. Along with thousands of others, I was taken in captivity to Ireland. It was no more than we deserved, for we had turned our backs on God and did not keep his laws. Neither did we obey our priests who reminded us of our salvation. As a beardless adolescent I was captured before I knew what to look for and what to avoid. I was like a stone lying deep in the mud.

Reader Psalm 70

Patrick God, who is mighty, came and lifted me up in his mercy and raised me to the top of the wall. That is why I ought to shout in a loud voice, and return something to the Lord for all his benefits here and in eternity, which the human mind cannot even begin to comprehend.

All Glory to the Father, glory to the Son,
glory to the Spirit,
ever Three in One.

Leader I arise today through a mighty power,
the Holy Trinity.

All   Affirming threeness, confessing oneness,
           in the making of all through love.

Leader I arise today through Christ's power in his birth
            and in his baptism.

All   His power in his dying, his rising from the tomb,
            and in his coming again.

Adapted from 'St Patrick's Breastplate'

Patrick After coming to Ireland I was put to work tending
             cattle, sheep and hogs, and many times during
             the day I would pray. More and more the love
             of God and the fear of God came to me, so that
             my faith was strengthened and my spirit was
             moved. In a single day I would pray as often as a
             hundred times, and nearly as often at night when
             I was staying in the woods and in the mountains.
             I would rouse myself before daylight to pray,
             whether in snow, frost, or rain; it made no
             difference and I felt no bad effects. Because the
             Spirit in me was fervent, I knew no sluggishness.

Reader   Joel 2:13, 28-29

There may be singing, dance or music

Storyteller

           Six years later God gave Patrick a 'word of
           knowledge': he had a mental picture of a boat
           ready to sail overseas. He trekked two hundred
           miles over unknown countryside before he
           found the boat and persuaded the crew to take
           him across the sea. When the crew landed they
           were stranded and without food. 'Christian, you
           are supposed to believe in God. Tell your God to

find us some food,' the captain yelled at Patrick. Patrick did indeed pray to God, and soon a herd of wild boar came right into their path, and they had more than enough to eat.

Reader Luke 11:5-10

There may be singing, teaching or the following story may be told

Storyteller

In his heart Patrick had a longing to be a hunter, or fisher of souls. So he trained to be a priest. Some say he trained at the Holy Isle of Europe, Lerins, near Nice, where true community, true holiness, and true excellence in study and worship were offered daily to God.

After a few years he returned to his parents in Britain. They begged him never to go far from them again after all the trials he and they had been through. It was said that Patrick set his heart on a ministry in a lush valley near his home. But God reserved that for David, whom he would raise up a generation later. God had other things in mind for Patrick:

Patrick But then I saw in a vision of the night a man who seemed to be coming from Ireland, carrying many letters. His name was Victoricus. He gave one of them to me and I read the opening lines, which were, 'The voice of the Irish'. While I was reading I thought I heard the voices of the people who live by the wood of Voclut, which is by the western sea. They cried as with one voice, 'We ask you, son, to come and walk once more among us.' I was heartbroken at this, and could read no further, and so I woke up. Years later, thanks be to God, the Lord granted them what they had asked.

I owe an immense debt to God, who granted me so much grace that many people in Ireland were reborn in God through me. Clergy were ordained everywhere to look after these people who had come to trust the Lord. It was essential that we spread our nets so that a great multitude should be taken for God, and that there were plenty of clergy to baptise and counsel the people, as the Lord tells us to do in the Gospel.

So it came about that Ireland, a land filled with people who never had the knowledge of God but worshipped idols and other foul objects, now has a people of the Lord who are called the children of God. It was not my grace, but God, victorious in me, who resisted all opposition when I came to the people of Ireland to preach the gospel and to suffer insults from unbelievers. If I should be worthy, I am ready to give even my life most willingly and unhesitatingly for his name. I am bound by the Spirit who witnesses to me. Christ the Lord told me to come here and stay with the people for the rest of my life, if he so wills, and he will guard me from every evil that I might not sin before him.

The Confession of Patrick

There may be singing

Intercession

Leader   Almighty Trinity, who in your providence chose your servant, Patrick, to be the apostle of the Irish, to boldly confront the kingdom of darkness, baptise those who were lost and in error and bring them into the light and truth of your Word, give us boldness, keep us in that light, and bring us to everlasting life.

First   We pray for young people who have lost their way or lost touch with you. Draw them to yourself as you drew Patrick to yourself.

Second   We pray for those who are in enforced labour and those who feel trapped by their circumstances. Free them, as you freed Patrick, from all that enslaves spirit or body.

Third   We bring before you the people of Ireland.
As Patrick sought to bring them to one Faith,
one baptism,
make them of one heart, one voice,
one love for you,
on one mission to the world.
May British people make themselves
one with their Irish brothers and sisters,
in penitence and love.

There may be free prayer and singing

All   The eternal Father,
the eternal Spirit,
the eternal Word,
shield us on every side,
protect us from every evil
and bring us to the land of promise. Amen.

Patrick Midday Prayer

Leader This day for our shield we call
All God's strength to direct us,
God's power to sustain us,
God's wisdom to guide us,
God's vision to light us.
Leader This day for our shield we call
All God's ear for our hearing,
God's word for our speaking,
God's hand to uphold us,
God's forces to save us.

From 'St Patrick's Breastplate'

Storyteller

Once a year at the spring solstice, the High King of all Ireland gathered the regional kings, with their Druids and bards, to the high Hill of Tara. There, at a giant celebration, they lit a bonfire with the aim of invoking the sun to shower beneficently upon them and their crops in the coming season. On that day, it was forbidden for anyone else to light a fire.

Patrick, knowing of this celebration, but unaware of the ban on the lighting of other fires, ascended the Hill of Slane, which could be seen from Tara. There, he and his fellow Christians lit a large fire to celebrate the resurrection of their Lord Jesus Christ, true God, Sun of suns. High King Loegaire was extremely disturbed, and ordered his staff to arrest them and bring them to him. His shamans intuited immediately what this was all about. 'If the fire of this new religion is not put out this night it will not be put out until Doomsday. Moreover, the person who kindles it will supersede the kings and rulers of Ireland unless he is banned,' they told the king.

When they came with their chariots to arrest Patrick, he, according to the medieval *Life of St Patrick,* quoted scriptures such as 'Some trust in chariots and some in horses but we will trust in the name of our mighty God' (Psalm 20:7).

Reader   Some trust in war chariots and others in horses, but we will trust in the power of the Lord our God.

All   We will trust in the power of the Lord our God.

Reader   They will stumble and fall, but we will rise and stand firm.

All   We will rise and stand firm.   *Psalm 20:7*

Storyteller

They also prayed the Psalm: 'Let God arise and scatter his enemies' (Psalm 68:1). A storm ensued – so violent that the horses and their riders fled. Although the king's men lay in wait to catch Patrick and his men as they left, all they saw passing them was a herd of deer. That is how the tradition grew that as these Christians prayed the armour prayer now known as 'Patrick's Breastplate', God shielded them from their enemies' eyes, and it is why that prayer is known as 'The Deer's Cry'.

There may be free prayer and singing or silence

Leader	In the middle of the day
All	Christ be our Shield and Encircler.

Leader	When the world around is hostile
All	Christ be our Shield and Encircler.
Leader	When our hopes seem to turn to dust
All	Christ be our Shield and Encircler.

PATRICK EVENING PRAYER

There may be singing

Storyteller

Patrick's first mission group disembarked at Strangford Lough and walked inland to rest. There the swineherd of a naturally good pagan named Dicu discovered them, and brought them to Dicu who lived here. Dicu, thinking they were bandits, resolved to kill them, but when he saw Patrick's face he instantly recognised goodness and changed his mind. Patrick, following Jesus' advice to missioners to stay in homes where they were made welcome, postponed his plans and stayed several days with Dicu. Dicu was discipled, baptised and became one of a praying 'back-up force' for Patrick's mission. Indeed, one of the first churches of Ireland was established at Strangford Lough and the Faith spread from there.

Reader   Psalm 96

Storyteller

Patrick visited the leading households of many northern tribes. It was said he used the shamrock's three-leaves-in-one to illustrate the Trinity. This is what he taught them about the true God of all people:

First

There is no other God, or ever was, nor will be than God the Father unbegotten, without beginning, from whom all things began, the Lord of the universe, as we have been taught, and his Son Jesus Christ, whom we declare always to have been with the Father, spiritually and ineffably begotten by the Father before the beginning of the world, before all beginning; and by him were made all things seen and unseen.

Second

He was made human, and, having defeated death, was received into heaven by the Father; who has given him all power over all names in heaven and on earth, and every tongue shall confess to him that Jesus Christ is Lord and God, in whom we believe and whose coming we expect soon, to be judge of the living and of the dead; who will give back to every one according to their deeds.

Third

And he poured forth upon us abundantly the Holy Spirit, the gift and pledge of immortality, who makes those who believe and obey children of God and joint-heirs with Christ; and him do we confess and adore, one God in Trinity of the Holy Name.

Storyteller

And so it came about, in Patrick's words, that Ireland, a land filled with people who never had the knowledge of God but worshipped idols and other foul objects, now had a people of the Lord who were called the children of God.

There may be singing or music and movement

Reader   Hosea 2:19-23

Leader   For our shield we invite
All   Heaven's might, sun's brightness,
                   moon's whiteness, fire's glory.
Leader   For our shield we invite
All   Lightning's swiftness, wind's wildness,
                   ocean's depth, earth's solidity.

Storyteller

Patrick suffered much, incurred opposition, but he never ceased to hold forth the Word of life. Thomas Cahill observes that 'Patrick found a way of swimming down to the depths of the Irish psyche and warming and transforming Irish imagination – making it more humane and noble while keeping it Irish.'

Reader   2 Corinthians 2:14–3:3

There may be singing

*There may be intercession groups, introduced by this confession that Patrick taught his followers to use repeatedly: Kyrie eleison, Christe eleison or
Lord have mercy, Christ have mercy
(Say or sing several times)*

Patrick Night Prayer

Leader	We lay this day at your feet.
All	May this night lie open before you.
Patrick	As a beardless adolescent I was captured before
	I knew what to look for and what to avoid.
	I was like a stone lying deep in the mud;
	but he that is mighty came and lifted me up
	in his mercy,
	and raised me to the top of the wall.
	That is why I ought to shout in a loud voice,
	and return something to the Lord
	for all his benefits
	here and in eternity.

There may be singing or music or a pause

Reader	Lord, thank you that you lift your people up
All	Lift us up, Lord, this night.
Reader	Those who feel as if they are in captivity,
All	Lift them up, Lord, this night.
Reader	Those who are like a stone lying in the mud,
All	Lift them up, Lord, this night.
Reader	Psalm 33:1-12

Any may name blessings of their Christian heritage

Leader	Our loved ones bless, dear God,
	and those who know you not.

Any may mention names

All sing	Christ be beside me, Christ be before me,
	Christ be behind me, King of my heart.

Christ be within me, Christ be below me,
Christ be above me, never to part.

Christ be in all hearts, Christ be in all tongues,
Christ all around me, shield in my strife.
Christ in my sitting, Christ in my sleeping,
Christ in my rising, light of my life.

After J. Quinn's adaptation of 'St Patrick's Breastplate'
to the tune Bunessan

Reader   Revelation 22:1-5

Storyteller

On the day of Patrick's death, night did not
wrap its black wings around the earth, and the
evening did not send the darkness which carries
the stars. The people said that to the end of that
year the night's darkness was never as great as
before. On the first night of his wake, angels
kept watch by his body. After they returned to
heaven, they left behind a scent of honey and a
sweet fragrance.   *Muirchu*

There may be silence and night lights may be lit

Leader   As the angels guarded Patrick,
may they guard us as we sleep,
hovering around our beds,
giving us visions in the night.

All   May the Spirit be glowing in us tonight
and in eternity.

Patrick's Creed

All Our God is the God of all humans,
the God of heaven and earth,
the God of the sea and the rivers,
the God of the sun and moon,
the God of all the heavenly bodies,
the God of the lofty mountains,
the God of the lowly valleys.

Leader God is above the heavens,
in the heavens and beneath the heavens.
Heaven and earth and sea,
and everything that is in them –
in all these God lives.

All God inspires all things,
gives life to all things,
stands above all things
and beneath all things.
God gives the light of the sun,
and strengthens the light of the night and the stars;
God makes wells in arid lands,
dry islands in the sea,
and places the stars in the service
of the greater lights.

Leader God has a Son and they are co-eternal
and similar in their essence,
and the Holy Spirit breathes in them.
The Father and the Son and Holy Spirit
are inseparable.

All The Father be with us for the rest of the night.
The Saviour beside us as we work.
The Spirit within, refreshing us.

FIRE – AN ALTERNATIVE PATRICK NIGHT PRAYER

*The ideal place to meet is round a living fire, outdoors or in
a house with a chimney. If this is not possible, gather in a
house or church with a living flame. As people gather there is
silence or singing of chants such as 'Kindle a flame'*

Storyteller
A fire was kept burning at all times in many a
monastery church of Celtic lands as a sign of
God's presence in the human heart. At Brigid's
monastery at Kildare a fire was kept burning for
a thousand years. Today there is a longing for
that fire of passionate Christian devotion to burst
into flame again.

Reader
Eternal Creator of day and night,
as darkness deepens, and we look for your coming,
cleanse us by your refining fire;
dispel the darkness of our hearts,
and kindle in us the Pentecostal flame.

Reader
The Lord is king, let earth rejoice,
let all the coastlands be glad.
Cloud and darkness are your raiment;
your throne, justice and right.
A fire prepares your path,
it burns all that opposes you on every side.
Your lightnings light up the world,
the earth trembles at the sight.

All
A fire prepares your path.

Reader
The mountains melt like wax before the Lord
of all the earth.

	The skies proclaim your justice;
	all peoples see your glory.
All	A fire prepares your path.
Reader	Let those who serve idols be ashamed,
	those who boast of their worthless gods.
	All you spirits, worship God.
	For you indeed are the Lord,
	most high above all the earth,
	exalted far above all spirits.
All	A fire prepares your path.
Reader	Lord, you love those who hate evil;
	you guard the souls of your saints;
	you set them free from the wicked.
	Light shines forth for the just,
	and joy for the upright of heart.
	Rejoice, you just, in the Lord;
	give glory to God's holy name.
All	A fire prepares your path.
Reader	Exodus 3:1-6
All sing	'In darkest night we pray.'
First	John the Baptist said: 'One greater than I will come who will baptise you with the Holy Spirit and with fire.'
	Echoes Luke 3:16
Second	Jesus said: 'I have come to bring fire on the earth.'
	Echoes Luke 12:49
Third	When the day of Pentecost came, all the believers were gathered together in one place . . .
	Then they saw what looked like tongues of fire which spread out and touched each person there.
	They were all filled with the Holy Spirit.
	Acts 2:1, 3

All sing   O thou who camest from above,
the fire celestial to impart,
kindle a flame of sacred love
on the mean altar of my heart.

There let it for thy glory burn,
with inextinguishable blaze,
and trembling to its source return
in humble prayer and fervent praise.

Jesus, confirm my heart's desire
to work and speak and think for thee;
still let me guard the holy fire,
and still stir up thy gift in me.

Ready for all thy perfect will,
my acts of faith and love repeat;
till death thy endless mercies seal,
and make the sacrifice complete.

Charles Wesley

Intercession

Reader   Kindle in my heart a flame of love
to my neighbour, and to my foe,
a flame of love to the brave, to the knave, to all.

Leader   Let us pray for situations where fires need to be lit.

*Silent or free prayer; a song such as 'Colours of Day'
may be sung*

Reader   Kindle in our hearts, O God,
the flame of that love which never ceases,
that it may burn in us, giving light to others.
May we shine for ever in your presence,

set on fire with your eternal light,
even your Son Jesus Christ.   *Columbanus*

Leader   Let us go in the undying fire of his love.

CREATIVE ACTIVITIES FOR PATRICK

A

1. Hold a St Patrick's Day parade.

2. Hold a St Patrick's Day dinner.

3. Decorate homes with shamrocks which, they say, Patrick used to teach the truth of the Trinity.

4. Make St Patrick flags. The St Patrick Flag is the white triangle on a red background that is included in the union flag of the United Kingdom of Great Britain and Northern Ireland. A touch of green may be added.

B

At longer St Patrick gatherings each of the following petitions may be allocated to a group to meditate on, discuss, dramatise or pictorialise. Alternatively, each petition may be used as a heading, and anyone be invited to pray on that theme

First   Father, give us winsomeness
               to woo a rising generation for you.

Second   Saviour, give us boldness
               to confront the seats of evil for you.

Third   Spirit, give us imagination
               to communicate the Truth for you.

Fourth Sacred Three, give us grace
to turn adversity into advantage for you.

Fifth True and only God, give us holiness to conquer
the corroding invasion of worldly charms.

There may be singing

Leader Christ the True Sun shine on us and our loved ones,
and make fruitful the work of our hands.

All Amen.

ST PATRICK'S EASTER SUNRISE SERVICE

*People gather in silence on a rise of dry land. They face
east when the sun will rise. A tomb sealed by a stone or
an empty cross may be placed nearby. As people arrive,
a round sun disk may be given to them to pin on a garment,
inscribed with the words:*

As surely as the sun rises daily, the True Sun shall rise upon you.
*Listen to the sounds of nature. As they salute the nearing
of dawn, let them evoke adoration of the One who is called
'The Morning Star' and 'The Bough of Creation'. As the
first hint of sun is glimpsed those present raise their arms
to greet the rising sun and the leader says:*

Leader As the sun rises upon us, let us welcome
the True Sun who shall rise for ever.

All Alleluia!

Leader Christ is risen from the dead.

All He is risen indeed. Alleluia!

There may be silent adoration or singing

Reader	Luke 24:1-12 or John 20:11-18

First	Rejoice, heavenly powers!
Second	Exult, all creation around God's throne!
Third	Jesus Christ, High King of Heaven, is risen.
Leader	Sound the trumpet of salvation!
All	Alleluia!

A trumpet, flute or pipe may be played

First	Rejoice, earth, in shining splendour.
	Radiant in the brightness of your King!
Second	Christ has conquered death! Glory fills you!
Third	Darkness vanishes for ever!
All	Alleluia!
First	Rejoice, O Church! Exult in glory;
	the risen Saviour shines upon you.
Second	Let this place resound with joy,
Third	Echoing the mighty song of all God's people.
All	Alleluia!

There may be singing

Reader	Matthew 28:2-6

If there is an Easter Garden, the stone is rolled away from the tomb entrance, or this action may be mimed

Leader	As the stone is rolled away from the dark and desolate tomb, so we roll away the stones that hide you from us.
First	The stone of despair.
Second	The stone of derision.
Third	The stone of denial.
Fourth	The stone of discord.
Fifth	The stone of domination.

Any	The stone of _____.
Leader	As Mary Magdalene met you by the garden tomb early in the morning, so may we meet with you today and every day of our lives. Reveal yourself to us as a Living Friend.
All	Renew our hope. Kindle our joy. Inspire us to share your Presence with others.

There may be singing

Leader   Christ was killed and raised from death at the time
         of the Jewish Passover in order to fulfil its meaning.
         As ancient Jews crossed over the sea from a land of
         slavery to a land of promise, so Jesus passed over
         from death and life, and we may pass over from
         the slavery of sin to the freedom of life in Christ.

         That is the meaning of our baptism. Joined to
         Christ, we daily bury the life of sin and rise up to
         freedom in God.

All   Dying with him we shall live with him for ever!

Reader   On this momentous day
         we place heaven with all its power,
         the true Sun with all his fire,
         between us and all the powers of darkness.
              Echoes words from the Rune of Patrick

Leader   As God's saints of old rose up from their tombs
         at the dawn of the first Easter Day,
All   So we join the uprising of saints old and new
         that a new Easter may dawn on the earth.

         Turn to face the direction indicated

First	May it dawn in the east _____ *(peoples may be named).*
Second	May it dawn in the south _____ *(peoples may be named).*
Third	May it dawn in the west _____ *(peoples may be named).*
Fourth	May it dawn in the north _____ *(peoples may be named).*
Leader	As Patrick lit up the resurrection fire, a fire that shall never be quenched,
All	May the fire of the True Sun blaze out in this world in the east, in the south, in the west, in the north, till all the world is alight.

There may be creative activities, intercessions and singing

Leader	Listen to the word from God: 'Go quickly and tell the others that he is raised from the dead and is going ahead of you.'
All	We will walk in the light of his presence.
Leader	The risen Christ said: 'My peace I give you.' Let us give one another a sign of this peace and share it with the world.

All may give a sign of peace such as a handshake, kiss, wave, hug or gift of an egg

Breakfast may follow

Samson

*Suitable for gatherings on the theme of wisdom,
anointings of the Holy Spirit, healing, miracles,
spiritual warfare, circling and Bible study*

SAMSON MORNING PRAYER

Storyteller

Almost every book in the Old Testament contains
a warning: how easy it is for God's people to back-
slide. Almost every book also features a warrior of
faith, raised up by God to restore him as sover-
eign amongst his people. That pattern repeats
itself in the history of the Christian Church, not
least in its beginnings here in Britain.

Samson was probably born in 486. His father,
Amon, and his mother, Anna, were officials in
neighbouring kings' courts, and they were
Christians. Anna was infertile, but longed for a
child. One day they travelled three days to see a
prophet. Before they opened their mouths, he
knew they wanted him to predict that they
would have a baby. He, however, wanted them
to give their will to God first of all. He asked
Amon to have a rod of silver made which was
the exact height of his wife, and give it to God.
After Amon had done that, he told them God
would give them a child. Then God told Anna
in a dream that she would have a son; he would

be a priest, and they were to name him Samson. No doubt this implied that he, like the Samson in the Old Testament whose birth also came as a result of prophecy, would be strong for the Lord.

Leader Light and peace has come into the world
through our Lord Jesus Christ
and through his saints.

All The light of Christ has come into the world.

Leader You led the ancient people of Israel to freedom
with a pillar of cloud by day
and a pillar of fire by night.

All The light of Christ has come into the world.

Leader You led the ancient people of Britain
out of darkness
through the holy prayers and powerful signs
of Samson and other saints.

All The light of Christ has come into the world.

Leader May we who walk in the light of your presence
acclaim your Christ, rising victorious,
as he banishes all darkness from our lives
and from our land today.

All The light of Christ has come into the world.

There may be singing

God's Word

Reader Psalm 125

Leader We bless you, Lord, that Samson's birth,
schooling and calling
were the fruit of prophecy.
We thank you that his prayer,

his heroic acts of witness,
his courtesy and wonderful love towards all,
won pagans to the Faith,
and patterned a new way of being the Church.
As we contemplate his life, give us a new zeal,
we pray through Jesus Christ. Amen.

Reader   Judges 13:1-7; 24-25

The Song of Zechariah

Leader   Blessed are you, Lord, the God of Israel.
         You have come to your people and set them free.
All   You have raised up for us a mighty Saviour,
         born of the house of your servant, David.
Leader   Through your holy prophets, you promised of old
         to save us from our enemies,
         from the hands of all who hate us,
All   To show mercy to our forebears
         and to remember your holy covenant.

Leader   This was the oath God swore to our father,
         Abraham,
         to set us free from the hands of our enemies,
All   Free to worship you without fear,
         holy and righteous before you,
         all the days of our life.

Leader   And you, child,
         shall be called the prophet of the Most High,
         for you will go before the Lord to prepare the way,
All   To give God's people knowledge of salvation
         by the forgiveness of their sins.

Leader	In the tender compassion of our God
	the dawn from on high shall break upon us.
All	To shine on those who dwell in darkness
	and the shadow of death,
	and to guide our feet into the way of peace.

| Reader | Acts 28:1-10 |

| Leader | In faith I trust in the God of power. |
| All | God is my refuge, a very strong tower. |

There may be singing

Storyteller

The *Life* of Samson is thought to have been written in the seventh century, not long after his death. Samson's nephew handed down much eye-witness material. It is therefore one of the earliest records of life in Britain.

The author mentions that Samson's parents took time to play creatively with him when he was an infant. That is something all children need, but so few receive. Since there were no state schools, Amon and Anna took him to Illtyd's monastery school, the most famous in the land, where he learned the psalms, philosophy, sports, and the ways of Christ. Illtyd was regarded as the wisest man of his time. Yet we learn that when he and Samson debated the meaning of Scripture, it was Samson who decided to fast and pray until understanding was given. He was the model of a serious Bible student.

In pairs each person asks if the other can shed light on a passage of scripture that is hard to understand.

There may be teaching or singing; groups may
prepare to act out each of the following prayers

Intercessions

Leader   Anoint young people to fresh callings
and anoint us for fresh service.

Reader   Call, call, call, great Chief of the high hills;
call, call, call, great Christ of the far paths.
Call, call, call, great Counsellor of the near gate,
set our spirits free to soar wherever you climb.
Set our feet free to trek wherever you go,
set our mouths free to say whatever you command.

First   Guard my eyes for me, Jesus Son of Mary,
lest seeing another's wealth make me covetous.

Second   Guard for me my ears
lest they listen to slander.

Third   Guard for me my tongue
that it spread not gossip.

Fourth   Guard for me my hands
that they be not stretched out for quarrelling.

Fifth   Guard for me my feet lest,
bent on profitless errands, they abandon rest.
There may be free prayer or singing

Leader   May the Spirit that came mightily upon Samson
come mightily upon you.
Go in the strength of God
to oppose all that harms.
Go in the seeing of God
to expose all that deceives.
Go in the mercy of God to bind up all
that is broken.

Samson Midday Prayer
Restoring Healing Ministry

Storyteller

Samson proved to be ahead of the other monks in the school of faith. Samson was a devoted student of Scripture. So acute was Samson's understanding that he wanted to dig deeper than his teacher. Once the two of them came across a doubtful point; though they had carefully studied all the books of the Old and New Testaments, they could not find a satisfactory explanation. Thereupon Samson decided to undertake fasts and vigils until God's understanding broke through. He was praying at nearly midnight when a heavenly light appeared and a voice spoke out of the light: 'Do not trouble yourself any further on this, God's chosen one, for in future whatever you ask God for in prayer and fasting you will obtain.' Then Samson returned quite happy to his cell and told Illtyd, his teacher, all he had seen and heard.

Reader   Psalm 119:9-16

First   You have sown in our hearts the precious seed
of your Word.
Nourish it by prayer, reflection and obedience,
that it may take root in our lives
and bring the fruits of wisdom, holiness and zeal.

Second   May your Word, O God,
be profitable to us for teaching,
for bringing awareness of what is right and wrong,
and for encouraging us in your ways.

All   Open our ears that we may hear.

Open our minds that we may understand.

Open our hearts that we may respond.

There may be singing or a pause

Storyteller

This insight was soon to be tested. It was a lovely summer's day. The brothers were weeding the fields of crops. A poisonous snake darted out from a blackberry bush and bit one of the brothers in the groin. He collapsed and the brothers gathered around in tears, expecting him to die.

When Illtyd was informed, Samson happened to be with him and they both shed tears. Samson, however, moved by the Holy Spirit, said: 'My father is well able to free our brother from this death of pain; may I go and pray over him?' At first Illtyd thought Samson must have been influenced by some pagan shaman and was trying to copy him, and he was uneasy. But Samson explained 'Surely you are aware that I have no father except God?' Then Illtyd agreed. The brother was cured, and that began a healing ministry in the church of Samson's time.

Reader   Luke 10:8, 9

Leader   We bring to our Healing Christ
a sick and broken world.
In silence let us focus on someone who needs healing of mind, body or spirit,
and picture Christ laying his healing hands upon them.

Pause or free prayer

On appropriate occasions anyone present may be invited to receive laying on of hands for healing

Leader   As we hold all these for whom we have prayed
before our God,
let us pray together.

All   Healing God, present with us now,
enter their body, mind and spirit
and heal them of all that harms.
In Jesus' name.

Leader   May the Christ who walks with wounded feet,
walk with us on the road.
May the Christ who loves with the wounded heart
open our hearts to love.
May the Christ who heals with wounded hands
stretch out our hands to heal.

SAMSON EVENING PRAYER
Slaying Dragons of Fear

Storyteller

Samson grew in stature, and the time came when he was ordained deacon by Bishop Dubricius. Both Dubricius and Illtyd saw the anointing of the Holy Spirit come upon him and stay upon him, in the form of a dove. These Celtic Christians were sensitive to these anointings, which often indicated to them whom they should ordain.

Reader   Zechariah 4:11-14

All may sing 'Come Holy Ghost our souls anoint' or another hymn

Leader	Open our lips, O Lord,
All	And we shall proclaim your praise.
Leader	Make our hearts clean, O God,
All	And renew a right spirit within us.

Storyteller

Illtyd's nephews had thought they would become the leaders of the monastery, because in those days leadership often went along the lines of heredity. The obvious stature of Samson threatened their ambitions. They were jealous, and they hatched a plot to poison him. God revealed to Samson what they were up to, and gave Samson supernatural protection. Later, the plotters confessed and were forgiven.

Reader   Mark 16:15-18

Reader   When others try to poison our lives
by misuse of chemicals,
by smear or innuendo,
may we not imbibe and spread the poison,
but let you transform it into sweetness
through the power of a new affection.

There may be singing, music or silence

Storyteller

When his father died, Samson persuaded his mother and other relatives to take vows and enter monastic life. It was revealed to his mother that he would be the founder of many monasteries, which he was.

Once Samson's family accompanied him on foot on a faith-sharing mission. They came to a place inhabited by a dangerous snake from which local inhabitants had fled. 'Put your trust in the One who said, "If you have even as little faith as a grain of mustard seed you will be able to remove a mountain and nothing shall be impossible to you",' said Samson. He went forward some distance alone, repeating psalms such as 'The Lord is my light and salvation'. The serpent was hissing and writhing and spewed a large stone out of its mouth towards Samson.

All The Lord is my light and my salvation, whom then shall I fear?

Reader Psalm 27:1-3

All The Lord is my light and my salvation, whom then shall I fear?

Storyteller

Samson marked a large circle in the earth around the serpent, and fixed his cross on the perimeter of the circle. He addressed the serpent: 'Advance only as far as you are allowed.' He asked his family to stand back and see what God would do. They saw the serpent slowly uncoil itself and crawl to the edge of the circle. But it never went outside it. Hour after hour it hissed and writhed and repeated this action, always stopping at the circle. Samson encouraged his frightened family with the words 'Those who really trust in the Creator need never fear the creature.' He spoke words that built up their faith. Finally, as dusk approached, Samson spoke directly to the serpent: 'We have a long journey ahead of us, but your time has come. I command you in the name of the Lord Jesus Christ to die in our presence this very hour.' The serpent reared its head, cast forth all its venom, and died.

Intercession

Hand out a picture or reproduction of a snake to each person

In silence each identifies a place, person or situation they are afraid of which the snake represents for them. Each chooses a place where they place the snake on the ground and draw a circle around it with a stick or a foot. While they pray over their snake two people take it in turn to repeatedly read aloud Psalm 27:1-3.

There may be singing

Leader   Circle us, Lord,
amid the dangers that threaten to engulf us
and our world.

Any may name a threat to be circled

The Lord's Prayer may be said

Leader   Circle us, Lord, for the rest of the day.
All   With Samson, the saints and the Saviour we will journey on in faith.

SAMSON NIGHT PRAYER

Storyteller

In due course Samson went to Ireland; then he was made a bishop. In those days bishops were not weighed down with bureaucracy, they were 'flying' bishops. God's Spirit led Bishop Samson, after short stays at Caldey Island and Padstow, to journeys of witness in Cornwall and the Channel Islands. One night Samson was preparing to celebrate the Easter Eucharist. He ate nothing but the blessed bread, and then stood throughout the night alone at the altar. He was lost in prayer and adoration when he was alarmed by a person of great size and splendour who stood in front of him. 'Take courage,' said this messenger from God, 'for God holds you dear. God commissions you to stop waiting around here, and to be a pilgrim beyond the sea where you will be greatly used in the Church.' It was an angel, who gently withdrew the following morning. After celebrating the Easter Eucharist, Samson made his way across the Severn sea.

There may be singing of the following or another song

All

Alone with none but you, O God,
we journey on our way.
What need we fear when you are near,
O King of night and day?

More safe are we within your hand
than if a host stood round.
Our lives we bow to your control
and yield to your command.

We live in peace, for from your hand
no power can snatch our soul.
Could earthly powers ever appal
a soul that heeds your call?

Storyteller

As Samson embarked on a Brittany shore he met
a man who had been weeping there for three
days. An inner voice had told him to await the
arrival of a man who could heal his sick daughter
and deranged wife. So it was that Samson's mission
to a new land began with a spectacular miracle.
What a boost! Samson went on to establish a series
of Christian communities in the region and his
monastery at Dol became large and famous. It
was there that he died.

Leader Into your hands we commit those
we have met today.
Into your hands we commit those
we can no longer be with.
Into your hands we commit those
we shall meet on our journey ahead.
Into your hands we commit those
we carry in our hearts.

Any may mention names

There may be singing or silence

Reader Ephesians 1:13, 14

Storyteller

At the annual celebration of Samson's life and
his birthday into heaven, the good God worked

signs and wonders among the people just as he had done through Samson in his lifetime . . . just as he does now, with us. Glory be to God who lives in the company of his shining ones through the ages.

All   We lie down tonight in the lap of your love.
We lie down tonight desiring your will.
We lie down tonight with prayer in our heart.
We lie down tonight and in you we are still.

Samson's Not Quite Night Prayer

Samson of Wales was named after the Samson of the Bible who, although he took vows of abstinence, was taken over by women and wine. According to the writer Gildas, most British clergy, not to mention the lay folk, got drunk during the time of Samson. So here we imagine, since Samson was very wise, a Night Prayer he might have suggested for visitors who were the worse for wear.

I'm not in a fit state to pray, Lord.
I'm somewhere in between
a big high and a big low.
I've been showing off.
I've drunk too much.
I've taken a few things I shouldn't have.
But it's not all bad;
I've had fun and you like fun.

I'm confused.
Do I have to choose between being all good
and being all bad?

I'm nearly out now.
Yet deep down I want you.
I've got a hangover,
but I don't want you and me
to be for ever hung up on each other.
I'd prefer not to sleep with my back turned to you.
But everything's too complicated to sort out now.
Sorry, Lord.

Now repeat between ten and one hundred times

Lord, have mercy on me.

If you're not asleep by now, you will be before you've finished saying what comes next.

Repeat between ten and one hundred times

I will lie down with God
and God will lie down with me.
Amen.

Trees – Kevin, Columba
and the Saxon Poet

*People gather outdoors near trees, or indoors with a
potted tree or a projection of a tree in the centre*

Leader　　The theme today is trees. Britain's first great
theologian, Pelagius, wrote to a friend: Look,
too, at the great trees of the forest; look at the
wild flowers and the grass in the field; look even
at your crops. God's spirit is present within all
plants as well. The presence of God's spirit in all
living beings is what makes them beautiful; and
if we look with God's eyes, nothing on the earth
is ugly.' We will try and take a fresh look at trees
through God's eyes, and through the eyes of two
great Celtic saints, Kevin and Columba.

　　　　　　There may be music

　　　　　　A picture of Glendalough may be projected or displayed

Storyteller

　　　　　　Kevin, the hermit of the outdoors, was praying
in the rugged Wicklow mountains about thirty
miles from Dublin. He sensed someone approach
him and offer to make his life more comfortable.
'I would clear away these hills and crags and
rocks and wooded dells where little grows and
no one lives,' said the messenger. 'I will give you
lush pastures for cattle to graze, a winding
stream and gentle fields on which you may grow
grain in place of this bare land.'

'Let them stay as they are,' Kevin replied, 'for I love the hunted creatures of the wild like any child; and any bird that climbs the sky here is free to wander just as I am, or to dwell in peace beside the lake. To make them homeless on account of me would trouble my conscience night and day.'

Kevin swore that the branches and leaves of the trees bowed down to him and sang sweet songs when he prayed there. He warned those who threatened to cut or burn the wood that they would reap what they sowed and their life, too, would be cut short if they did this. So although his life was hard, it was alleviated by the heavenly music of the trees.

Leader   A recent pilgrim to Kevin's home at Glendalough prayed thus:
Let me not spoil one leaf nor break one branch.
Let me not blunder, plunder, pollute, exploit,
but rather see and hear,
and touch and taste and smell,
and in my sensing know you well,
Creator God.   *Marie Connolly*

There may be recorded sounds of nature or music or silence

Storyteller

Kevin was convinced that the messenger was an angel sent from God.

Who knows how many angels sing when the trees rustle in the wind? Macrina Niederkehr wrote this in her book *A Tree Full of Angels:*

Reader I see the first rays of sunlight shimmering through a silver maple tree. I stand gazing as one in the midst of a vision . . . and then in a twinkling I'm certain. I am standing before a tree full of angels dazzling me with their glorious presence. Bright wings of fire all aglow! Such beauty! Celestial bodies trembling in the trees. Trembling in awe over the beauty of the world that I take for granted.

First Psalm 96:1-3

Second Psalm 96:11-13

There may be singing, mime or dance

Three people stand at the front to represent three trees. These could be visually presented by wearing an apron with the tree depicted on it, or by holding up a picture of the tree. The three trees are: oak tree (wisdom), apple tree (bitter fruit) and bare tree (suffering of Christ's Cross)

Storyteller

Kevin was not the first of our early Christian apostles to cherish and save the trees. Oak trees have grown in Britain for thousands of years. They were thought of as a sign of wisdom. For they grow slowly and they don't rush in where angels fear to tread. Columba established a large community in the oak-wood Plain of Derry. Many are the tales of his love for Derry and its oak woods. He wrote:

I would give all for one little cell
in my beautiful Derry.

For its peace and for its purity.
For heaven's angels that come and go
under every leaf of the oaks.
I love my little Derry,
my Derry, my fair oak grove,
my dear little cell and dwelling.

The local king gave Columba a plot of land in the oak grove near Derry. But like other Celtic monks before and since, it went against the grain for him to cut down trees. He would not build the church in the place of choice if it meant cutting down an oak. And he left instructions that those who came after him should not cut down the trees. And if a tree fell in a gale, it was to be left for nine full days, out of respect, before it was cut up and taken to the poor as firewood.

In Derry (Londonderry) people wear the oak leaf to commemorate Columba on 9 June.

An oak leaf is given to each person present

Leader Let us pray for the oak trees and the other trees of the world.

Reader May the forests continue to grow,
may the trees continue to breathe,
for they also serve who only stand and wait.

People may go to a tree, touch it and repeat a prayer for the trees

A person depicting an apple tree comes into the centre

Storyteller

The Bible begins with the story of a tree (Genesis) and ends with a glimpse of a renewed creation in which is a tree whose leaves are for the healing of the peoples (Revelation). Trees can heal and be healed, as this story of Columba tells us.

In the grounds of the monastery at Durrow there was a tree that provided local people with a big supply of apples; however, these tasted so bitter that they complained. One autumn day, Columba went up to it and, seeing it laden with fruit that was going to give more displeasure than pleasure, he raised his hand and spoke to the tree: 'In the name of almighty God, bitter tree, may all your bitterness depart from you, and from now on may your apples be really sweet.'

Columba's biographer commented: 'Wonderful to tell, more swiftly than words, all the apples on that tree lost their bitterness and became wonderfully sweet.'

Apple blossom or apples may be distributed

A hymn such as 'O Lord my God' may be sung

A person depicting a bare tree or cross comes into the centre

Leader Let us weep for the rain forests gone
and the trees felled without thought.
Let us weep for the spoiling of creation
and the suffering caused to our Creator.

Reader O Son of God, do a miracle for me
and change my heart.
Your taking flesh to redeem me
was more difficult
than to transform my wickedness.

It is you, who, to help me, went to be scourged.
You, dear child of Mary, are the refined
molten metal of our forge.
It is you who make the sun bright,
together with the ice.
It is you who create the rivers and the salmon
all along the river.
That the nut tree should be flowering,
O Christ, it is a rare craft.
Through your skill too comes the kernel,
you fair ear of our wheat.
Though the children of Eve ill deserve
the bird flocks and the salmon,
it was the Immortal One on the Cross
who made both salmon and birds.
It is he who makes the flower of the sloes grow
through the surface of the blackthorn,
and the nut flower on other trees.
Besides this, what miracle is greater?

> *Adapted from Tadhg Og O Huiginn (d.1448)*
> *translated by K. H. Jackson*

*There may be music, silence and the event may end
here or continue*

Storyteller

The large wooden cross-beam on to which Christ
was nailed was often called a tree. Another word
used for this was rood. In older English churches
you sometimes see a screen between the main
part of the church and the part where the choir
stalls and altar are. These sometimes have carvings
of the tree on which Christ died and are called

the rood screen. Celtic Christians understood that this tree on to which Christ was nailed, was affected by the crucifixion of Christ, because in some way the whole of creation was affected. The Bible, for example, says there was an eclipse of the sun at the time Jesus was dying. In the ninth century a famous poem was written called 'The Dream of the Rood', in which the Saxon poet looks at the tree on which Christ died. Here is part of that poem:

Reader   Wondrous was the tree of victory . . .

I saw this glorious tree
joyfully gleaming, adorned with garments,
decked in gold; the tree of the Ruler
was rightly adorned with rich stones;
yet through that gold I could see the agony
once suffered by wretches, for it had bled
down the right hand side . . .
I lay there for a long while
and gazed sadly at the saviour's Cross;
until I heard it utter words;
the finest of trees began to speak.

I remember the morning a long time ago
that I was felled at the edge of the forest
and severed from my roots.
Strong enemies seized me,
bade me hold up their felons on high,
and made me a spectacle. Men shifted me
on their shoulders and set me on a hill.
Many enemies fastened me there.

I saw the Lord of humankind
hasten with such courage to climb upon me.
I dared not bow or break there
against my Lord's wish, when I saw the surface
of the earth tremble.
I could have felled
all my foes, yet I stood firm.
Then the young warrior, God Almighty,
stripped himself, firm and unflinching.
He climbed upon the Cross, brave before many,
to redeem humankind . . .
They drove dark nails into me;
dire wounds are there to see,
the gaping gashes of malice;
I dared not injure them.
They insulted us both together;
I was drenched in the blood
that streamed from the Man's side
after he set his spirit free.

From 'The Dream of the Rood'
Translated by Kevin Crossley-Holland

CREATIVE ACTIVITIES

1. Project photos of Kevin's bed and of Glendalough.

2. Sing (guitar chords given) the following:

> A   G   A
> What could I do? What could a tree say?
>
> G A   D
> I'd no earthly power.

```
          A        G        A
They mocked us both and bruised us both
    G       A        D
on this his triumphant hou - r.

Bm             A        G        A
But on me, just one more old broken tree,

G       A              D
our Lord sets all folk free.
```
Andrew Dick

A Memory Verse

Christ himself carried our sins in his own body
to the tree, so that we might be finished with sin
and be alive to all that is good. *Echoes 1 Peter 2:24*

A Prayer

When Irish Christians were lying in bed worrying
about some trouble, they would imagine the tree
of Christ's Cross being placed between them and
the trouble. This is a prayer written in Ireland:

> I come to rest in the name of the Father,
> lying on my bed in your name,
> O noble King.
> I place the tree upon which Christ was crucified
> between me and the heavy nightmare,
> between me and each evil thing.

A song or music such as the following may be suitable:
'The trees of the field shall clap their hands with
joy'.

A Litany with the Saints

Leader St Fursey saw four fires – may we put out the fires of falsehood, greed, discord and cruelty. Lord, hear us.

All Lord, graciously hear us.

Leader St Brigid lit a fire of resurrection outside the church –
may we keep the fire of resurrection
in our hearts.
Lord, hear us.

All Lord, graciously hear us.

Leader As St David gathered bundles of souls, so may we. Lord, hear us.

All Lord, graciously hear us.

Leader May we, like St Chad, show that a true leader is a servant.
Lord, hear us.

All Lord, graciously hear us.

Leader May we, like St Patrick, surmount all kinds of trials.
Lord, hear us.

All Lord, graciously hear us.

Leader May we, like St Cuthbert, storm the gates of heaven.
Lord hear us.

All Lord, graciously hear us.

Leader May we, like St Brendan, voyage with you into the endless adventure.
Lord, hear us.

All Lord, graciously hear us.

Leader	As St Columba left his homeland
	as a sign of repentance,
	may we leave behind our selfish ways.
	Lord, hear us.
All	Lord, graciously hear us.
Leader	As the Spirit moved St Samson
	to spread the good news of the kingdom,
	may the Spirit move us.
	Lord, hear us.
All	Lord, graciously hear us.
Leader	Make us, like St Oswald, a people of prayer,
	compassion and valour.
	Lord, hear us.
All	Lord, graciously hear us.
Leader	As St Ninian's Whithorn community
	became a shining household,
	may we become a lighthouse of the world.
	Lord, hear us.
All	Lord, graciously hear us.
Leader	May we, following Aidan's example,
	understand and love the people of our land.
	Lord, hear us.
All	Lord, graciously hear us.
Leader	As St Hilda brought out God's gifts
	buried in the people,
	so may we.
	Lord, hear us.
All	Lord, graciously hear us.

Poem on Caedmon

ONE

That night frost stretched
the fields into stiff white sheets;
from post, strut and roof glinting
ice-fingers pointed to the ground.
But within walls, reed-woven,
mud-baked, we warded off
the wind-beast's bellow and bite.
Herded in the wool of our own warmth,
near red-gold flames that licked
logs, then leapt to find the hole
to heaven, we defeated winter's pikes.
That festive night we filled
our bodies' troughs with roasted meats,
with mead that honeys the senses, muzzes
the mind. As ever I kept quiet,
stoked myself with the comfort rising
from the rush-strewn floor, the goodwill
steaming through talk and laughter.

My contentment crumbled into ash
when to claps and shouts the wooden board
was lifted for fingers to pluck its strings
and make its sounds a weft for words.
I had always shrunk into the shell of self
when the harp was passed round.
How could I relate stories in song?
I was so cack-handed with speech
that if man or woman questioned me

in house or field I stood wooden
as the figure of twigs stuck in the earth
to scare crows from the seed,
wrestled to pull from my throat
a few straggled straws of words.

Face on fire with fervour
each person told a tale that struck
strongly as the sea breaking on the shore
below our cliffs. Bound in a spell
I longed for those times when men
did not snail-creep through life
in mean places but strode with certainty,
lived in the light of halls hung
with gold, hunted dragons from bogs
that glistened darkly with stinking evil,
destroyed terror with the thrust of blades.

The spell snapped when the harp came near.
I wanted to crouch on haunches like a dog,
listen unseen, but hissing fear
towered up, pinioned me in its claws,
and I knew I would mutter lumpish words,
make mis-shapen lines, stutter
to a halt, be a laughingstock.
I stayed till my neighbour grasped
the harp and my heartbeat was louder
than the songbeat, then stumbled to the door,
fled from dwelling into moonlessness.

TWO

Chilling darkness wheeled over me
and silence clattered in my ears
but when I saw the stars had pricked
through the thick cloth of night
quietness became the flurry and slow
fall of duck-feather snow.
I found my way to the stable
where the cows were in my care till dawn,
knelt down, nested in the straw
to unbuckle my body from the bitter cold.

I was more at home in a stall with cows
than housed with humankind. My fingers
still know by heart what rhythms
draw milk from heavy, aching udders,
milk whose sweet scent dwells
in the seedheads of August grass,
hot dung, crushed straw,
milk, high in a bucket, its warmth
swooshed as I drink for nourishment.
I can recognise the call or yearn in mooing,
have tugged calves, jelly-coated
from the wombs of groaning mothers,
and watched the newborn still wet
from tonguing try out unsteady legs.
That night the chomp of cud-chewing,
the tail-switch and burry breathings
from the mound of each animal,
eased me into the flow of sleep.

THREE

Suddenly a tall light stemmed
from the flattened straw. It was alive,
sap-succulent as shoots of corn
and near my hand were feet, unshod,
freshly-washed. I looked up,
saw a man whose face was the shining
of many candles, whose command was sharp
as an axe-head's fall on a naked branch:
'Sing, Caedmon, sing me a song.'
My courage failed and I trembled
as the calf does when it finds itself
unfurled outside the body's cave
at the verge of our thorn-thicket world.

'I cannot sing!' I cried. 'Words
baffle me. I can no more craft
poetry than create gold for the girding
of fingers. I ran from the telling of songs
at the feast to escape being pelted with scorn.'
I longed to creep away, to hide
the slug of my shame under a stone.
But in a voice softer than rabbit fur,
finer than spider thread, he replied:
'Delve for the hoard of words in yourself,
Caedmon. Uncover it and sing to me.'
Then fear lost its grip, fell
off my back, died, and hope
gushed through me like a thawed stream.
'What shall I sing to you?' I cried.
'Sing of the creation of life on earth.'
His words lapped in my ears like the tide
on emerald weed at the sea's edge.

Was it he who gave me power
to draw gleaming words from the thick
and grainy dark, link them in lines?
I spoke of God in a steeply-pointed,
russet crown, separating heaven
from earth, cream from milk, of him
sifting land out of the sea,
kneading its toughness into wet dough,
peaking mountains, rolling out plains,
baking rocks in ovens underground,
cutting long river rifts.
Then I sang of the Maker covering ground
with quilts of grass, embroidered
with coloured flowers, studded with trees
bearing fruits. I told how he
held up the round fire of sun
to make day and the silvery yellow
disc of moon to make night,
how he measured out the years,
started the miraculous movement of seasons.

I sang of the stocks of fish he laid
in the sea where he wrought huge whales,
of the waves washing creatures up
on trackless sand where some unwound
wings and flew into the sky, some
uncoiled legs and learnt to run.
Lastly I told of the two clay figures – he
moulded with love in his own shape.
There was no fumbling – the words
came naturally as leaves upon a tree,
and though I'd spanned many years – it was the

first time I'd found a fitting voice.
When I stopped the man thinned into dawn
and I was tumbled into an ocean of sleep.

FOUR

I awoke to cow-lowing, felt
peaceful as the chalk skim across the sky
till my dream swarmed through my head
like a hiveful of excited bees.
I made more lines about Adam, Eve
and the sly serpent twining round
the tree, luring them to bite
the plump ripeness of forbidden fruit,
about God chasing them from paradise
to forests dark and dense with disorder
where they hacked and hewed to make clearings.
My new skill filled me with joy
bright as ragwort, foxglove, speedwell.

Then I fell down in a quake of fright:
Was the gift unbound in cold-bolted night
meant for one so clumsy in mind?
I was dazed by this jewel as if
I might drop it, tread it into muck
while I dug up turnips; sheared sheep.
I soothed, milked the complaining cows,
saying: 'I will go to the reeve. My prize
is a burden I cannot bear alone.'
The reeve had knowledge to match his rank,
had travelled and been in the King's hall.
He said: 'We must take your dream

for those who live close to God to judge.'
And so I forsook my small patch
flaked with snow, my wooden house,
the cows and sheep I called my friends,
followed the reeve along a path
where frost-blue grass blades stood
like stiff hairs, where icy eyes
glinted roundly from the mud. I saw
strange moors heave against the sky,
stared down from hostile cliffs
on gulls, tiny sail-folded craft
flecking the swirling green of the sea
and I quivered in the frail ship of self.

FIVE

At last when I was heartsore for home,
we reached the monastery, a kempt world
enclosed by high grey walls
where men with bald pates,
shorn locks and wearing black robes,
toiled. I was taken to a building
of stone, the mightiest in height and length
I'd ever seen. Cleanliness hung
in the air and pine-sweetness, holy breath.
I saw on floor, wall and roof
shadows from the trembling flames
that sprouted from rows of wax stems.
I saw radiance take life
from silver crosses, bowls, stands,
adornments, and my small mind grasped
I was come to God's sacred hall.

Many, who had been steeped in the dye
of God's learning, gathered here.
They were led by the great Abbess who said:
'Caedmon, tell the song of your dream
to these knowledgeable people.' Her smile
was sun spilling from the pod of sky
on the gloom of heather and bracken moor.
At that moment I seemed reborn
and I told my poem without stammering.
The wise mother whispered with her flock
and when she spoke again it was sweet
as the fall of rain on green moss:
'Caedmon, this poem is a gift
from God. Go with these two monks,
listen to a holy tale, and if you can,
create another song of celebration.'

I was given meat and milk, then led
to a place that housed strange treasure:
pages bearing sets of black-marks
for words, some decorated with scrolls,
circles, knots, and lines plaited
round bird or beast heads. The patterns
had colours fierce as blackberry juice,
bright as winter hip and haw,
clear as the sky-blue stamped on butterfly.
I heard a tale of David who killed
Goliath by slinging a single stone.
That a weak shepherd boy could outwit
the evil of a cloddish giant, strengthened me.
I began to pick words for a poem.

I wove lines together far into
the night and next morning, carried
the new garment of song to the Abbess.
She found it fitting, said:
'Like a grey dove on a tree, grace
has settled on you. Your work should be
crafting word pictures with pleasing sounds,
for as bread feeds hungry bodies
so your poems will nurture minds.'
She asked me to cast off the skin
of my wrinkled life, become a monk.

Six

I have lived here since that day,
sewn into song stories of men
ever in battle with dragons of wickedness,
with fiends of despair, ever on the brink
of kindling the fire of their own destruction,
yet finding hope flowering
on the driest soil and goodness in grains
strong as the salt in the rolling sea.

Now I must leave this world,
ask you to make me a bed of quiet
in the house where each of us shall die.
Soon you will lay my emptied flesh
and bones deep in clay's sunlessness.
But I shall shake off the dark and rise,
a lark spinning song into boundless
blue, come to rest in light.

Myra Schneider, from New and Selected Poems
(Enitharmon, 2000)

APPENDICES

Acknowledgements and Storytelling Sources

The storyteller's material on Martin is provided by Kate Tristram by kind permission.

Accessible, easy-to-read sources in English for the saints in this volume:

Floris Books, Edinburgh, publish a series of little books on Celtic saints which include:

Saint Brendan

Saint Bride (Brigid)

Saint Mungo

Saint Ninian

Saints of Northumbria: Aidan, Cuthbert, Hilda, Oswald

Saint Patrick's World (translated by Liam de Paor, Four Courts Press), includes the *Lives* and the Writings of St Patrick.

Celtic Spirituality (translated by Oliver Davies, Paulist Press) includes *Lives* of Brigid, David and Patrick.

Bede's World (Penguin Books) includes Bede's *Life of Cuthbert.*

Llanerch Press publish *The Life of Samson.*

Early Christian Lives (includes Sulpicius Severus's 'Life of Martin of Tours', Penguin Classics, 1998)

They Built on Rock by Diana Leatham (Hodder & Stoughton); tells in her own words the stories of Brigid, Columba, Columbanus, Cuthbert, David, Martin, Mungo (Kentigern), Ninian, and Patrick.

Wisdom of the Celtic Saints by Edward C. Sellner (Ave Maria Press) includes the story of Ciaran of Clonmacnoise.

The Anthology *Celtic Fire* by Robert Van de Weyer (Darton, Longman & Todd) includes the stories of Hilda and Illtyd.

Flame in My Heart (Chad)

Themes